IN HABIT

IN HABIT

An Anthropological Study
of Working Nuns

SUZANNE CAMPBELL-JONES

With a Foreword by
BRYAN WILSON
All Souls College, Oxford

FABER & FABER London & Boston

First published in 1979
by Faber and Faber Limited
3 Queen Square London WC1N 3AU
Printed in Great Britain by
Latimer Trend & Company Ltd Plymouth
All rights reserved

British Library Cataloguing in Publication Data

Campbell-Jones, Suzanne
In habit.
1. Monasticism and religious orders for women.
I. Title
301.5'8   BX4205
ISBN 0–571–11324–9

For S, S and S

CONTENTS

FOREWORD

Until recently, religion has been regarded as a delicate subject for sociological scrutiny. Even the most human aspect of religion, its organizational forms—well recognized on theological grounds as no more than human inventions, devised and created by men—enjoyed the overspill of the sanctity of divine things themselves. They, too, came to be regarded, by the lay public as well as by their own members, as inappropriate subjects for sociological inquiry. Of course, religious orders and congregations had it very much within their own power to disallow the intrusion of inquirers, and the idea that inquiry amounted to intrusion applied no less to the investigation of the serious scholar than to that of the sensation-seeking journalist. The sacred sphere of the religious community was well separated from the profane world: laymen had no access. Although religious orders were never secret societies, their activities, as laymen viewed them, often appeared to be surrounded by an atmosphere of sacred secrecy, and this impression persisted even in the case of those religious congregations which sent out their people to undertake such secular work as nursing or teaching.

The early sociological studies of religious orders (and here *orders*, which exact solemn vows, subsumes *congregations*, which require only simple vows) were largely concerned with typological analysis. It was the refinement of the concept of the religious order as an ideal type that preoccupied these writers. The use of ideal-type constructs, strictly as heuristic devices, has been as indispensable to sociology as it was to theoretical economics. But the use of the method has exacted its own price—a tendency for sociologists to flirt with essentialism. Recurrently, sociologists have confused typologies with systems of classification, and an undue amount of energy has gone into the construction of sets of empty theoretical pigeon-holes, into which new 'cases'—of orders, sects, cults, or other collective phenomena—might be conveniently pushed. Once this labelling was done, the sociologist all too readily assumed that his job was done. Empirical inquiry was sacrificed for deductive logic, as sociologists contented themselves with answering such riddles of their own devising as, 'When is a sect not a sect?', or, 'Is X organization a religious order or a cult?' Ideal-type analysis, properly done, still has its place in sociology, but its use conforms to Weberian tradition only when the types are used as heuristic models with which empirical material is compared, or when carefully constructed types are compared one with another. Undoubtedly, such comparison clarified the vital differences between, for instance, the religious order and the sect, which transcended the similarities of circumstances of origin, similar styles of protest against the Church and the social order, and, frequently, a common measure of asceticism. But the point of such comparison has now become familiar enough, and what has been needed for some time has been less attention to ideal types and much fuller empirical studies of individual orders and congregations, the comparison of their internal structures, and their ways of fulfilling their mission. Happily, this is exactly what this book provides.

There is a variety of important questions to be asked about religious orders, some of them developed within the sociology of religion, and some arising from the more general concerns of the sociology of organizations. The issues of authority are self-evidently significant, especially so in institutions that demand total or near-total obligation. So, too, are such matters as the process of socialization of novices; the maintenance of commitment; the balance of pressure for individual adaptation or institutional change; and the function of ritual (taken both in the anthropological sense, and in the more specifically religious sense of recurrent and solemnized action with reference to sacred objects or objectives); and the relations of religious organizations to a changing external world.

It is the change in the relation of the religious order—and of the Church in general—to the wider society, that has induced religious bodies to seek the assistance of sociologists in interpreting the situation in which they now find themselves. If, until recently, centuries-old orders could continue their work according to the formulations of their founders, content with the legitimations provided by the Word of God and the endorsement of the Church, and clear about their own role and the meaning and purpose of the religious life, now, within the course of little more than a decade, the old certainties have all been questioned, and the old assumptions have ceased to be self-evident. Just how a religious order, rooted in what, in the past, were regarded as timeless truths, should adapt to a changing external world, has become a question of which the orders themselves have become increasingly conscious, and one that has also become pressing. Once such a question is even raised, let alone entertained, it demands a response: forcing it into the consciousness of the orders has itself been a way of putting on the pressure for change. And change might be at many, or all, levels—from basic matters such as the interpretation of vows, to such materially minor (even if spiritually and symbolically important) matters as dress, style, comportment, and contact with lay people.

The crisis that followed the Second Vatican Council, which was undoubtedly far more serious than anything for which the Roman Church was prepared, left few pillars of the faith unshaken. Old dogmas were replaced by new doubts. The Church, used to making normative pronouncements to which the lay world was expected (or half-expected) to conform, or, at least, to which it was to give lip-service, now lost its own conviction about its authority. Instead of interpreting the world for others, the Church now found itself looking to others for an understanding of society and its processes of change. Those others were necessarily scholars whose basic grasp of social reality rested much less on normative assumptions and much more on empirical evidence: namely, the sociologists. The Church was suddenly aware that its own role was no longer determined by its own 'explicit performances', that—to put the matter more sociologically—its own declarations were no longer sufficient as legitimations for its acts. The Church became accessible to the sociologist: indeed, sometimes, he was not merely welcomed—he was invited, as when the Vatican itself sponsored small conferences of sociologists to clarify for the Church the processes of change occurring in society and in the condition of religious belief.

Within the Church, women's congregations were perhaps less immediately and less dramatically affected by Vatican II than either the diocesan priesthood or the men's orders, among whom defections, declining number of vocations, and agitation for a married clergy all became commonplace and worldwide phenomena during the late 1960s. The religious congregations of women had grown vigorously in the nineteenth century, when they provided the surplus population of women with an outlet into a variety of newly developing careers, particularly in teaching and nursing. But as women's rights grew, and as more professional openings for women occurred, it became increasingly possible that the congregations would fail to attract so many women. Sociologists, and indeed churchmen, might have foreseen that possibility: there is little evidence that they did. It is perhaps no longer possible to determine whether general changes in the social condition of women and the later militant 'liberation' movement were of more consequence for the congregations than were the wider processes of secularization and the destruction of barriers. All of these things were refracted in the new light thrown on Roman Catholic affairs shed by the Second Vatican Council itself. In the event, the numbers in women's congregations began to decline in the late 1960s, and this was followed by the ferment of internal reappraisal as the orders became aware of the pressures of social change. The process continues, and if some orders have found something approaching a new *modus vivendi*, it would be too early to say that new patterns of communal life have as yet been stabilized. But the chief irony that has entered the soul of the situation is perhaps that the religious community, which thought of itself as changeless and of its order as possessing a timeless validity, has come to acknowledge a world in which change for its own sake sometimes appears to be the only value to which most of us subscribe.

Obviously, high standards of personal devotion and dedication to selfless service in the name of God persist in women's congregations, as elsewhere in both regular and lay religious bodies, both Catholic and Protestant. The quality of spiritual life (of which, neither in sociological nor theological terms have we wholly adequate measure) may flourish unimpaired within the orders. Indeed, it might be argued—since so much more now depends on individual consciences, and so much less on conformity to routine procedures—that the quality of spiritual life has improved. However that may be, the actual changes that have been made are of momentous importance to the Church and of great interest to the sociologist. What has apparently happened, as Dr Campbell-Jones so ably documents in rich and telling detail, is a fundamental shift within religious communities in the balance of communal control as against self-control. Of course, religious have always had to acquire intense commitment to a distinctive and demanding code of morality and decorum. But, in the past, those codes were reinforced by the rhythms and patterns of the life of the community itself. Today, with the external and visible signs of invisible grace having become so much less congruous in the secular society, the order has perforce come to rely on a much more generalized and abstract sense of moral commitment, applicable to a wider variety of circumstances, less confined and less particular to a community, and less fixed to specific sets of concrete situations. The great merit of a comparative study, such as this book provides, is that it throws into high relief the nuances of just such sociological issues as these.

The two congregations that Dr Campbell-Jones examines were established with very different constitutions, and she shows how the more rigid and elaborate of these codes has required much more radical revision than the more general provisions of the Fransiscan congregation. The religious orders offered, and continue to offer, their members opportunities for spiritual development, and above all the ordered life of service and devotion. All of them put, as they have always put, method, regularity, and consistency at a premium. Traditionally, their strength and purpose was to provide the social control that bridled human folly and human frailties—whether they tended towards undue rigour and asceticism, or towards the failure of steady spiritual resolve. The changes that have followed Vatican II have brought the orders to accept a new balance between, on the one hand, regulated communal control and, on the other, individual strength and persistence of purpose. Whereas private devotions were previously often a part of a public or quasi-public performance (if we allow that, in this sense, the community constitutes a public, albeit a very special and supportative public), that general process of the privatization in religion, of which sociologists write, and which in this sense is a reinforcement of the essentially personal nature of religious commitment, has now penetrated the cloister and the convent. The modern nun is exposed to more profane environments, and exposed with less of the supportive framework that the congregation once provided. Of course, religious orders have experienced radical changes in the past: they changed significantly with the emergence of the Canons Regular and the various orders of Friars in the Middle Ages. That, too, was a shift from communal to increased self-control, but there are differences. Then, the new balance was expressed by the emergence of new orders of a new type. Today, the changes take place *within* each already established order. Then, the orders were growing, and new forms arose from augmented strength. Today, the orders and congregations are in decline and the internal changes are more of an accommodation to the times than a gesture of confidence.

Social change provides the occasion for this book, but given the paucity of studies of religious congregations and orders, and the small number of sociologists in the field, one ought not to overlook its more general contribution to our knowledge of these organizations. Access to the orders has come late, and has come only when things have already been undergoing transformation: but we are fortunate that, once that access was granted, it was granted to an observer with the objectivity and sympathetic detachment of Dr Campbell-Jones. She conveys convincingly to the reader the ethos of the convent, of which she was obviously a most sensitive observer. The two orders— cloaked in protective anonymity—need have feared nothing from so scrupulous and perceptive an investigator. Serious and personal questions to the sisters were not avoided, and they themselves emerge more sympathetically for having answered—and, thus, for having been asked. Far from derogating the order's understanding of itself, the sociological analysis in this study extends the range, sharpens the focus, and enlarges the perspective: there are new intimations for churchmen—and churchwomen—to pursue. For sociologists who wish to comprehend the workings of groups such as these, Dr Campbell-Jones has provided a model of clarity and order, and it is my conviction that a study of this kind must act as the very best letter of introduction to allay the doubts that churchmen have often entertained towards sociology as a discipline.

B. R. WILSON

All Souls College,
Oxford

CHAPTER ONE

Science as Gossip:
A Sociological Perspective

A veiled figure walking between yew trees appears as a recurring image in T. S. Eliot's *Ash Wednesday*. A figure clothed in silence and colours of white and blue. She is the 'lady of silences' whom we shall never know. She is the intercessor between the lost souls of the waste land and the spirit-beings who can offer hope. The veiled figure of Mary is handed down to us in the frescoes of Italian churches and the pure colours of Renaissance paintings. Pure, distant and haloed, she symbolizes the Christian ideal of the chaste virgin queen, an eternal mother unsullied by the reality of everyday life. Something in the contrast between the ideal and the real world encourages a vicarious curiosity about Mary and her immaculate conception, as it does about the nun and her vow of chastity.

A friend of mine, a young psychiatrist, pinned a photo-poster on the wall of his cell-like room in the hospital where he worked. It was in startling contrast to his other posters—languid Mucha prints and decorative Klimts. It was a picture of a nun stooping to fix her suspender. A flash of pink thigh above the black stocking and even blacker habit gave the poster an erotic quality like the postcards of the naughty 1890s. The psychiatrist laughingly analysed his choice as appropriate to his profession. His curiosity about people took him to the inner life of the individual. Mine was captured by the social significance of the poster. That black religious habit symbolized so much. It was prescribed by an organization. It had rules and regulations. Why did the nun follow them, who decided on them, what was her relationship to other people outside her group? I was as curious about the image of Mary in white and blue as I was about the black garbed figure in the poster: two contrasting representations, one idealized, a cultural stereotype of goodness, the other shocking and deviant, each containing messages for which society holds the key.

A general interest in people motivates every one of us and it is often as far as potential professional voyeurs get in explaining their desire to become journalists, sociologists or social workers. One of the more theatrical sociologists, John O'Neill, has described sociology as

a skin trade. The sociologist works with people just as the hair-
dresser, the dentist, priest, judge or prostitute does. Students of
sociology, he says, have a libidinal and expressive concern for people.
He was writing in the late 1960s when youth was still concerned and
politically activist, flushed with the communitarian ideology of the
revolution of that decade. As a skin trade sociology is clean, professional; even an interview is structured by a schedule which defuses
any chance of personal interaction between subject and 'scientist'.
The young students soon grow disenchanted; they lose their naïve
hope that in learning about 'society' they will be able to improve
human relations. John O'Neill set a plea for sociology to be tested
against everyday life. 'I want to restore its symbiotic connections
with the body-politic',[1] he said, in the language of the skin trade.

We all exchange information about ourselves and the people around
us. Some of us tend to mystify that information, encircle it within a
'discipline' and call it a science. Social relationships thrive on gossip
and whether we call it history, ethnology or comparative religion, it all
amounts to the same thing . . . high-level gossip. Historians dress
their gossip in the valued robes of serious research; sociologists take
on grand theory, quantification and abstraction; anthropologists
cling to the uniqueness of their researches. The very destruction of the
cultures they study enables them to justify the romance of travel and
the discomfort of foreign places for the record of a disappearing
world. In thus demystifying my research the only justification I can
offer for the role of key-hole Kate is that in learning something about
the lives of others we learn something of our own, which is the naïve
position from which all students begin and at which all too few end.

This book is a record of a disappearing world, the world of the
religious life. It is a gossip about the manners and customs of a group
of people. It attempts some explanation of why women in particular
should dedicate their lives to the welfare of others and the worship of
a God. People continue to seek relevance and reassurance that their
brief years have been well-spent. Religion offers a framework for that
reassurance. There are still a million women living a form of religious life today, celibate, restrained, dedicated to the dogma and
doctrine of the Roman Catholic Church. The nuns I met were representative of a few thousand living in the Western world. Their life
has been subject to the social and technological changes of the
twentieth century; changes which culminated in the meeting of the
Second Vatican Council in the early 1960s. Known as Vatican II, it
was inaugurated by Pope John in 1959 and effected the first major
changes in the Church in a hundred years.

I undertook the study of nuns as a piece of anthropological fieldwork, not clinically investigating through questionnaires but taking

part in the life of the people studied as a participant observer. Ioan Lewis recently described the anthropologist as some sort of cross-cultural private-eye relentlessly pursuing clues to lay bare the soul of his foreign hosts.[2] The presence of an anthropologist has an effect on the host society. The fieldwork experience makes a deep impression on the anthropologist, but few have documented this relationship. The publication of Malinowski's diaries came as a shock to some for they felt that he had based his classic fieldwork techniques on a 'soft' experience. In fact he gives an honest account of his feelings of confinement in an alien culture, of his almost obsessional longing to be back in his own cultural surroundings.[3] Colin Turnbull has, more recently, dramatized his traumatic experience among the Ik, a people struck by famine whose depraved behaviour shocked and revolted him and exposed his own weakness and his altruistic ideals.

Until I began these researches my knowledge of nuns and their beliefs was restricted to occasional encounters in English literature and the history of art and one dramatic meeting when in hospital having my second child. At a crucial point in the labour the midwife appeared. I saw only commanding pale eyes set in a wizened face pinched by the enclosing habit, and heard a voice full of the confidence of years of experience instructing my movements. The nuns gliding down the hospital corridor, like the distant veiled figure walking between the yews, were as foreign to me as African tribesmen. A natural curiosity was intensified by my anthropological training. Later, on hearing that an anthropologist was coming to her convent one sister collapsed into gales of laughter. 'I thought they only studied apes,' she giggled, when she recovered. Not apes, but people, groups which can be as strange to an outsider as any primitive hunters and gatherers, the language unfamiliar, the rituals bizarre, the people shy and unforthcoming.

The relationship between the anthropologist and his 'people' is more complex than that of other researchers. So strong is the identification that anthropologists are frequently known by their tribes, as in Lienhardt the Dinka, Spencer the Samburu. They become spokesmen for their people. When more than one anthropologist visits a field, bitter wrangles sometimes erupt as to the accuracy of data and the importance attached to different aspects of the culture. When the anthropologist begins his researches closer to home, in a Mediterranean village, a factory in Lancashire, a commune in America, the likelihood of his findings being challenged is even greater. He builds up an elaborate methodology, designs questionnaires to cross-check the information he gathered more informally. Constructing a picture of the lifestyle and beliefs of a community is rather like undertaking a pointillist painting. Hundreds of individual contributions are crowded together until in the final analysis all are blended together in the eye of the researcher.

Anthropologists can be distinguished from sociologists by their preference for exotic cultures, by their felt need of immersing themselves in that culture and arriving at a holistic, descriptive account of what makes it tick. They will tend to look for contrasts rather than similarities with other cultures and will concentrate on the interconnectedness of the various social events, economic goals and political arrangements which distinguish 'their' tribe. In support of these aims they may quote Jean-Jacques Rousseau who advised, 'One needs to look near at hand if one wants to study men: but to study man one must learn to look from afar: one must first observe differences in order to discover attributes.' The sociologist, so the stereotype goes, will examine some aspect of Western industrial society with the aid of mathematics, statistics and the computer, thus dehumanizing the whole process and attaining a worthy objectivity. Moreover, he will be unlikely to develop any theory of his own about the how and why of his particular research but will leave that side of things to other colleagues who devote all their time to concept analysis and theory-building.

My researches, and those of many others, do cross the rather artificial frontiers of academic disciplines. It can be a dangerous exercise. I chose two congregations of nuns with the help of an organization in London which advises potential candidates for the religious life. I asked to be put in touch with a progressive thinking congregation. This is the term used to describe an organization of women who have dedicated their lives to God under 'simple' vows; strictly speaking, women cannot belong to an order. The congregation would be engaged in pastoral work. I did not want to study contemplatives who are disengaged from the world. I talked to a bright young nun with a degree in sociology who suggested a teaching congregation which was known to be very progressive and friendly, and as a result I arranged an interview with the Mother Superior of a convent in south London.

It was autumn 1968, wind and traffic churned the dry leaves, a gaunt Edwardian house was set back from the road. All the woodwork was painted brown. The gate-post needed mending, tiles were lifting unevenly in the covered porch by the front door. The doorknocker and handle had been fixed so that you could only enter by ringing a bell and waiting to be let in. I shivered. Footsteps. A smiling girl dressed in a white blouse, blue cardigan and skirt and a short veil almost like a scarf perched on the back of her head stood before me. She was a nun, cheerful, friendly, natural, a total contrast both to my expectations and the house. I was ushered into a large

room on the left of the front door (the key position for the visitors'
room I was to discover later). The room was furnished with comfortable well-used armchairs and a sofa. A piano stood in one corner,
a television in another, above the fire some carvings from Africa, on
a low table some issues of *The Tablet* and a bible. Coffee and biscuits
were brought in and then the Mother Superior arrived. She too was
a surprise, the short veil and wooden cross being the only items of
dress which would have distinguished her from the average smart
fifty-year-old. She wore a crisp white embroidered blouse, grey skirt,
sheer stockings and town shoes. She waved her hands as she spoke
and totally lacked the formality and restraint in manners and speech
which I had expected. But then my expectations were largely founded
on the Hollywood ideal of the sister of mercy and Fred Zinnemann's
portrayal of *The Nun's Story*. After an hour with the Mother Superior
I could feel excitement building up. She was reassured by the aims of
my research. I was not intending to delve into the sisters' very personal
lives, to question their renunciation of sex, or to ask for intimate
details. She would ask the Mother General in Rome for permission
for me to begin work. It was granted. The identity of this congregation and of all the sisters who helped in the research has been disguised. It would be unkind and unjust for anyone to attempt to
identify them, for it was their generosity in revealing the secrets of
their organization which made the research project possible.

During the following year I visited eight different convents within
this congregation. In the first few months I spent many days in the
south London convent attending chapel with the sisters, eating with
them, even helping out in the kitchens. Individual interviews were
conducted often at a moment's notice with no planned questionnaire
but with a framework of questions in mind. The interviews were
tape-recorded when the sisters allowed it. I had already had some
training in the techniques of recognizing non-verbal behaviour and
recording conversations without the aid of a tape-recorder. I built up
a series of verbatim accounts of the life and experience of the sisters.
The minimum length of an interview was an hour, the maximum
length of stay in one convent was ten days. I travelled the length and
breadth of England and went to Rome. At the end of the year I had
interviewed more than fifty sisters of all ages and abilities; many of
them had talked far into the night on any subject concerning them at
the time. With their help I was able to build up the picture to include
life on the missions, and life in Ireland, America and Europe.

It is quite impossible to describe a social situation with complete
objectivity. If that social situation is within your own cultural experience objectivity is even harder to achieve. Religion has such a
hold over the hearts and minds of its believers that it invokes an

emotional response which cannot be ignored. Like so many contemporaries educated in England, I took on the formal bag and
baggage of Anglicanism without becoming heavily involved in the
religious experience, but how was I to record the beliefs of Roman
Catholics with a degree of objectivity? If a Roman Catholic had
studied these congregations of nuns, he or she would have come to the
work fortified with a life-long education in Catholic theology and
Church history. In many ways they would have had a great advantage
over me; the private language of their religion would have been
available to them. They would have had the faith in God shared by
the sisters. But they would also have preconceived ideas about the
behaviour of nuns and the orthodox practice of their religion. I came
as an outsider with a common Western culture but no shared religious experience. The nuns explained their beliefs to me, did I have
to sympathize with them?

Ever since Plato and Aristotle 'drew the battle lines between realism
and nominalism'[4] Western philosophers have debated this essential
tension between worldly (practical, contextual) and other-worldly
(absolutist, non-contextual) thought. When the nun says that God
exists or that the human soul carries on to a life hereafter, it is an
expression of the absolutist nature of Western thought. The anthropologist can answer in the same terms: 'That is how people are. They
think and speak in the ways that I have described.' You do not have
to wonder how seemingly logical, intelligent people can hold such
unflinching beliefs in a deity whose existence can never be proved.
You simply accept it as real for them. This device has a good pedigree.
Kant took belief in God as a postulate which cannot be established on
theoretical grounds. A century later Wittgenstein confronted the
problem of the existence of God with his own 'subtle kind of positiv-
ism'. He said, 'The meaning of a religious proposition is not a
function of what would have to be the case if it were true, but a
function of the difference that it makes to the lives of those who
maintain it.'[5] Like that other Wittgensteinian proposition, 'Language
is its use', the spotlight is turned away from the right or wrong, the
truth or falsehood, the existence or non-existence and towards the
context of the word or the belief. You do not seek the meaning of the
word, you ask for its use. You do not question the belief, you look at
the context. Its use lies in the pattern and rules which apply to it.
Rules are sociological phenomena. Look at another culture or a group
within your own culture and you have no possible means of criticizing
their beliefs. The whole point about miracles is that they are *miracles*.
The sisters would say, 'It is not for us to understand miracles.' All the
outside observer can do is to take this statement in the context of the
religious beliefs of the particular social system in which they operate.

Concepts may not be clear, in which case it is the context which needs reinterpretation. Ernest Gellner alerts us to these dangers. 'The over-charitable interpreter, determined to defend the concepts he is investigating from the charge of logical incoherence, is bound to mis-describe the social situation. To make sense of the concept is to make nonsense of the society.'[6]

The researcher has to be aware not only of where he stands, but of his own evaluations, his own place in the 'field of vision'.[7] The nuns thought carefully before they allowed an anthropologist into their communities. Some of those communities had never before allowed an outsider within the religious enclosure. Neither of the congregations I approached had ever allowed their Religious Rule and Constitutions to be seen by an outsider, indeed Canon Law forbade it. An anthropologist can never give back all that he has taken from the people he studies. He is always, in the last analysis, an exploiter. He can only attempt to articulate theories at a general analytical level where they are not subject to the variability of social action. It is at that level that his findings may be relevant to other institutions. But even theory is insufficient, I believe, for the full understanding and explanation of social phenomena. If sociology is to move from the purely descriptive to an analytic level then a comparative methodology is essential. The comparison must take place within a clearly delineated field of inquiry and a well-defined analytical framework. As many variables as possible are then held constant and independent variables emerge and can be tested. These principles guided my choice of a second congregation with which to compare the teaching congregation.

I looked for a congregation with one startling difference and as many similarities to the teachers as possible. The startling difference was 'conservatism'. The vocation sisters told me that these other nuns were so conservative that I would be most unlikely to gain entry. The Mother House was in England so I wrote directly to the Mother General. A reply came from the Secretary General suggesting I visit the Mother House and explain my research to one of the sisters. That first visit could hardly have been in greater contrast with my visit to the teaching congregation. I drove from London into the well-groomed countryside of southern England. The main gate to the convent opened onto a tree-lined drive. Farmland rolled away into the distance. Figures from a Millet landscape, with long skirts, heavy aprons, heads covered by thick veils, picked apples in an orchard. Several cars stood in the main courtyard of a spreading red-brick house with mullioned windows and low sloping roofs. A small figure answered the heavy ring of the door-bell. She was a young Chinese girl dressed in the working habit of a novice. She directed me to the visitors' parlour. A nun passed us dressed in purest white, head down, hands tucked under her scapular. I waited in a warm, well-furnished room, wood-panelled, thickly carpeted, decorated with holy pictures and mementos from the missions. The window gave a panoramic view of the green hills and trees characteristic of the South Downs. They served as a backdrop to the formal gardens of the convent. An elderly nun introduced herself as Mother Mary Peter, Secretary General for the congregation. She apologized for Mother General's absence, but she would explain the congregation to me and find out about my requirements.

The congregation was a member of the Franciscan Third Order. This turned out to be a crucial factor in explaining their attitudes to changes in the Church during the 1960s. I shall refer to them as the Franciscans, or the Franciscan congregation for easy identification. Like the teaching congregation they had been established in England around 1900, but their main pastoral care was nursing. They now ran several large hospitals and many smaller institutions, such as homes for unmarried mothers, for the disabled and for mentally defective children. Like the teaching congregation they also had missions in various countries all over the world and had grown steadily in number and in capability. But whereas the teachers had felt the need to reorganize their congregation under the impetus of Vatican II, the Franciscans remained virtually unchanged. The teachers earned the reputation of being amongst the most progressive Catholics in England. They radically altered their lifestyle, economic base, governmental structure and even their form of religious belief. Save for some minor alterations in custom the Franciscans preserved all the traditions of their congregation. They remain today in full religious habit, in silence, in enclosure. Although they had felt all the pressures for change both from society and from the Church which their teaching sisters had experienced, they resisted those pressures and are still successfully drawing candidates for the religious life, thriving as a congregation, and carrying on their valuable caring work.

The 1960s had seen the religious institutions of the Roman Catholic Church under greater pressure to change than at any time since the sixteenth century. The promulgations of Vatican II forced them through a period of introspection and self-examination. These institutions, which had survived the post-war changes in Western European society, now had to face internal pressures, originating in the ideas of powerful Catholic thinkers. Why had the Franciscans resisted those pressures, and why had the teaching congregation accepted the call to change to the extent of revolutionizing their organization? Why does one organization respond to pressures for change and another resist? These are not questions which apply only to nuns, to religious orders; they apply to any organization which persists over time and especially over generations of time. The goals established in one era may be irrelevant in another. Numerical growth usually means greater complexity, possibly bureaucratization. I describe the religious organization as a bureaucratic one and I would claim that my explanation of the nuns' responses to change is equally appropriate to secular teachers in schools, to clerks in banks, to the workers in British Leyland or the Ford Motor Company. The religious congregation has the rather nebulous goals of teaching or nursing but this does not invalidate their efficiency in organizing for those ends. It is quite appropriate to compare the foundation of a community of nuns with the beginnings of the Women's Peace Movement, for example. When it won the Nobel Peace Prize in 1977 it was only two years old. It began with the fire and dedication of two women who drew to them the women of Northern Ireland and the compassion of the world. Within two years they had commitments totalling two million pounds sterling. Their movement has seen a meteoric rise in numbers and economic responsibility, but it is comparable to that of the foundress of the Franciscan congregation who began with two nuns in a tenement house and within her lifetime saw a thriving congregation of several thousand sisters scattered over the world.

It would be equally valid to compare the development of religious congregations with similar institutions for secular women. For example, the Mothers' Union, for generations a bastion of Anglican respectability, propelled itself into the 1970s with a new charter. It changed the criteria for membership, admitting the divorced, the separated, unmarried mothers, and even men—thus redefining the aims of its foundress, Mary Elizabeth Summer, who set out to strengthen, safeguard and promote Christ's teaching on the nature of marriage and family life. It now emphasizes that parenthood is not the exclusive concern of mothers. It arranges sex education courses in schools, provides for single-parent families, battered wives and immigrants. The acceptance of new goals and the formulation of a radically new charter and new membership is all part of this organization's response to change in the wider society during the twentieth century. Like the congregations of nuns, it had existed for a hundred years and had survived two World Wars and an economic depression; now it was facing up to the decline in committed Church membership, the break-up of the family and the changing position of women in Western society.

While the Mothers' Union, like the teaching congregation, went for radical change, that other stronghold of respectability, the W.I., celebrated its Diamond Jubilee in 1975 by congratulating itself on how little it had changed. On examination I found that the National Federation of Women's Institutes, which is the full title of the W.I., had been passing radical resolutions since its inception. In 1943 it was demanding equal work for equal pay. In 1927 it was urging the government of the day to 'take necessary steps without delay for stopping the further pollution of our seas and coastal shores and thus removing the terrible menace to the life both of our sea birds and fish'. In 1923 it was drawing attention to child-cruelty and baby-battering, which were as prevalent then as they are today. Now the W.I. challenges the general assumption that women are second-class citizens and demands rights for women almost as vociferously as the more revolutionary 'Women's Liberation' groups. Yet their image and their main concerns are still with wholesome food, corn-dollies and flower-arranging. The possibility that a remarkably conservative institution can harbour such radicalism and not need to change was the primary finding of my study of the Franciscans. They had all the appearance of a deeply conservative institution, yet they remained effective in a changing world. I found that they incorporated certain innovatory elements in their social structure, both in their government and in their ideas, which were lacking in the teaching congregation and which enabled them to make small adjustments and innovations throughout their development and which pre-empted radical change.

Obviously one cannot carry the comparison of secular organizations of married women with the religious organizations of celibate women very far; there are too many basic differences. Despite all my care in choosing the two congregations of nuns I am aware of a certain imbalance in the material collected. In addition to gathering information as an observer I collected historical data in the form of biographies, minutes of Chapter meetings and histories of the congregations written at different times. In the case of the Franciscan congregation I had to place greater reliance on this secondary material for they were less open or willing to be investigated. The imbalance in the empirical data was as much a function of the structure of the two congregations and particularly the degree of change which they had experienced throughout the 1960s as any other factor. On every visit to the Franciscans I was welcomed, given hospitality, and every effort was made to find sisters to be interviewed or material and films to be seen. But I was given neither freedom of access nor the ability to participate in any but a very restricted sense. Attendances at the chapel were restricted to the midday office, and I was strictly chaperoned on visits to other parts of the convent. The congregation, through its Mother Superior, kept a rigorous eye on the amount of information divulged, and religious enclosure was preserved at all times. Given these restraints, I still managed to interview a cross-section of the community and to visit a hospital as well as the main convent on many occasions throughout the year. Mother General permitted me to see the documents of the congregation and directed me to the wealth of historical data on the Third Order of St Francis of which this congregation was a member.

One distinction between the congregations which was clarified by the historical perspective lay in their relationship to the Church. A religious congregation is defined by the Canon Law of the Church; its members have to have Church approval before they can be accepted; its Rules and Constitutions have to have Church approbation before they can be adopted. This 'external legitimation' for the practices of the congregation is the major difference between a religious congregation and a religious sect. The sect contains its own legitimations and relies on no external source. In other respects the sect is very similar to the congregation. Members of a religious congregation take simple vows which are distinguished from the solemn vows of members of religious order by being taken for 'life' rather than 'in perpetuity' and because they can be revoked. Strictly speaking, women who live in religious congregations are called religious sisters or just religious, but the common term 'nun' is used in colloquial speech and writing. Both solemn and simple vows involve the three vows of poverty, chastity and obedience which are regarded as essential to the religious state. A religious congregation may also be called an Institute which simply means that it is an organization with a written Rule approved by the Vatican. Both these congregations were Institutes in this sense, but they were lay Institutes since clerical Institutes include priests. The Franciscans regarded themselves as having a special relationship with the Pope. It enabled them to take a more independent line than the other major orders but it also led to years of unease between the friars and the Church in which many groups (though not the congregation under study) overstepped conventions, were excommunicated and damned as heretical. Excommunication is the Church's ultimate weapon. The excommunicant is deprived of heavenly grace. An expelled religious is automatically excommunicated unless he or she receives dispensation. One of the features of Vatican II was a greater leniency to those who asked for a release from religious vows. Church and congregation could avoid the ultimate sanction and the defector was saved from damnation.

An active religious congregation can never be totally isolated from the world outside. Institutions which do become insulated from the rest of society have been classified as 'total institutions' by Erving Goffman.[8] He has pointed out that modern man tends to sleep, work and play in different places under different authorities and with different co-participants. Prisons, mental hospitals, boarding schools and religious congregations carry out these basic aspects of everyday life under the same roof, under one single authority, in the same company and under a tight schedule operated by explicit formal rulings and a body of officials with the one aim of fulfilling the explicit goals of the organization. This encourages isolationism until the institution becomes insulated from the rest of society. Goffman himself finds many differences and exceptions between the religious congregation and his other 'total institutions' and I certainly find it difficult to accept a description which would see the congregation as totally isolated. It is dependent on the outside world for recruitment of new members, and for economic stability. At times the congregation is strongly influenced by events in the outside world, at other times it remains impervious to them.

In the nineteenth century the teaching congregation had a tendency towards dualism. They arrived in a hostile Protestant England as missionaries. Catholics welcomed them in secret; they dared not wear their habit for it provoked vicious attacks. Their vows were seen by the nuns as a barrier against this hostility and the weakness and temptation in the world. Religious enclosure was a protection from a hostile environment. Even the choice of isolated positions, in parklands or the suburbs, was a protective mechanism. When the sister did meet the outside world, even in her apostolic work, she said a prayer to place herself under the special protection of the Virgin Mary. The position of the visitors' parlour near the outside door was a similar device. It was not reflecting the thorough dualism of a group like the Manichees, it was more a tension between this-worldly and the other-worldly.

The enclosed religious regards worship as the only way of *meeting* the suffering of the world outside. The active religious describes the vows as an expression of freedom which is worked out in terms of tension and temptation. I found that the actual degree of isolation and insulation varied between the Franciscan congregation and the teaching congregation. It was expressed in the boundaries between this world and the next, between life and death, between the nun and the secular world as they changed over time and in response to organizational demands.

The teaching congregation maintained a rank discrimination which never existed in the Franciscan congregation. Their distinction between lay sisters and choir nuns was derived from the earliest orders in medieval times when ladies entered the convent with their maids. Progressives within the congregation and the legislators of Vatican II released the lay sister from the kind of humiliation described to me by Sister Patrick. 'It was terribly hard, the rank. When you entered the chapel and things, you didn't go by age, you went by when you entered the convent and whether you were a choir nun or a lay nun. However young the choir sister was, we were always put below them, no matter how old we were. Sometimes there were girls from my home town, I knew where they had come from, and to think that I had been put below them! You know, it used to hurt me terrible. But I got over it. Other orders would be a lot worse.' However, Sister Patrick found a new life in middle age. She trained as a caterer, wore short skirts and, just as she had accepted the old ways without question—for the love of God—so she accepted the new. Adapting to the outside world did have many unforeseen consequences; some caused great amusement. When the teaching congregation allowed its nuns to wear standard dress instead of the religious habit they left the length of skirt to the individual sister's discretion. A visit to Lourdes by sisters living in London brought problems. What was acceptable in the milieu of working-class London where all the younger women wore thigh-length mini-skirts was shocking to the pilgrims they accompanied to Lourdes. Vice versa, when they wore long skirts which were just acceptable to the pilgrims used to nuns in the traditional habit, their neighbours at home laughed at them. In contrast, the Franciscans consciously retained a distinctive white habit— traditional, yet made from easy-care fabrics. They avoided the various distinctions of social manners and customs which existed outside the convent.

Each convent community is a practising ritual group and its rituals tend to confirm community spirit. It is quasi-familial; Superiors are called 'Mother', the nuns 'sister'. Just as the abbot is the paternalistic figure in a Benedictine monastery, so the Mother Superior is the maternalistic figure in a religious community of nuns. The rituals of the convent do not stop at the chapel door; every mealtime, every recreation time is taken together, mother and sisters. The individual is subsumed in a group identity. In the teaching congregation I met women who had great talents—musical, artistic, organizational— which they had not merely neglected, but actually crushed in the service of their religious life. The Franciscans tended to employ the talents of their members, and the teaching congregation now encourages its sisters to develop talents for the service of the community and pastoral care. But in the traditional convent individualism was cast off with all memories of the outside world as the aspiring nun entered the convent. One of the mechanisms for maintaining the corporate group was a *rite de passage*. The girl shed her clothes, her baptismal name, her legal rights and her freedom of action in a ceremony in which she dressed as a Bride and wedded herself to the Church. A heavy door shut out the world she knew. It could not be seen from windows designed just high enough to be over her head. No communications were allowed with friends or relatives. Religious organizations demand the total commitment of members. They use both alienative and indoctrinating procedures to achieve it. The commitment is normative, that is, there is no utilitarian gain and no coercion—or is there? How do convents arrive at the right choice of girl when they are recruiting new members? Is the decision to become a nun a truly voluntary decision?

Congregations carefully screen their entrants before they accept them for the first of a number of training periods in which they 'socialize' the entrant. She is schooled in the ways of religious society. Entering a religious congregation is a privilege for a Catholic girl; parents are proud if their daughter is accepted. She is especially suitable if she has recognized a 'call from God'.[9] The pride of families and theological justification that you have been chosen by your God leaves the 'voluntary' nature of religious vocation open to question. A nun goes through humiliating and degrading procedures to gain her place in a religious community, but she sees them as aids rather than as punishments. A nun and a prisoner both undergo stripping, abasements, even torture, and the nun sees this process as a means of liberation, of enhancing her better self, whereas the prisoner will find it degrading. Shaving his head will enrage a mental patient, but will be welcomed as the ultimate sign of renunciation of the world and membership of a spiritual élite by a monk. Much of the difference lies in whether society at large considers the procedure opprobrious and stigmatizes the recipient. Entering a convent, at least in Christian society, is voluntary and even honoured. It is reinforced by the sense in which a religious congregation is a collection of virtuosi whose strivings to lead a sanctified life are sanctioned by the Church at a level not considered necessary for the 'ordinary' membership.[10] The practice of ascetic denial grants the religious an élite status in relation to their lay brethren.

To look at the religious congregation through a sociological perspective involves us in a number of issues central to society and to women as members of that society. Today, in Western Europe and America, organized religion involves only a very small proportion of the population, yet it permeates culture and social relations to a considerable extent. The nations' presses still report the opinions of Popes and Bishops, and the findings of inquiries into religious belief. Even modern industrialized man tells the census that he believes in God even if he is tired of the Church. Roman Catholic statistics can tell us that over seven hundred million or 18·3 per cent of the world's population were baptized Catholics in 1977, and that the figures could underestimate the true numbers. There is a tendency for religion to be put outside the tenets of general sociological explanation when studied by theologians or 'religious sociologists'. I hope to harden the case for reorientating religion within the general theoretical and methodological concerns of sociology, which is no more than the classical theorists, including Comte, Spencer, Durkheim and Weber, did.

In both these religious congregations it was not only organization which changed over time but also religious beliefs and their expression in ritual and symbolism. With the radical transformation of the 1960s there was a change in the form and timing of the *rites de passage* which marked the young nun's exit from one world and entry to another. In the traditional convent every hour of the day, week and month of the year, was structured by a religious observance of prayers and services. God was at the top of the bureaucratic hierarchy and could only be reached through exact prayer and the medium of a priest and Holy Rite. With the revolution of the bureaucratic organization in the teaching congregation, God took His place as a member of the small group, symbolizing the cellular structure which had been adopted, and He could be reached without intermediaries. The form and meaning of the Mass—the central ritual of the Catholic Church—changed, with less emphasis put on the sacrificial aspect and more on the communal event. The whole question of the relationship between religion and social structure has to be raised again. The relationship is that of plausibility. There comes a point at which the faith gives way, beliefs become implausible and the society changes. It is a dialectical relationship. Sometimes religion will be an independent variable and in other situations a dependent variable. Peter Berger comments, 'It seems quite inappropriate that ideas concerning the gods, the cosmos and eternity, should be located in the social systems of man, bound to all the human relativities of geography and history.'[11] But in fact it is part of the very function of religion that it has a social nature. It may even have a specific function such as the legitimation of political authority: the Kings and Queens of England have been well aware of that! The universality of religion is due to its social function rather than to some metaphysical validity.

On my first visit to the teaching congregation I had been struck by the appearance and behaviour of the nuns. Not only did they wear ordinary dress, but they travelled, they talked of tourist sights and good food. They grew animated as they talked, they read the daily papers and the latest novels. Where was the constraint of silence and the religious enclosure which I had expected? Was a suburban house to be seriously compared to the traditional convent? The modern house is described by Marcuse and McLuhan as a machine that mechanizes living in a mechanical world. I found every modern convent had a television, every nun was a consumer. John O'Neill is

concerned by the lack of privacy and individuality in 'one dimensional society'. He decries modern architecture for destroying the
boundaries between public and private space. 'In a strange, dis-
ordered repetition of ancient symbolism, the modern household is
hooked into the centre of the universe through its television navel and
suspended by an aerial . . . between heaven and hell.[12] Through the
picture-frame windows of the modern house the metabolism of
family life is projected into the public realm and from there it com-
pletes its circuit back into the home through a magical aether popu-
lated by waxes, deodorants, soap-suds and tissues'.[13]

The way we treat our bodies, the way we organize our houses are
symbolic of our social lives. When the nuns changed their lifestyle
they also changed their convents and they altered their attitudes to
their bodies and to the religious symbols, the rosary, the sacred
heart, which expressed those traditional attitudes. We are not so far
away from the young psychiatrist and the poster on his wall. But I
shall begin in historical time, with the growth of women's religious
congregations in the nineteenth century and the spur of incipient
feminism.

CHAPTER TWO

The Lady or the Lamp:
Nuns and other Working Women in
Victorian England

The religious congregation is not isolated from society at large. The active nun is even dependent on society for her livelihood. More important, the status of women in society affects the nun's perception of her relationship to God, her role in the Church and the aims and direction of her work. When this work is the education of girls it becomes crucial. When, as in the case of the teaching congregation, manners and customs become stereotyped, locked into the past, and the organization entrapped by its own rules and regulations, the imbalance between religious life and the outside world threatens its very existence. Ironically the radicals of the 1960s looked back to their founder, to the austere Augustinian canon who laid down the principles and precepts of their religious life in the 1820s. It is a common enough feature of Church history, where numerous breakaway groups have appealed to the primitive Church for validation. It also makes the character and personality of the founder doubly important in producing many of the features which differentiate congregations. The expectations of women in society, the aims of the founder and the development of the congregation to a consolidated and stable state, either appealed to or mitigated against the success of a congregation in remaining viable and appropriate to the world it sought to serve.

I cannot name the founder of the teaching congregation for it would expose their identity. He was a bishop heavily involved in the laws and work of the Church in the Netherlands. The sisters did not know very much about him; their only biography was a short 'life-story' written by one of the sisters. I found it in the Novitiate, forty or fifty typed pages held together by red string and wrapping paper showing snowmen and angels! The only nuns who had read it were in positions of authority; they formulated future policies with constant reference to the founder's writings. In the traditional convent his notes and writings were read at mealtimes and every sister had an abridged copy of his Rule for religious life. His views could not fail to permeate the congregation despite the neglect of his character and personality—an interesting contrast with the Franciscan congregation which continually speculated on the character of St Francis and delighted in his portrayal in pictures, in literature and in historical biography.

The founder was the only son of middle-class Catholic parents. He was known as a quiet, shy boy, a devout Catholic who was seen teaching Catechism to poor children when he was ten years old. He made his first communion in the same year and was sent away to school. At thirteen he entered a Jesuit monastery. It was a boyhood marked by appeals to the supernatural for guidance. At seventeen he made a novena—a nine-day prayer—to St Joseph to decide on his future. With the approval of his contemporaries and his parents he decided on the priesthood and joined an Augustinian abbey at the age of nineteen. He avoided military service but as his spiritual director said, 'You have been spared service in the Imperial army to enlist in the militia of the King of Kings.'[1] During his year of Rhetoric he was in charge of the acolytes at the altar and lived with the boys in a small house. His fondness for, and appreciation by children was soon noticed, and by the time his preparation as a priest was complete he had decided to dedicate his life to the education of the poor. This ambition was hampered by the official campaign against French-sponsored Catholicism in the Netherlands, which followed the Napoleonic advance through Europe. At the time of his ordination the Pope was in captivity and the Church in turmoil. He began writing pamphlets on religious freedom and the necessity for Catholic education. A society was formed which promoted Protestant books for the education of children which he countered with a Catholic society to put Catholic books within the reach of everyone 'with the object of combating ignorance about religion, causing morality to flourish again, opposing the fatal system of dogmatic toleration which is being propagated more and more, and frustrating plots that are being made against Catholic practices'.[2] His work in politics was recognized by the Catholic hierarchy with an appointment as synodal examiner and titular canon to the city in which he operated. He was elected president of the diocesan commission on education and became an Archdeacon and Dean of Chapter. He first set down his principles of education when he was Superior of a Catholic college in 1825. They give an insight into the man, the educational philosophy of his time and his attitude to his fellow men, all of which are important to the style of organization of the congregations founded by him.

The foundation of a new religious congregation depends on an individual with pioneering spirit and the approval of the Vatican.[3] The earliest Christian groups and the first monks, solitary hermits in the desert, recognized few ties with the established Church and even claimed sacramental powers to themselves. It was to control this proliferation and to keep a spiritual monopoly that the Church insisted on a form of registration. It bound Superiors and abbots of religious houses to its own centralized governmental system of bishops and cardinals. The Roman Catholic Church is a plurality of organizations under one supreme head, the Pope. He rules through various tribunals and offices. Religious congregations are directly answerable to the Sacred Congregation for Religious, a body based in Rome but in touch with its members through local dioceses. Central authority can act to protect the congregation from undue interference at a local level, but it can also control the growth of houses at the grass-roots level—no approval, no funds, no access to spiritual power.

Papal authority does not act in an exactly similar way on each congregation, though there is very little difference between these teachers and the Franciscans. The degree of autonomy allowed is limited by Canon Law and by the Charter or Rule approved by Papal authority. Every congregation has an archive in which it keeps the books of Rules, formal statements of intent and papal pronouncements. The influence of the papacy on congregations is therefore both controlled by written laws and restricted to certain specific areas. But it is backed by the force of Canon Law—the ecclesiastical law governing the conduct of Christians and upheld by the moral authority of the Church. Breach of Canon Law is an offence against God and the Pope; such a 'sin' can lead to expulsion from the community of Christians and the extinction of the soul.

Every congregation has a Superior General who is the embodiment of internal authority but is answerable to the Papal representative for the proper running of her convents. She is elected to office and her election is both presided over and ratified by the Local Ordinary (who is usually a bishop or a bishop's representative with ecclesiastical jurisdiction over a specific, geographically and legally defined area). The dependence of a religious congregation on its local ordinary will vary slightly. Some congregations, like roving Franciscan groups, are exempted by the Pope from his diocescan jurisdiction. Generally Papal approval has to be sought for the establishment of new houses or the suppression of old ones, for the establishment or transferral of the Novitiate or Generalate and for numerous financial transactions. It also has to be sought to depose a Superior General or to dismiss a professed sister.

The founder of the teaching congregation was an Augustinian canon. Throughout Church history religious groups have answered a variety of needs. The great monasteries of the Benedictine and Cistercian orders required large endowments, imposing charters and acts of foundation to get started. In contrast the Augustinian canons came into existence without ritual or formal acts of foundation, and without the obligations of stability, enclosure and special duties entailed in the Benedictine Rule (St Benedict devised his Rule for his monastery at Monte Cassino in A.D. 540). In the fifty years from 1075 to 1125 there was simply a flowering of small groups of men recognizing and following the 'Rule of St Augustine'. St Augustine had not left a formal rule as such but a set of principles. The first 'Augustinian abbey' was established at St Ruf with four priests who came together to live a religious life in a church donated by the Bishop of Avignon. Pope Urban II, himself a Benedictine monk, approved. The Benedictines had taken good care of the supernatural obligations of the religious life; they had played the part of Mary in the Church. Now, with an eye on the primitive Church which had always encouraged both forms of religious life, the monastic and the canonical, the contemplative and active, or Mary and Martha roles, the canons set to play the Martha part, to look to the more worldly aspect of religious life. Their slogan was 'modest services for men of moderate means and moderate needs'[4] and with foundations costing a quarter of that of a Benedictine monastery endowments flooded in and a new movement established itself.

A hundred years later in 1206 an Augustinian canon called Dominic created a great new monastic order. The contrast between the two orders of mendicant friars, the Dominicans and Franciscans, is almost startling, and it can be traced in the differences between the teaching congregation and the Franciscans today. Dominic had witnessed the failure of three Cistercian abbots in Languedoc to combat the Albigensian heresy. He was convinced that they had failed because they never really made contact with the people they had come to protect and convert. He spent fifteen years until his death in 1221 trying to restore evangelism to the Augustine canons and promote an active apostolate. He gave his friars a set of strong organizational principles, clear objectives and strict discipline. The origin of the rosary is attributed to the Dominicans, which in itself is a sufficient contrast with the early Franciscans. The rosary represents the practical reiteration of basic Christian principles in an aided prayer which even the humblest and most illiterate could learn and use,[5] rather than mysticism and the supernatural.

To return to the founder of the teaching congregation we have to leap over five centuries, which takes us over the reformation of Luther and Calvin to the relentless attack on the Church by the rationalist philosophy of the eighteenth century. The 'Enlightenment' notably in France was sustained by a hatred of all the Church stood for—corporate, ecclesiastical and cultural. It culminated in the French Revolution which has been described as 'the most vivid and dramatic instance in history of the destruction—temporary though it proved to be—of a universal religion within a single area'.[6] Something of the strength of that hatred is captured by de Tocqueville: 'something was taking place in France that the world had not seen before. In earlier ages established religions had been violently attacked, but this had always been due to the rise of a new type of religion and the fanaticism of its adherents. ... In France, however, though Christianity was attacked with almost frenzied violence, there was no question of replacing it with another religion. Passionate and persistent efforts were made to wean men away from the faith of their fathers, but once they had lost it, nothing was supplied to fill the void within.'[7]

The dechristianization decrees of 1793-4 aimed at eradicating Christianity from France. The Jacobins expropriated all Church property, terminated all clerical and monastic vows, paid state wages to those priests who would swear loyalty to the new French state and beheaded those who would not. They made all the social, visible aspects of the Church, like marriage, death and baptism, matters for the State and above all segregated schools and colleges from the Church. In fact the attempts by revolutionaries to rid the people of religion and destroy the Church not only failed but had a reverse effect. People clung to their religion even tighter. A new breed of devout, evangelical clergy moved among them. Bishops, no longer caught up in the affairs of state, directed their attentions to the efforts of these clergy and to the direction of their flocks. It was a great time for founding new congregations. In France alone the numbers of women's congregations doubled between 1815-30 from 1,829 to 2,875. All efforts were directed to the great need of the time—schools. The revolutionary governments of France had ordered schools to 'avoid everything that pertained to the doctrine and rules of all religions and sects whatever they may be'. Churchmen understood that in the secular state schooling had become a crucial issue—Catholic children must have Catholic schools. Men like the founder of the teaching congregation dedicated their lives to this end.

The founder's educational ideas remained an integral feature of the educational policy of the congregation until the 1950s. It is interesting to note that Froebel wrote *The Education of Man* in 1826, just one year after the Canon set down his first principles for a Christian education. They represent diametrically opposite views. The Canon saw the child as a wild creature which had to be tamed and trained to be fit for society. Froebel took the opposite view, that a child is born complete and good and it is for educators to preserve those features. The Canon wrote in 1825, 'we must help souls to attain perfection, because they are born in an incomplete state; we must help them to perfect themselves, because they are born partially developed; we must help them to put themselves in tune, because they are born discordant.' While Froebel wrote, 'the child's nature being what its Creator intended it to be, that is, in its essence good . . . what we have to do at first is merely to help its normal growth, by securing for it a proper environment, and by supplying it with, and enticing it to use, the fitting means for the activities which its nature needs for development . . . every precumbering, restricting, encroaching kind of instruction must operate hurtfully upon the normal child-nature, and should be carefully kept from it. I educate children by play.'[8]

The teaching sisters were familiar with their founder's educational concepts. Froebel's educational principles, on the other hand, were slow to take effect in England. The first Froebel Society was set up in 1875 but English training colleges had a very restricted and restricting view of their task and his ideas were not acceptable. The 1930s saw the further propagation of Froebel's ideas through the 'new school' movement of A. S. Neill and Bertrand Russell. But the 1930s was also the age of Dr Truby King and the 'exact science of motherhood'. It was not until after the Second World War that Froebel's educational ideas became popularized and formed an integral part of teaching practice. Only in the 1940s did the first Froebel- and Montessori-trained teachers enter the congregation, to find their training in direct conflict with the aims and practice of their religious training. The educational ideas of the founder were important not only for their ideological content but for the conflict they were to produce in those 'progressive' teaching sisters in the 1950s and 1960s.

The founder said that education was of no value unless it was established on religion and piety towards God. One achieved this end by a system of rewards and punishments, by order and method. Rewards included the wearing of a cross on a ribbon and eating meals at the Headmaster's table; punishments included the eating of dry bread while standing in the middle of the refectory. His philosophy was derived from Fénélon, de Sales and Jouvenci. The study of religion was the keystone of his educational system for he said, 'The fear of the Lord is the beginning and base of wisdom'. He applied education to poor and rich alike, but his teaching congregations grew out of an attempt to help the poor. He established 'lace factories' in which boys or girls could learn a trade, how to read and write, and gain a practical knowledge of mathematics.

The first religious congregation set up by the founder was a brotherhood founded in 1817. The brothers gave poor children bread and taught them to weave while they instructed them in Christian doctrine. Within two years a fee-paying school was set up next door to the poor school and a trend towards the education of the middle classes was begun. Having initiated his plans for the education of boys the Canon turned his attention to the girls and began by estab-

lishing a congregation of women religious. It started in the efforts of
an active, conscientious woman who lived near the Canon. Together
they established a small religious house of dedicated women who set
up a workshop and a school for girls. Soon two other schools asked to
join them, and by 1840 there were two fee-paying schools, a free-
school, a poor house and a house for women working amongst the
poor under the overall control of the Canon. They worked out a
rudimentary religious Rule and a local bishop gave his approval to
this congregation of women who had pledged and dedicated their
lives to God and the education of girls. The teaching congregation
began, therefore, as a diocesan foundation; it was not until the end of
the nineteenth century that it applied for Vatican approval of its
Rule and Constitutions and was granted full status as a religious congregation. By that time the original foundation had grown so large
that it separated into one group dedicated to the education of the
poor and the other—the one I visited—to the education of middle-
and upper-class girls.

The founder claimed that girls should be educated in much the
same way as boys. Girls, he said, should be educated for they were
destined to be the mothers of the future. He wrote, 'The bad education
of women does more evil than that of men, since the dissoluteness of
men often springs from the bad education they have received from
their mothers and the passions with which other women have inspired
in them at a more advanced age'![9] The Christian family, he said, was
founded on the moral worth of the wife and mother, therefore girls
must be educated to fulfil that role. The sisters were urged to consider the example they set the children in their care: 'in order to
make the child good, how good one must be; to make him pure, how
pure one must be!' The founder and his congregations always had a
reputation for friendliness and lack of formality. He wrote to his nuns
that they should show the children 'feeling so full of affection, you
will constantly prove yourselves so penetrated with solicitude for
them, for the sake of God and of their souls, that, in all their troubles,
anxieties and sorrows, they will address themselves to you as they
would to their mother or to their best friend . . .' The display of
affection for children, their fellow sisters and strangers is characteristic of this teaching congregation. It was part of his notion of femininity; the role of women in society was to make domestic life happy
and loving, to be 'the joy and ornament of the home, to maintain
harmony and the spirit of order and economy in it, to give society a
tone of politeness and decency'.

The founder did not neglect the care of the body in his educational precepts. Girls, he said, should have good posture and a cheerful
disposition, they should eat well and dress sensibly. Believing that a

happy soul is expressed by the body, the founder urged his nuns to point out to their charges: 'How badly a gloomy, proud and disdainful face suits a well-bred person and causes unpleasantness, whilst an even temper, a sweet and joyful appearance, a simple, gracious and reserved manner often do more for happiness than the great talents of the mind.' He set out suggestions for graded physical exercises, like a keep-fit manual, to be performed in the open air all the year round. He also set down elementary rules for hygiene and care of the body. By her formative years, say twelve to fifteen, a girl should know all she had to know to take up her life as a mother; she should have sufficient cultural background, and the arts of needlework and housekeeping, and most of all she would have—religion. This was quite advanced thinking, but unfortunately it did not apply in England. The first English house of this congregation was not set up until 1870 and the first school not until 1875.

During the nineteenth century in England the development of Catholic primary education tended to be parish-orientated under the administration of the Bishops, and secondary education became the work of the religious orders. By 1850 there were twenty different congregations of nuns engaged in education in England.[10] The historic teaching orders, the Dominicans and Benedictines, had had schools of long standing but they were all based on the contemplative ideal. A new kind of teaching congregation more fitted to the scientific and technological world of Darwin, Stephenson and Brunel grew up which dropped the strict enclosure, organized themselves on a central basis and multiplied communities all over the country. The Sacred Heart congregation and this teaching congregation were examples of the new-style community; both had their origins on the Continent and aimed to bring up Catholic girls in a Catholic educational system. When the sisters of the 1960s began to question their aims it was as much a response to the new pressures of twentieth-century England as the initial foundation had been a response to the nineteenth.

It is no surprise that the founder's primary emphasis was on equipping girls to be good mothers. In her study of the education of girls in nineteenth-century England, Pauline Marks[11] found that while working-class girls tended to get the same kind of education as working-class boys, middle- and upper-class girls were given a different education from their brothers, one which was considered more 'feminine'. In the first half of the century the daughters of socially aspiring families were taught at home either by their parents—usually their mothers—or by a governess. There were a few denominational schools and charitable foundations like Christ's Hospital, otherwise they were small profit-making girls' boarding schools. There girls

were expected to be 'obsessed with fashion, to develop delicate com-
plexions aided by starvation diets, to improve their posture with aids
like straight laces, back boards, iron collars, and wooden stocks, and
to keep their feet firmly in position while repeating information
learned by rote'.[12] Accomplishments rather than education was the
aim for girls who were to grace drawing-rooms with their singing,
dancing, playing and painting. Their parents' one aim was to make
them a good 'match'. Jane Austen was a good anthropologist!

Certainly the Victorians had an obsessive preoccupation with the
'home'. The rapid growth of industrialization had led to a separation
between home and workplace amongst middle class as well as amongst
poor workers. As capitalism demanded increasingly competitive behaviour from men at work, so increasingly their home became a
status symbol and a refuge to be preserved. The founder of the
teaching congregation was expressing the common values of his
society when he stressed the importance of the mother/wife. Women
were given the special role of maintaining order, keeping everything
and everybody in the right place, preserving the coherence and
stability of Victorian society.[13] Ruskin wrote, 'the woman's power is
not for rule, not for battle—and her intellect is not for invention or
creation, but for sweet ordering, management and decision. She sees
the qualities of things, their class, their places.'[14] Women created this
order by 'being good'. While they could not actively change their
men, they could, by example and passive goodness, save men from
their baser instincts. The 'sanctity' of home was described in a
religious idiom with Bible readings and family worship.

Religion permeated Victorian life, and while there were still many
philosophers who wrote as though the age of religion was over, the
nineteenth century actually saw unprecedented religious revival. In
England, the revival of Catholicism was only one expression of the
resurgence of all those communal, corporate, social and aesthetic
qualities of religion which had been under attack for the previous
three centuries. Nisbet calls it a great irony: 'the fact that the nineteenth century—coming, as it does, hard on the heels of the Protestant
Reformation, the Age of Reason, the Enlightenment, and the Revolution—should be one of the richest of all centuries in philosophical and
literary expressions of religious community'.[15] After the formalism
and rationalism of the eighteenth century there was a return to
mass-appeal, to religious enthusiasm, revivalism and fundamentalism,
especially in England and the United States. The foundation and
growth of the teaching congregation has to be seen in this context.
England and Wales had a population of 20·8 million in 1851, of
which 7·3 million regularly attended a place of worship.[16] While
you might not agree with Marx that 'Religion is the sigh of the

oppressed creature, the heart of a heartless world, just as it is the spirit of an unspiritual situation. It is the opium of the people',[17] it most certainly set the standard of moral behaviour for the population at large. It gave the answer to those imponderable questions of life and death, suffering and success.[18] The founder of the teaching congregation gave this advice to those who cared for his poor children, 'teach these poor disinherited ones to join their hands in trusting prayer, to beg the Father for their daily bread and to count on Providence. Tell them, above all, that Jesus was close to them in the acomplishment of their heavy tasks. Inculcate in them a taste for work, for that useful work which can improve their lot and procure more comfort for their families'. Marx was right, and he was fascinated by the relationship between religion and society. The Jesuits said, 'Give me a child to the age of seven and I'll teach it truth.' The founder of the teaching congregation said, 'on the knees of a mother, truly conscious of her mission, are formed the good men and women so much needed in the world.'

While there was no cultural conflict between the educational aims of the founder and those of early nineteenth-century society there was considerable opposition to the idea of education for girls in the second half of the century. Poor girls, like poor boys, were given a minimal education. In the words of Gladstone this meant '. . . sound religious instruction, correct moral training and a sufficient extent of secular knowledge suited to their station in life . . .'[19] Poor girls were lucky to get any education at all. The aim of all socially aspiring women (quite different from ladies!) was the one-servant household; then they were in a position to make use of the type of education propounded by the Canon. But the aim of that education—marriage—was denied to a substantial number. For various demographic and social reasons there was a surplus of women in Victorian times—girl babies survived better than boy babies, many adult males migrated or died in wars. The position of middle-class and lower-middle-class spinsters and widows was anomalous. An unmarried woman was somehow deficient. If she was not supported by her father she could be in severe financial difficulties. All this has been well-documented in the novels of Jane Austen, George Eliot and other socially conscious writers of the Victorian age. The only socially acceptable profession was teaching. But that was teaching as a governess in a home. Home was not always a haven of kindness and morality, and it was in response to the plight of governesses that the Governesses Benevolent Institution was set up in 1843. It was the first of many institutions which challenged the structure and content of education for middle-class girls.

The Victorian age was also the age of the great reformers, and the second half of the nineteenth century saw substantive changes in education, particularly in the schooling of girls. Girls began to be given the same education as their brothers, and by the 1870s a few were being admitted to the universities; Girton and Newnham colleges were opened. Frances Buss had founded the North London Collegiate in Camden Town, London, in 1850. She was one of the more revolutionary educationalists, believing that girls should have not only the same educational opportunities but the same employment opportunities as their brothers. This thinking brought direct conflict with the more conservative elements in society who saw it as a threat to the 'position of women' as wives and mothers. Anne Clough, principal of Newnham, was prepared to educate her girls for their traditional role in society by simply giving them a better education, while Dorothea Beale, first a teacher at Queen's College, Harley Street, and then headmistress of Cheltenham Ladies College in 1858, sought to remedy the appalling education in existing boarding schools for girls and to educate 'dutiful and piously religious women'. This took the form of a demanding curriculum including mathematics, logic and classics interspersed with the teaching of religion.[20]

By the time the teaching congregation set up its first school in England its educational ideology was more in tune with Miss Beale than with existing boarding schools or the more advanced educationalists. The girls in its convent schools were first and foremost educated to be mothers, but with sound religious knowledge—Catholic religious knowledge—and 'sufficient' mathematics and French. A Catholic writer deplored the education given to girls in England: 'the want of thoroughness and foundation; want of system, slovenliness showing superficiality; inattention to rudiments, undue time given to accomplishments, and want of organization. The reason for all this is not hard to find, with the suppression of the convents at the time of the Reformation, many of the ideals of Christian womanhood had disappeared. Hence respect for the feminine intellect, after two centuries of decline, had now reached its lowest ebb. Girls were no longer offered any serious instruction, for they were deemed incapable of assimilating it.'[21] In fact the French Revolution had the curious effect of encouraging the English to be more tolerant to Catholics. They welcomed refugees from France and the Low Countries. Many of these ran convent schools and the standard of education was, in general, considered higher than that in non-Catholic schools. By the time of the 1851 census there were an estimated 622,619 Catholics in England, or about 3·46 per cent of the population. Not revealed in the figures were the numbers of Irish Catholics, but these were poor and lived in the rapidly expanding industrial towns.[22] They would be lucky to receive any education at all. Growing numbers of Catholics reawakened the fear and prejudice of Popery in the English population. On the re-establishment of the Catholic hierarchy in England (bishops, cardinals, etc.) *The Times* carried this vehement comment: 'each new diocese is an added insult to the English people,' while the Prime Minister made an inflammatory speech on 4 November 1850 expressing alarm that the papacy was infringing the sovereignty of England. Rome's action was, he said, 'profane, blasphemous, and anti-Christian'. The Catholic priesthood was 'subtle, skilful and insinuating, emissaries of darkness' who schemed to undermine English freedoms.[23] This speech was followed by a Guy Fawkes day on which the principal effigies burnt were those of the Pope, Cardinal Wiseman and other leading Catholics. Priests were pelted in the streets and windows of Catholic churches were smashed.

If the reaction to Catholicism was prejudiced and based on ignorance of Catholic practice and belief, the reaction to the growing numbers of convents was equally extreme among non-Catholics. One of the paintings at the Royal Academy exhibition of 1873 depicted a beautiful young girl standing in a niche in a wall, eyes turned heavenwards in gentle resignation. A monk was hard at work closing the niche with trowel, bricks and mortar, while four or five nuns stood by waiting for the immolation to be complete. The scene was taken as reality by some of the visitors, and no wonder, when on the streets outside scandal sheets were sold with salacious titles like *Revelations of a Convent*, or the *Story of Sister Lucy*, in which depravities and horrifying events were retold for the delectation of pious Protestants.[24] In 1872 a Bill was put before the House of Commons asking for 'safeguards for the interests of families, and for the personal freedom of inmates, found necessary wherever such institutions exist throughout the civilized world'. The M.P. Mr Newdigate said that he could produce girls who would testify to being abducted and incarcerated against their will in convents all over France where, he said, the civil authorities were empowered to inspect convents and so rescue these unhappy girls.

When the first four sisters from the teaching congregation arrived in England in 1870 they wore ordinary dress. They had been warned that the religious habit would draw unwelcome attentions. They wore long fustian dresses and cloaks and, in this disguise, set up a house in south London. The local people were hostile and suspicious, but Catholics came and loaded them with presents. There were difficulties with the local diocese. The Bishop would not give them his full support, so they moved to the north-east of England where a sympathetic diocese encouraged them to establish a school. The early years were very hard. The sisters had to endure poverty, illness and the jibes of local people. To make matters worse they did not qualify for a visiting priest as there were only four of them and they had to

tramp over muddy fields and brave the taunts of the locals to go to
Mass. After two years, more sisters joined them from the Continent
and they established a school for about fifty girls and a convent. Soon
they began to recruit young girls in England who were sent to the
Mother House to be trained as novices and teachers and returned to
work in the school and gradually built up the congregation's strength
in England. It was a sense of missionary endeavour, the protection of
their vows and the advice of their founder, which gave them the
determination to fulfil their apostolate. They had to sustain their
beliefs in the face of anti-Catholicism and the charge of anti-feminism.

The nuns had to maintain a balance between their apostolate and
their religious life. Their first duty was to live for God and to strive for
perfection. Perfection in religious terms was the same as 'good' in
secular terms. The only way to achieve perfection, they were told, was
through the Rule. The Rule had been given by the Lord to those who
governed it. Before he died the founder wrote a long letter to one of
the convents in his teaching congregation. It illustrates the importance
of restraint, striving, perfection and the part played by the Rule in the
everyday life of the nun:

> Love your Rule, love the duties of obedience more than your
> health, more than your rest, more than your honour or your reputa-
> tion . . .
> Sacrifice one's personal tastes for the good of all and for the har-
> mony of the whole community; interest oneself in one's task, do
> one's duty to the best of one's ability; always be exact and on time;
> restrain oneself constantly in many things, in words, attitudes; in
> one's bearing, in the innumerable details of propriety, of mortifica-
> tion and religion, in order to contract good habits and not to lose
> them. While forbidding excessive austerities for those who teach and
> giving the requisite and abundantly calculated time to recreation,
> sleep, amusements and small family feasts, one must carefully avoid
> all excess and practice to the letter of St Paul's precept: 'whether
> you eat or drink, whatsoever else you do, do all to the glory of God.'
> One must also take pleasure in living inside one's house, not seek to
> go outside, behave prudently towards outsiders, concentrate one's
> affections within the religious family, so as to preserve oneself from
> divers dangers which weakness and lack of mortification only too
> often cause one to hide from oneself in dealings with the outside
> world . . .

A religious congregation is a closed group. Demands are constantly
made on that group identity. The rule of St Benedict tried to protect
the group by saying that if a monk had to go outside into the world
then he was forbidden to mention anything he had seen or heard

within the monastery walls.[25] The founder of the teaching congregation was full of advice about the dangers 'out there', some of which were very real to the sisters in the nineteenth century. The active religious life was a life in which the riotous self had to be quelled with external aids to the general good and to the good of God; those aids most highly recommended were the vows, a life of prayer and a life of community as stipulated by the written Rule. Obedience was central to the Rule, obedience to the Superiors within the congregation who in turn fulfilled the duties of their office with the same sense of obedience to a yet higher authority until the infinite authority of God was the only Superior remaining to be acknowledged. This was a hierarchy reflected in the Church and in society, and it was reiterated daily in the prayers of the sisters.

In the nineteenth and early twentieth centuries the prayers of both religious and secular believers were devotional, that is, a form of prayer used in prayer books regularly through the year. The weekly exercises are an example. There was a special devotion for each day of the week. On Sundays prayers were directed to the Holy Trinity. This devotion recalled the individual to her place in the whole Church and her possible fate after death. The Rule instructed the sisters that their courage came from the Father, their confidence from the Son, and divine love from the Holy Ghost. On Mondays the Holy Ghost was remembered again as the 'giver of light', the guide to their ultimate salvation. On Tuesdays devotions were made to the Son, Jesus Christ, the 'Divine saviour and spouse'. One of the great attractions of religious life at this time was the word, 'leave the vanities of the world, come to Me and I will be yours. I will no longer call you servants, I will call you my friends; you shall be my Spouses.' (*Constitutions*, 1891). The sisters were spouses of Christ and had to preserve this special relationship through purity and obedience. For purity, special assistance could be counted on from the angels, and Tuesday was given in prayers to them. The founder told his nuns, 'it is to the zealous care of your Guardian angel that you are indebted for having so often escaped the snares into which your imprudence, your rashness, your corrupt nature would have caused you to fall.' The world was full of men ready to tempt or catch the unwary.

Not only the individual but the Institute itself was in potential danger, and Wednesdays were given to prayer to support it:

Protect, most careful Guardian of the Holy Family, the chosen people of Jesus Christ. Keep us, most loving Father, from all pestilence or error and corruption. Be merciful to us, most powerful protector, from thy place in Heaven, in this warfare with the powers of darkness; and, as though didst snatch the

Child Jesus from danger of death, so now defend the holy Church of God from the snares of the enemy and from all adversity. Guard each of us by thy perpetual patronage, so that, sustained by thy example and help, we may live in holiness, die a holy death, and obtain the everlasting happiness of Heaven. Amen. (*Manual of Prayers.*)

There was a strong element of dualism throughout this period in the congregation's history—an element reflected in the isolated rural position of the convents, in the attention given to the boundaries of the community, and in the nature of the interior struggle it was supposed each individual would be having against her worser self. The constant emphasis on the exact observance of the Rule is a feature of this protective, inward-looking attitude to the world outside, and the dangerous elements of human nature. The Saturday devotion re-emphasized the purity of the group and the dangers that lay about it. The sister should thank the Virgin Mary for placing them:

> far from the dangers of the world, sheltered in a sacred home where she reigns as Queen and on which she unceasingly pours forth the most abundant graces . . . Deign, oh most Blessed Mother ever and always to rule and to watch over this flock that thou hast chosen; to defend it always from the attacks of the wolf and in the end to lead to the heavenly Shepherd. (*Founder's writings.*)

The isolation of an active congregation was never emphasized to the same extent as in a contemplative order, but the active sisters played their part in making reparation for the sins and wickedness of the world out there and devoted their Friday prayers to this end. If men were indifferent to God's generosity then the sisters would try to make it up to him.

Friday was the day for devotion to the Sacred Heart, and while I shall look at this devotion again for its symbolic content, it is relevant to our concerns here for its special meaning for women and for personal asceticism. A woman, St Gertrude, first reported hearing the beating of the Sacred Heart. But she was told in a vision by St John the Evangelist that it was a revelation reserved for later times. In 1675 a nun of the Visitation order had a vision in which Christ showed her his open breast in which there was a heart surrounded with flames and asked her for a cult of reparation and love, to be achieved by frequent communion, communion on the first Friday of the month, holy hour and during the octave of Corpus Christi. The Visitation sisters and the Jesuits propagated the devotion until 1765 when Clement XIII gave it official approval. In 1865 this approval was extended by Pope Pius IX to the universal Church. The founder propagated the cult in the early nineteenth century because he felt very strongly that the supreme sacrifice of love made by Jesus Christ (to save the world by his death) had not been fully appreciated. 'The immediate object of this devotion,' he said, 'is the Heart of Jesus with the infinite love of which that Heart is the symbol.' He was one of the first to encourage an active congregation to take on a devotion to the Sacred Heart, though by the end of the century it had spread to almost every religious community in the Church.

In stressing their isolation in purity, in emphasizing the role of the nun as an élite spouse, a member of a consecrated group dedicated to the reparation of the sins of the world, the nun was making a positive step in redeeming an anomalous position in society. Women who were not married, especially Catholic women who engaged in teaching, were much abused and even feared in a social climate which placed motherhood and the home above all else. The dualism inherent in the nun's way of life was a reflection of a society which had elevated the home and the 'chastity' of its occupants—particularly its female occupants—to 'mystical levels of sanctification'. There is an uncanny resemblance between the nun and her counterpart, 'the carefully cosseted married woman (and her forerunner the even more carefully guarded pure, innocent, unmarried daughter) living at home, never going into public places except under escort and then only on the way to another private home, surrounded by orderly rooms, orderly gardens, orderly rituals of etiquette and social precedent . . . in stark contrast to the woman of the streets, the outcast, the one who had fallen out of respectable society'.[27] Women were divided into two groups—the pure and the fallen. The dangers against which the founder warned his nuns were dangers which afflicted their married sisters. But what of the unmarried, of the surplus (sometimes put as high as 40 per cent in the 20 to 24 age-group, though a figure notoriously hard to assess)? The anxiety about the 'spinster' or 'old maid' and the education of girls for anything other than motherhood was expressive of the fear that the symbolic boundary between pure and fallen, home and work, would be broken, not by the employment of women, for they were already labouring in Victorian England, but by the employment of Ladies! When Florence Nightingale refused to marry and began her nursing crusade she flew in the face of conventional manners and morals. In joining a convent the nuns gained a protection which Florence Nightingale spurned, though her purity was legendary.

Biographies of Florence Nightingale reveal the dilemma of a woman unable to realize her potential within the social conventions of the Victorian home. She was not fitted for a religious life which presented the only possibility of a working life for ladies, and she was an 'upper-class' lady. Miss Nightingale recognized in the 'lady' and 'nurses' controversy which dogged her progress in creating efficient hospital organization, that it was the upper-class ladies who were the best equipped to carry out her work. The middle-class ladies had neither the education nor the powerful connections. 'She had never felt handicapped by her sex or wished to be a man . . . statesmen, cabinet ministers, public servants had willingly sat at her feet, and she assumed that any woman who chose to take the trouble could achieve the same position.'[28] Her courage and indomitable will gave spinsterhood a positive value in a society which had sanctified motherhood. The growth of the active women's congregations in the nineteenth century must be seen as much as a result of Miss Nightingale's work as it was of the religious revival, for Anglican and Catholic sisterhoods flourished by the end of the century.

In the nineteenth century the foundation of congregations of active nuns answered both a religious and a secular need. The monastic life of silence and seclusion was not unlike that prescribed by the most modern educators—like Dorothea Beale, for example, who urged strict silence during school hours. 'Great quietness is insisted on; this is not only desirable in itself, but necessary for the community . . . it is almost necessary for the general discipline and it is a means of teaching self-restraint. Surely one thing that women should learn is to keep silence, when they feel inclined to speak; it also helps to form a habit of strict obedience, of conscientious regard for little things . . . it prevents gossiping and enables girls to attend a large school without being exposed to temptations often incident thereto.'[29]

The founder of the teaching congregation died in 1865 and his successor carried on his work. She saw her life's work as the 'bending of children to the religious life'. Her congregation was dedicated to the Christian education of girls. The Rule which received Papal Approbation in 1870 remained virtually unchanged for ninety years. The world-view of the Augustinian canon, legalistic, dualistic, in which the children were incomplete, wanting, weak in the face of temptation, was outdated and even produced conflicts in his nuns which had to be answered by radical changes. In contrast the other congregation, the Franciscans, with a very different style of foundation and a different personality as founder, were not caught in the web of conflicting values. The Canon said that to win souls for an awesome God they must be directed, coerced, taught self-restraint and obedience. He was a man of his times, a protagonist in the fight for Roman Catholicism and a member of the Church establishment. His congregations were both embedded in the social history of their time and in Church bureaucracy.

CHAPTER THREE

The Fiery Furnace of Love:
On Following St Francis

The teaching congregation owed its foundation to a deeply religious man who none the less was a pragmatist. His work had given him high office in the Church establishment where he both defended its dogma from Protestantism and atheism and propagated its doctrines through education. The teaching congregation was, from the start, part of the established Church, embedded in Church bureaucracy and the needs of Catholics in the nineteenth century. The Franciscan congregation had in effect two founders: a young girl, Mother Mary Francis, and an Italian saint whose flame had burned bright through the centuries. Its origins lay in revolutionary action, in mysticism and in an intense 'personalized' relationship with the founder which is described as charismatic. Franciscan congregations are not embedded in Catholic bureaucracy. They owe their legitimation and obedience directly to the Pope. Franciscans put humility and poverty before obedience. They go out to meet the world and join with the sinful, the neglected, the poor. By personal example they bear witness to the love of God. While the Canon had stressed obedience the Saint stressed religious individualism. Their followers too are characterized by a willingness to follow the Canon or the Saint. A woman today who is interested in women's rights may work for the Equal Opportunities Commission or she may join at the battlefront of women's aid with Erin Pizzey, who, in her fight for the protection and shelter of battered wives, confronts bureaucracy and the law with dogged individualism. These are the extreme contrasts between the teaching nuns and the nursing nuns. They both follow a Rule ratified by Canon Law, but in practice the Franciscan revolutionary spirit and St Francis's charismatic appeal has been brought under the control of the Church.

The type of Rule followed by a religious congregation may vary from the highly specific, virtually utilitarian, to vague precepts on spirituality. The Rule encapsulates the 'spirit' of the congregation. It sets out the aims of its existence, the values it should inculcate in its members, and the tone and direction of prayers. It may even recommend desirable personal qualities and behaviour. The stated aim of the teaching congregation in 1891 was for 'the individual perfection of each member of this religious family and the Christian education of children' (Article 1.1891). Each member took the three vows of Poverty, Obedience and Chastity and lived their lives according to the Rule. The teaching congregation had here a very specific aim which remained with it until 1968. The Franciscan congregation followed the Life and Rule of St Francis and the additional requirements of their foundress. These requirements were 'the sanctification of members by the practice of virtues' and to 'co-operate to the spiritual good of souls by nursing the sick, maternity work, the education of orphans and helping ecclesiastical colleges' (Rule 1927). Indeed, if the sisters were on the missions they would be expected to engage in any work required of them. The Franciscan congregation had a much more diffuse and general aim which has carried them through to today. Throughout the Rule that aim is biased towards group activity and the achievement of sanctification through various good works. While the legal precepts laid down in a Rule derive from Canon Law, the particular characteristics, aims and customs which distinguish one congregation from another derive from the founder. Neither St Francis nor Mother Mary Francis were conventional personalities.

In 1917 a young Catholic girl confided to her spiritual director her desire to become a religious in the poorest possible community. The priest did know of such a place; it was a cold, damp house with no bathroom, just a tin bath in an outhouse, and sacking hanging over the cracks in the walls. Five nuns lived there and looked after a bevy of orphans, begging from the local shops for clothes and food to feed them. This tumbledown, heavily mortgaged house was all that was left of a brave attempt. In 1870 a group of women had taken the Third Order Franciscan Rule and, acting as Tertiaries, had begun a mission amongst the poor in the North of England. Out of that group grew a congregation of religious women taking vows. The congregation split several times into various groups providing about ten small houses with very little means of support between them. By 1909 eight of these houses had been suppressed. The one remaining one in Hampshire eked out a living in severe hardship. It was to this house that the young girl made her way. The old sisters accepted her and she began a Novitiate in the tumbledown house. Three of the sisters took to her at once; she seemed to have a special quality; they looked on her as someone sent by God. The other two were less ready to accept a young, strong-willed, shockingly modern girl as the right material for the religious life. But they taught her all they knew and the novice was schooled from morning to night in the harshest conditions, without a fire to dry out by if she was wet, and little food. She had given up a comfortable life and a loving family, yet she welcomed the deprivations of the convent. Like St Francis, she said, she found joy in rain and cold and hunger. Within three years she had taken her vows and she had assumed charge of the orphanage.

Sheer hard work and a dynamic personality transformed the orphanage into a children's home full of happy children well-integrated into the community. That same dynamism brought music to the convent, decorated it in light and bright colours, put flowers in the windows. Within ten years the convent was out of debt and had grown in numbers, and new recruits left for nursing training in London. Older, infirm nuns moved out to a sister house on the Isle of Wight. The young girl, now with the religious name of Mother Mary Francis, was made Mistress of Novices and Mother Assistant. Within another five years it became obvious that more work was needed to absorb all the energies of the thirty-four active sisters who were now working together. Mother Mary Francis suggested that they begin training as midwives. She saw one of the chief evils of society in the breakdown of family life. If they undertook maternity work they could make an effective contribution towards the Christian ideals of marriage and family. In 1935 they began training, anticipating by one year a Papal Instruction which appealed for women religious to work in mother and child care. Mother Mary Francis held up the ideal of spiritual Motherhood which became a basic inspiration for her congregation's religious life. Her followers consider it a gift from God, a specific charisma.

A nursing home was built which set out to uphold Christian ethical and moral principles. But this upset the local bishop who felt that the vows of chastity were incompatible with work in midwifery. He asked the sisters to move their convent out of his diocese. Protestant propaganda claimed that the real reason for nuns running maternity homes was to cover their own 'mistakes'. Catholic bishops who read the scandal sheets still circulated in the 1930s might well have been worried. In fact the relationship between the bishop and the Franciscan nuns was a friendly one; he just stood by his principles. The novitiate was moved out of his diocese and a home for unmarried mothers was opened. By the beginning of the Second World War there were nearly one hundred sisters in the congregation. The numbers continued to grow rapidly and under Mother Mary Francis's guidance they began missionary work and opened convents all over the world. In 1947 the Pope approved a Rule and Constitutions which established the congregation, like other Franciscan congregations, under Pontifical Rite, and Mary Francis was given the title of 'Mother Foundress'. Her inspiration had been the life of the 'Seraphic Saint' himself. From the outset the congregation had a mystical quality to it, alternatively described as charisma or inspiration by the sisters themselves. The choice of apostolic work was almost left to chance. It was always described in the most general terms, but always related to the poor and needy. The choice of midwifery led the sisters to a veneration of the Divine Motherhood; their Rule and their Mother Foundress led them to St Francis.

The story of St Francis of Assisi is too well-known to need repeating at any length. The details of his life and the emphasis placed on various aspects of it vary according to the teller, but invariably involve effusive accounts of his personality. He was born in 1182 of reasonably wealthy parents. In a series of 'visitations' he received his calling to follow Christ and amazed the people of Assisi by stripping naked in the main square. It was a dramatic statement, overwhelming the people with his poverty and nakedness, where before he had dazzled them with his riches and extravagance.[1] At first he restored the fabric of derelict churches, believing that this was his calling. Then he saw the possibility of a deeper meaning and went to the people. Again it was in the form of a dramatic gesture which established him as a saint of the people. He went to the lepers. In the twelfth century leprosy implied a complete separation from ordinary men. The leper took part in a ceremony like the rites of the dead and was banished to a lazar house or a solitary hut. Once a year, at Eastertime, he was allowed to come to Church dressed in a distinctive habit, waving a rattle. He was not allowed to touch anything and people avoided the area where he walked. Various religious orders gave alms and cared for the lepers, but all avoided personal contact. St Francis went to them, touched them, cared for them personally. It was unheard of.[2] It was an action which impressed not only Francis's contemporaries but men of all degrees who lived centuries later. Rudolf Steiner described his visit to the lepers as moral power triumphant over the demoniacal. He saw, in St Francis, 'a human being with a tremendous store of psychic life, in the shape of something which we have found in the ancient peoples of Europe as bravery and valour, which are transformed into soul and spirit and afterwards act psychically and spiritually'.[3] Steiner was describing St Francis the mystic, the idealist, the symbolist, as though all that he did had an inner symbolic meaning. If he went out to the lepers it was because they represented Christ for him. To rebuke them was to rebuke Christ. To love them was to love Christ. The heart of the Franciscan message was 'give up your possessions and go *out* and love your neighbour, whoever he is.'

St Bonaventure was the first to use the word 'seraphic' in connection with Francis. He says, 'Francis came in the Spirit and power of Elias, raised above all human things, and burning with seraphic fire' (*circa* 1265). He was 'smitten with the beauty of Christ; he desired so earnestly to be transformed into Him that his soul became like a fiery furnace of love sending out flames on all sides . . .'[4] The miracles associated with Francis are played down now, but the stigmata had a profound impact in the thirteenth century. St Francis came to his knowledge of Christ through the supernatural, not through laws and theologians. His movement was millennial in the sense that he led men to Heaven through reforms on earth. One group of followers were more directly millennial. Angelo da Clareno, leader of the Fraticelli, said, 'We see the founder himself weared out with his hopeless struggle to save his dream from the shackles of officialdom.'[5] The Fraticelli actually believed that they were the true representatives of St Francis on earth. The early friars were all individualists striving to attain the high ideals of Christian manhood that they believed Christ himself had exemplified. St Francis's first biographer, Celano, describes him as 'herald of the heavenly king' and 'minstrel of the Lord'. He led his brothers against the evils of the world like a 'knight errant from the age of chivalry'. In the early years these brothers were easily distinguished from other monks. Monks led well-ordered, routine lives of fellowship in a monastery. The Benedictine Rule in particular stressed the recognition of self through community. The friars represented a type of religious individualism. The friary was not looked on as a permanent home. There was a marked absence of ceremonial, and absolute simplicity in the living quarters. Sceptical commentators say that the reason no rules about eating and drinking were laid down in the original Rule was that most of the friars were starving.

St Francis had a sense of drama, a charismatic personality and a feeling for his times. He lived in a period of social unrest and religious faith, though the Church itself was in some difficulty. There were two major heresies, the Albigenses and the Waldenses, and the monasteries were corrupt. People went on organized Crusades and long pilgrimages, built huge Gothic cathedrals and paid public penance. Religion was important in an age when the natural and the supernatural were easily superimposed. Reaction to the corruption of the Church and the harsh living conditions of the poor was expressed in revolts, heresies and conflicts. Francis presented a new formula. It did not attack the Church or her dogma directly (the Pope was Cardinal Protector of the Order he founded) but it could not easily be identified with the Church either. This formula was one of humility, simplicity and prayer. It had a special appeal for the young who, nurtured on the medieval romances, had a love of symbolism, mysticism and poetry— faculties St Francis had to offer. In following him they left the misery of the towns and wandered like vagabonds in the countryside. St

Francis sought to reform through individual virtue. It was a message which appealed to all classes, from kings to peasants, but his Third Order had a special place in the religious life of the ordinary people. The social effect of those groups of men and women striving to lead a Christian life was considerable.

In the early twentieth century, there was also a degree of social unrest, and a sharp division between rich and poor. The problems which Francis had attacked eight centuries before were still present. Could moral degradation, cupidity and lack of honesty be tackled by Franciscan example, individual effort and the reform of self? Knowles has suggested that the rediscovery of St Francis in the late nineteenth century was probably a feature of the later stages of the Romantic movement.[6] The upper classes in England and Europe had a passion for medieval Italian life and art. They saw the story of St Francis in the verses of Dante and the frescoes of Giotto and the Italian primitives. His love of nature, the poor and the sick, appealed to their own sentiments. There is a proliferation of literature about St Francis in this period. The young girl who became Mother Mary Francis could not avoid being affected by it. Father Cuthbert, writing in 1899, said, 'St Francis was to fight against the evils of Christian society and deliver Christendom from the dangers that lurked within its own walls.'[7] The evils Father Cuthbert saw in 1899 were commercial selfishness, drunkenness and the desecration of the marriage vow. It was this breakdown of Christian marriage which moved Mother Mary Francis to found her congregation. The Franciscans had worked among the wretched and the poor in the thirteenth century; she was set to make her contribution to the legend in the twentieth.

The Rule which St Francis left was quite unlike either the Benedictine or the Augustinian Rules which formed the basis for religious institutes. His was a spiritual document rather like the Sermon on the Mount. It did not set up a formal, liturgical, monastic style of living but demanded individual sacrifice and presumed constant mobility. Three main groups organized themselves under this Rule, the Friars Minor, the Poor Clares and the Third Order of St Francis which was originally for lay people in family groups. The Franciscan missionary sisters took the vows of the Third Order, not those of the Poor Clares. Groups of men and women had always lived around the Premonstratensian Canons and the Benedictine monasteries and there were the Humiliati and the Poor Catholics who lived a life of penance. The Franciscan rule recommended a simple style of dress, moderation in food and drink and a rich prayer life. The ideal Franciscan was portrayed as someone who loved his neighbour above all else, who had a peaceable disposition, who would be prepared to sacrifice taste, will, ideas, even life if need be. St Francis's Rule was very much open to interpretation, which was both a strength and a weakness. The history of the Franciscans through the centuries is a history of reform and modification. The recent history of the Franciscan sisters founded in 1917 is likewise a history of modification of aims, or organization, yet they retain the value of sacrifice, of 'the fiery furnace of love'. The congregation is subsumed under the personality of St Francis. It is as though he still lives to cast his personal magic over his followers.

The term charisma has today a popular usage which bedevils its value as a precise descriptive word. In Christian vocabulary charisma is a gift from God, a grace, an inspiration. When Max Weber began his sociological definition of charisma he began with St Paul's Epistle to the Romans. 'The gifts we possess differ as they are allotted to us by God's Grace and must be exercised accordingly; the gift of inspired utterance for example, in proportion to a man's faith; or the gift of administration, in administration.' Such was the Church's monopoly on the supernatural that it could not afford rival mystics. By recognizing special qualities and bringing them within the general orbit of approved Grace, it was able to control potentially disruptive elements by labelling them charismatic and semi-institutionalizing them. The rebel's impact is diffused by being given official approval, whether it is the canonization of St Thérèse of Lisieux or honours handed out to popular entertainers. In the Franciscan congregation special talents were used to the full, where they belonged to artists, singers, academics, administrators; they were all seen as God-given. In the teaching congregation special talents were crushed, buried with the 'life outside'. In the Franciscan congregation charisma operated alongside other forms of authority, traditional, legal. It was the secret of St Francis's success. Other rebels had scoffed at the pomp and circumstance of the Church and the monasteries but they had been labelled heretics and rebels and failed to make any appreciable impact. St Francis accepted the legal authority of the Pope. He did not lose the power of his charismatic authority, and he operated within the bounds of the legal authority of the Church. He was then acknowledged as part of the wider society. Or, from the point of view of the Church, itself founded on charismatic authority, the inherent strains in the legal authority structure of the Papacy erupted in the person of St Francis, who criticized that authority. The conflict was resolved by rationalizing the source of conflict, by introducing a change in its own structure, by creating the mendicant orders.

Religious orders are essentially bureaucratic organizations in which offices, officials in administration and the Rule and Constitutions have their authority 'legitimated' in a number of ways. These have included the external legitimation of the Roman Catholic Church; a belief in the absolute value of superiors' demands (nuns will go anywhere without questioning); a belief in the legality of commands, and an affectual commitment to the God to whom members' lives are dedicated. Weber distinguished three 'pure types' of legitimate authority according to whether authority claimed legitimacy on rational, traditional or charismatic grounds. Rational authority, as contained in a system of rules independent of the personality of the office-holder, can only be seen in the context of the office from which it is derived. For example, a Novice Mistress who is appointed for a term of three years loses all authority over novices once her term of office is over. Traditional authority is owed to the person who occupies the traditionally sanctioned position of authority: the Pope or the founder of an order whose authority is bound by tradition. Charismatic authority demands of each follower an individual belief in the charisma of the leader. Weber's essential contribution to the definition of charisma is that charismatics are individuals who are *perceived* by a group of followers to be charismatic.[8] The charisma of St Francis depended on recognition by his followers. The Mother Foundress of the Franciscan congregation was described as having divine inspiration, grace, charisma, exemplary qualities of personality. A bureaucracy is primarily concerned with the operation of legal or rational authority. A Mother General in a religious congregation expects her directives to be carried out by those who receive them not only because she holds the office of Mother General but also because traditionally Mothers General are obeyed. In the Franciscan case the Mother General is obeyed because she also has a degree of personal charisma. It is the degree to which traditional and charismatic elements are interwoven with legal/rational authority which distinguishes Franciscan organization from other organizations and particularly from the Augustinian-based organization of the teaching congregation. The degree of charismatic authority is crucial to the Franciscan capacity for innovation.

In his initial analysis of charisma Weber defined it as some boundless, limitless authority. It was extraordinary, a total contrast to the 'rationality' of a permanent bureaucracy.[9] Charisma, he said, is a highly individual quality, its powers limited by the bearer and his mission alone. In fact it cannot be totally limitless because charismatic leaders can also fail. In the same paragraph Weber labels St Francis and a pirate as charismatic rulers, each spurning rational methodical methods of economy. Pure charisma, flowing from the personal strength of its bearer, is seen when proved by the making of miracles, the winning of battles or generally bringing 'extraordinary well-being' to followers. The key feature is the recognition of charisma by others: 'whether it is more active or passive this recognition derives from the surrender of the faithful to the extraordinary and the

unheard-of, to what is alien to all regulation and tradition and therefore is viewed as divine . . .'[10] St Francis had been a leader before he
began his extraordinary acts. He was already idolized by the young
people in the town in which he lived and had even led a group on a
crusade. It was with the attention of everyone on him that he re-
nounced his worldly belongings, stripping naked in the town square,
emphasizing his 'divine' inspiration to lead a different crusade.
(Norman Cohn tells us that 'streaking' was a device frequently used
by charismatics. It was an expression of disgust with worldly values.
Bockelson, the Anabaptist leader, made as his first public act a frenzied
naked run through Munster which he followed by a three-day silent
ecstasy.[11]) Francis was a dangerous personality. He persuaded men to
change their ideas as a direct response to their relationship with him.
Charisma revolutionizes men from within, unlike bureaucratic change
which must revolutionize by technical means, from without. This
does not imply any psychologism, merely that charismatic leadership
has a revolutionary potential which does not rely on external pressures
or some rationalization of positions.

Charismatic leaders are supported by a social structure of charismatic domination: they have a personal staff of ultra-loyal adherents.
Sometimes this even blocks the spread of charismatic appeal. Jesus
and his disciples are an obvious example. The relationship between
leader and followers, particularly in the 'inner circle', relies on a
sharing communistic ideology and economy. It is inherently unstable.
Once any materialistic bias creeps in and the effectual base is lost, the
relationship between leader and followers is transformed. The conflicts in the Franciscan order can be accounted for by the accumula-
tion of material possessions and institutionalization associated with
Brother Elias, the second Superior General. Many small groups
begin to fail when they accumulate property and possessions. The
followers of a charismatic inevitably try to retain their collective
excitement and seek ways of doing so. At once the 'purely' charismatic
relationship is lost and conflict arises. The followers of a war leader
form their own state, the followers of a prophet form a sect, the
followers of St Francis formed a religious order.

Is there any possibility for a continuity of charismatic domination
even over generations? Weber would say yes, for charisma is not entirely lost, it is transformed. In some cases it may even be transformed
beyond recognition, but it will be identifiable at any analytical level.[12]
What happens when the original leader dies? A successor has to be
found. In a bureaucracy a top man probably moves into the leadership according to certain general rules. Where the leadership has had
a considerable degree of charismatic authority the election of a
successor is virtually impossible. See what happened in China when

Mao died! What is possible is that a successor is seen to have some charisma. In choosing a set of attributes which can be defined as charismatic the followers are already on the road to transforming the charismatic authority of leadership into an institutional mechanism.[13] The dying leader might elect his successor, as in the choice of St Peter by Jesus, and the new leader is acknowledged by the followers. Or there might be an organized search for a new leader, similar to that for a replacement traditional leader, a new king when the old one has no outright successor. But this inevitably causes delay and stress to the already loose confederation of followers. They may resort to divine revelation, oracular divination or even the acknowledgement that charisma is hereditary by blood or by magical means. The divine kingship of the Tudors and Stuarts was claimed by blood-relationship and by the ceremony of coronation with all its magico-religious symbolism. Weber pointed out that the symbolic expression of apostolic succession in ordination and episcopal ordination, which includes coronation and annointment, has become more important than the underlying concepts. 'Here we find that peculiar transformation of charisma into an institution as permanent structures and traditions replace the belief in the revelation and heroism of charismatic personalities; charisma becomes part of an established social structure.'[14] This is the charisma of office.

The charisma of office contains two essential ingredients: firstly, the notion that the original leader, acting out his special powers and acting upon the personal loyalty of his followers, imbues the leadership of his group with some special qualities; secondly, the notion that these special qualities are retained in the institution and survive a number of different encumbents. One of the most radical forms of the depersonalization of charisma and its transformation into a qualification is the Catholic theory of the priest's *character indelebilis*.[15] A priest is established in office by the performance of a magical act which confers on him the magical qualification of forming sacraments from consecrating bread and wine. In the thoroughgoing bureaucracy of the Church this magical qualification rests in the office of priest; it is a transformation of the charisma of Jesus Christ. It also protects the Church from the possibility of a depraved personality polluting the organization. In a religious organization the personal charisma of the original leader is carried in a symbolic system which includes the sacred, the magical and the mystical. The Franciscan congregation show every visitor the relic of St Francis on display in their chapel. Like a fragment of the true Cross, its authenticity is undoubted and its magical qualities are as real as any tribesman's amulet.

The history of the Franciscan order is rich with mysticism and magical confirmations of decisions taken and organizations set up. The first Rule, of which no copy exists today, was confirmed by Pope Innocent III in 1209. He reached his decision after delaying a number of days until a strange dream revealed it to him.[16] Twelve men took the tonsure and the Franciscan order was born, dedicated to live like the twelve apostles (note the number twelve!). St Francis had had a dream which he related to his 'apostles'. 'Take courage, beloved, and rejoice in the Lord, and be not sad because you seem to be few. Nor let my simplicity nor your own, dismay you, for the Lord has revealed to me in truth that he will make us grow into a great multitude and will give us a great increase even unto the ends of the world ... I have seen a great number of men coming to us and wishing to live with us in the habit of a holy life and under the rule of the blessed religion ... I have seen, as it were, the roads filled with the multitude of them coming together in these parts out of almost every nation.'[17] His dream came true. There were 5,000 friars at the pentecostal chapter of 1222. But conflicts and dissensions were already racking the order. The instability of charismatic authority was tested. Francis, by now a sick man, fought to keep control.

The main problems were with poverty, privilege, study and the priesthood. Francis had wanted his flock to subsist under the very poorest conditions, but the numbers were now so huge that local leaders would not be held responsible for keeping men under starvation conditions. They said they needed proper food and clothing if they were to carry the message. The growth in numbers had attracted men, leaders, who wanted authority to exercise their leadership, but Francis insisted on one rank only. The priest-friars wanted altars, books and the other trappings they considered necessary for performing the sacraments; up to 1221 they borrowed these from parochial clergy. Other men, attracted to the order by its simplicity and poverty, wanted to combine preaching and study; they needed books and a quiet place to read. To Francis the ideal frair was 'idiota et subditus omnibus'; if a learned man wanted to enter the order then he should cast off his learning as Francis had cast off his clothes. Study, Francis felt, would erode not only his supreme poverty but his humility too, for the illiterate and simple would be bound to look up to a learned man.

Francis lost his case in Chapter, and the Rule which was confirmed by Pope Horonius III in November 1223 remains the official Rule of the Order to this day. Francis lost to the great numbers of men he had attracted and to the established Church. The towns were getting edgy about the numbers of mendicants and put pressure on the Church to take some action. In 1217 a provincial structure was organized by the Vatican in which Italy was divided into six provinces and a minister appointed by the Pope from among the leading friars to take charge in each area. France was divided into two provinces, and Germany, Spain and the Holy Land each had a minister in charge. Decrees were passed to define the authority of these ministers, methods of appointment and dismissal, and their relationship to Francis. It was these eleven men who forced through the Rule. They were led by Ugolino who was later to become Pope Gregory IX. In 1223 the provinces were further divided into custodies. The network of organization was growing and tightening and large friaries were established—a far cry from the small rock-hewn hermitages of the original followers. Francis's response is interesting. He retired to Mount Verna, where, in 1224, he kept vigil, until he came down to his brothers with the stigmata and more visions, divinely inspired, on which he based his Testament. The Testament was to become a crucial document on which the call for reform and subsequent splits in the order were based. It was a document which embodied the charisma of Francis.

Remembering that in medieval times the line between the natural and the supernatural was very vague indeed, the immediate acceptance of the visions and the stigmata by the public is not surprising. Indeed, it confirmed in people's minds the succession of Francis to the original Christian charismatic leader—Jesus Christ. With the stigmata he became a living image of Christ crucified. The impressive symbolism contained in this image was a weapon with which to face the opposition. The stigmatized Francis was a highly dangerous man to the Church. His charisma was very powerful and even though he died within the year, his personality, after death, could attract followers. In terms of the 1221 Rule this was now a deviant charisma—he wanted to lead in the 'wrong' directions. When Francis died in 1226 the Vicar General, Brother Elias, announced his death and described the stigmata. This confirmed the legend for the world. The successor to Francis as leader of the order was Brother John Parenti, a supporter of the clerical party. He was one of those who had allowed privileges to grow and encouraged the students. Meanwhile, Brother Elias with the help of Cardinal Ugolino was setting up a shrine to Francis at Assisi. In 1227 Ugolino became Pope and in 1228 Francis was canonized; a foundation stone for a huge Church was laid at Assisi, and Thomas of Celano was invited to write a life of the saint. Elias was kept busy sanctifying the saint, while John Parenti and the Pope ensured the smooth running and proper control of the vast numbers of men in the Franciscan organization.

Canonization brought the extraordinary events of St Francis's life under the general umbrella of the Church and at the same time defused the emotive appeal of the rebel leader. Etzioni has made the point that character assassination and canonization are similar processes working in opposite directions. In the case of St Francis, canonization channelled the interests of his followers in the direction approved by the Church. The authority of the Testament was officially declared as only of secondary importance; the commissioning of an official biography and the building of a great Church and shrine which would be visited by the faithful controlled the 'dangerous' elements. 'Devotion to the charismatic symbol is rechannelled to the organization and its goals.'[18] Canonization, like character assassination, manipulates the public image of the charismatic.

St Francis was canonized within two years of his death. The Church now waits fifty years before conferring canonization. The delay is both a control on the exploitation of canonization by deviant charismatics and an effective instrument for institutionalizing certain types of personality.[19] Today the most important elements of sainthood are the 'natural virtues' of 'prudence, fortitude, strength of soul, temperance and justice'.[20] The miracles and mysteries which were the stock in trade of charismatics take second place. The saint symbolizes the organizational values of the Church. The personality of the saint even becomes a 'model personality' for socialization. The history of the Franciscan order and the fate suffered by various biographies of the saint, emphasizes this form of manipulation. The order was plagued by dissension and even at times open riots and fighting. The problem lay in Francis's insistence on his personal and charismatic appeal as the sole source of legitimation for his movement, an insistence which took no account of the huge numbers he had attracted and the threat they presented to both Church and society. Francis's first Rule (his own, not the one ratified in 1223) was little more than a few guiding principles which he had chosen by opening the Bible at three different places and making a random selection. He appealed to the supernatural for legitimation. The basis he had chosen was poverty, healing and preaching to the poor. To become a friar a man would have to give up everything and live a life dependent on others. He worked on the premise that if a man laboured in the fields then he would be given food to eat. There were no rules about fasting or prayer. In his Testament, which he drew up while achieving the stigmata, another appeal to supernatural legitimation, he urged his brothers never to seek Papal authority for alteration to his Rule. The Chapter of 1221 in which a Rule was given Papal approval, in which even corporate property was allowed, both defeated Francis and paved the way for the feuds of the next two hundred years.

In comparing the Franciscans with the Benedictines, Michael Hill comments that the relative stability of the Benedictine order is due to the Rule and the Order being virtually synonymous. Any change that has to be made in the organization of the Order can be legitimated by an *ad litteram* interpretation of the Rule without provoking conflict.[21] The Franciscans never really made up their minds about the Rule and any appeal to legitimation from it invoked a conflict situation in the Order. It was only when splinter groups were given official recognition, first the Observants and later the Capuchins, and when the 'spirit' of the Franciscan ideal was finally incorporated in the institutional framework of the organization that stability was achieved. Charisma had been routinized, transformed in the Weberian sense, and incorporated in the office of Superior General as a valid source of authority and a potential legitimation for social change.

Legitimation is an agreement between the bearer of authority and those over whom it is held and who obey. It is 'the primary link between values as an internalized component of the personality of the individual and the institutionalized patterns which define the structure of social relations'.[22] Any such relationship is open to manipulation and change. It follows, therefore, that the legitimations of authority are also liable to change, or may have an element of change built in. Consensus on the agreed image of authority will vary in degree and intensity. Pressure groups build up who find their image disagreeing with their perception of reality. In religious congregations the initial values undergo slight changes as they become institutionalized and bureaucratized. Dissident groups clamour for changes which will retain the purity of those initial values. In the Franciscan order it was first the 'spirituals', made up of remnants of the first followers who called for a return to original principles. Later John of Parma tried to restore the Testament as a principle guide.

The source of legitimation will discriminate between different types of authority and changes in that authority. In the case of legal authority, where obedience is owed to the legally established impersonal order, change will only occur when the legal blueprint can be seen to diverge sufficiently from the values and norms it upholds for a dissident group to emerge and challenge the legitimacy of that authority. In the case of traditional authority, where obedience is owed to the person of the chief who occupies the traditionally sanctioned position of authority, change will occur when the chief subverts his position. Where the traditional authority rests on notions of precedent, these notions themselves can provide a basis for change independent of personality. In the case of charismatic authority, where obedience is based on personal trust, the only restrictions are the beliefs in charisma and the situation in which charisma operates. A leader in such a position can institute any change provided he retains his charismatic influence. An organization which retains charismatic legitimations for its authority structure retains the flexibility to innovate.

It was, then, the conflict between the legal authority of the 1223 Rule and the charismatic authority of St Francis which troubled the Order in its formative years—a history of conflict exacerbated by the Order's relationship with the established Church. The call to a life of absolute poverty was not new to Francis. It was a call put out by other schismatic and critical sects. Indeed the identity between radical Franciscans and heretical sects did much to provoke hostility. In the 1250s the Franciscans became associated with the heretic Joachim of Fiore. Joachim wrote a history of the world depicting three stages:[23] the Age of the Father (Old Testament), the Age of the Son (New Testament), the Age of the Holy Ghost, when men would really understand the meaning of the scriptures. The new age would be preached by an order of barefoot monks who would succeed in destroying the Anti-Christ, an event scheduled to take place in 1260. The Trinitarian aspect of this prophecy had already been condemned by the Lateran Council of 1215 when a Franciscan monk published the *Eternal Gospel* which described the role of the Franciscans in its fulfilment. This really alarmed the Papacy, and John of Parma and his group of spirituals were forced to resign the leadership of the 'barefoot monks'. St Bonaventure was appointed successor and he set out to place the affairs of the Franciscans in a stable and harmonious relationship with the Church. He began by publishing a new biography of St Francis. Called the *legenda major* it effectively wiped out the personal memories of the three companions, Brothers Leo, Angelo and Rufino, and the legends of Celano. It restricted the saint's biography to 'acceptable' events.

The Church was understandably anxious to control not only the spread of an unruly, anti-establishment organization, but also the use of charismatic claim to legitimacy; particularly one which was so similar to its own. However there was one important difference. In the early history of the Church of Rome there was no doubt in people's minds of the authenticity of the Pope's authority. Not only was the fusion of St Peter with the office of Pope managed successfully but St Peter himself had an excellent pedigree. According to the Gospel of St Matthew, the Messiah, the Son of God, had said to him, 'You are Peter, and on this rock I will build my church, and the powers of death shall not prevail against it. I will give you the keys of the kingdom of heaven, and whatever you bind on earth shall be bound of heaven, and whatever you loose on earth shall be loosed in heaven.'[24] The disciples were not only commissioned to carry the charismatic message far and wide, but they were given an appointed leader. St Peter in turn left his followers in no doubt of his succession.

In A.D. 34 he became bishop of Antioch, and in A.D. 40 he moved to Rome. By A.D. 57 he had instituted the fasts of Advent and Lent and in 59 he consecrated Linus and Cletus his successors.[25] In those days not only were the historical facts undisputed but there was the bodily presence of the Saint in Rome, even after his death. 'The body within the tomb, which would one day clothe the door-keeper of heaven, was the link between the presence in heaven and the church on earth.'[26] Men came to Rome to visit the body of St Peter and prostrate themselves before his 'persona' on earth—the Pope. Unfortunately for the Franciscans this transformation did not take place. The cult of St Francis in many ways prevented the depersonalization of his charisma and its routinization in office. The loyal followers even blocked the working of charismatic authority. His living memory made it virtually impossible for the vast organization he had left behind to remain unified. Only with the death of the original charismatic group and the eradication of their memories was the charisma brought under control, and even then the Testament remained.

The charisma of St Francis was dysfunctional for his organization and dangerous to the Church. Joachimism had revived the volatile and unmanageable elements of the Franciscan legacy. From the Church point of view the Franciscans had to be contained because they were a living reminder of the early Christian groups and their ethic of poverty and self-denial. Poverty, for Francis, was an ideal, something to be aimed at as an end in itself, a basic prerequisite for the Franciscan life. Francis had glowed with a vision of a world movement but he lacked the organizational ability to carry it out. His rival Dominic, on the other hand, who founded the other great order of mendicant friars on Augustinian principles like those of the teaching congregation, had exceptional organizational abilities. The legal rational aspects of the Dominican order have been recognized by constitutional historians as a model for democratic constitutions in secular states.[27] Dominic deliberately based his organization on the university towns, which were the intellectual and urban centres of Europe. There he reached the people in poverty and established an intellectual supremacy for his friars of whom St Thomas Aquinas was the jewel. Charisma plays no part in Dominican organization. Dominic was canonized because he was an exceptional cleric, not because he was a stigmatized charismatic leader whose authority needed to be channelled to the Church's advantage.

Dominic was canonized in recognition of his work on behalf of the Church, as an ideal for others to follow. Francis was canonized to tame his potential as a revolutionary. Contrary to expectations the great majority of saints were clerics, successful bureaucrats, holders of the 'ideal qualities' of Church and society.[28] In his book on altruistic

C

love, Pitkim Sorokin points out that the type of man who is canonized varies through the centuries with the demands of the Church. When hard pressed, its martyrs are those who actually gave blood for their faith; when times were more stable and the supremacy of the Church established, the eminent executive is accorded the honour of canonization or martyrdom. Once canonized, the saint is ensured a certain place in the remembrances of the faithful.[29] Images of saints are manipulated, lost, revived. They are not impermeable to change but they are established on the Church's rolls. St Francis's modest hut may have been buried under the splendour of the Basilica at Assisi but his message was kept alive in the pilgrims to his shrine. The personal appeal of the saint is alive today in certain Franciscan nuns and friars. His written testament remains a valid legitimation for changes and revivals and by this authority small groups of religious can still, legitimately, set up convents and friaries in remote corners of the world without the constraint of an overbearing organization.

The history of the Franciscans in England is relatively peaceful. Apart from the theological school at Oxford, the friars lived in very dilapidated houses and tramped the countryside barefoot and ill-clad.[30] When they did take on land and buildings it was only sufficient to grow fruit and vegetables, and the buildings were cheap. They always carried a small breviary with them so that they could fulfil their religious obligations on the road. Today every Franciscan missionary sister who leaves the convent is presented with a small, light-weight breviary. The Franciscan historian John Moorman has said that the Franciscans in England remained closer to the original ideals of St Francis than others throughout their development. They were largely from the Capuchins and Poor Clares who had always claimed to be the true heirs of the Franciscan message. By the time Henry VIII began the dissolution of the monasteries many of the friaries were in an appalling state of decay and they just quietly disappeared from the English scene. It was only in the nineteenth century that they were able to move back. When they did return, each separate branch of the order had stabilized and had its own version of the Franciscan message to deliver. Each kept the 1223 Rule but published it alongside the Testament. The very vagueness of these two documents assists today's friars in living a religious life adapted to the needs of the twentieth century. More importantly, the charismatic authority of St Francis has successfully transformed the office of Superior General, in whatever order it operates, to offer additional scope to the traditional authority.

As we have seen, Mother Mary Francis was recognized as an exceptional personality from her first entry to the tumbledown house in the south of England. From the start she was an undisputed head and innovator, she interviewed every new recruit to her organization personally and directed every new foundation and new apostolate. Even the special relationship with the Pope was reflected in this Franciscan congregation. It was established by Pontifical rite in 1947 and when the Mother Foundress celebrated her Golden Jubilee as a religious sister in 1970 she was awarded the Cross *Pro Ecclesia et Pontifice*—the highest Papal award for which a woman is eligible. Her congregation had grown with a speed which equalled the original Franciscan order, and still the Mother Foundress visited every convent, hospital and mission scattered all over the world. In a tribute to her energy one of her sisters wrote, 'behind all these enterprises is our Mother, her spirit informing the works, inspiring the Sisters who undertake them.'

The Mother Foundress's place as Superior General of the congregation was taken by another sister in 1970. The succession was clear and unambiguous. She was chosen 'because she is born of your (Mother Foundress) spirit, which is ours too'. This successor was the Foundress's first novice, her first successor as Novice Mistress and first Vicaress General. All the problems of succession to a charismatic leader were mitigated by this choice. The new leader was one of the original charismatic band, singled out for succession from the earliest days, yet with a reputation of her own as a builder of hospitals, competent, reliable and in tune with her foundress. In the few years since her succession the Mother General has achieved her own style of leadership, one based as much on personal charisma as on constitutional right. She established herself 'taking all hearts by storm, born with healing in her wings and peace in all her paths'. She personally supervises every new foundation, from the humblest field mission to the building of enormous hospitals in Australia and Singapore. She knows every postulant who enters the Novitiate. She is a formidable presence in council, and in Chapter it is her authority alone which allows any marginal activity or possible 'bending' of the Rules. This is a Mother General who spends a large part of every year travelling the world, yet knows every nun under her care personally. Her style of government is in complete contrast to that of the teaching congregation, where the Mother General is a fairly shadowy figure who lives in the Generalate and makes triennial visitations to the larger convents in her care.

In the Franciscan congregation the Mother Foundress is still alive but there is no conflict between her charisma and that of her successor. She plays no part in the government of the congregation. She writes occasional articles for the magazine but she has retired from active life completely. Her role now is in prayer and intercession with God. She is at one remove from the real world, interceding with the supernatural world beyond and in no conflict with the present leader—in such contrast with St Francis. Her charisma has been channelled both into the office of leader and into the religious goals of the organization. The potentially disruptive nature of charisma is controlled, but its innovatory possibilities enable the congregation to achieve a flexibility and mobility characteristic of the early friars and well-atuned to the twentieth century.

CHAPTER FOUR

Wise Virgins

Religious congregations and the monks and nuns who make up their membership are marked out by their chastity. Whatever else is extraordinary in their lives, it is their renunciation of sex which captures the imagination of 'everyman'. The glittering 'fiery furnace' of St Francis's love, the solemn dedication of the Augustinian canon are the magnets which draw the group together. The religious Rule and the relationship with the Church offers a framework for the group to grow and develop its potential as a caring community in the external world. Each convent can only be seen as a part of a network of social relations involving lay people, clerics, fellow nuns. Bernard of Clairvaux remarked: 'If you are a foolish virgin—if indeed you are a virgin—you need the community. If you are a wise virgin, the community needs you.' The sense of community, the consecrated virginity are the positive values of renunciation. The religious congregation must have the undivided commitment of its members to survive. The 'sacerdotal celibacy' of the convent commands an exclusive right to the sexuality of its members just as traditional Christian marriage demanded exclusive rights and undivided loyalty from wives.[1] Just how a religious congregation makes its appeal to the laity, and who those girls who take the virgin's veil are, is the subject of this chapter.

Not only social scientists but zoologists and ethnologists are concerned to find out why people and animals behave the way they do. What is it that prompts a young girl to leave her family and friends, to renounce sex, marriage and babies for the religious life? Why should she even expect to marry and live happily-ever-after? To what extent is her action altruistic and to what extent is she forced into it? The rules and values of the religious life are more demanding than those of society at large. To what extent is the nun's commitment whole-heartedly given and to what extent is it won by a series of indoctrinatory and alienatory procedures? I have already described the structure of leadership in the religious congregations, the authority structure based on the laws of the Church and the writings and charisma of the founders. A Superior General and any other official in a religious congregation can issue instructions, even commands, with every expectation that they will be carried out or obeyed. The Mother Superior's relationship with her nuns is one of control and consent—a relationship of compliance.[2] It is a relationship between those who have power and those over whom they exercise it. Power is not synonymous with authority, but if it recognizes and is recognized by legitimate means then it can be. Power is simply a matter of one person getting another to carry out his commands, for which he might easily use force. This would not seem to be a course open to a Mother Superior, although on reading Diderot one wonders. His heroine, Sister Suzanne, whose adventures are supposedly based on fact, is nearly broken by starvation, deprivation and solitary confinement for her inability to conform to the religious life.[3] But the use of force to gain compliance should be exceptional in a religious organization. The compliance relationship will be characterized by the nature of the controls prevalent in the organization. Amitai Etzioni has devised a threefold typology in which three kinds of power—coercive, remunerative or normative—can be combined with three kinds of involvement on the part of those controlled—alienative, calculative or moral.[4] Organizations generally conform to one of these analytic types.

A coercive organization is characterized by the use of coercive power or control and a high degree of alienation from its members, the controlled, for example in concentration camps, prisons or custodial mental hospitals. Religious organizations have employed coercive sanctions on their members' behaviour. The medieval Church crushed dangerous heresies by mutilations, total expulsion and even death. A utilitarian organization employs remuneration as the major means of control and calculative involvement characterizes the orientation of the controlled. The major industries, trade unions and the schools, are good examples of utilitarian organizations. The active religious orders do remunerate their members in kind; a roof and food for life are not to be minimized, but they are not remunerative in the money-sense. Technical training, ambitious careers and material rewards are tempered by 'religious humility'. Normative organizations have to rely predominantly on normative powers to gain acceptance for and achievement of objectives. Normative is one of those 'key-words' used by sociologists which have a rather limited and precise meaning and have only been in use since the 1880s! In the case of the religious congregation it means that the Superiors rely on the expression of religious objectives and the high moral involvement of members to gain compliance.

The real test for normative control is: what happens when you don't obey the rules? What sanctions are used against you by those giving the orders, and what pressures exist to hold you to the rules? Any nun's first answer would be her own will to fulfil her vow of obedience. The nun's commitment to her congregation is a highly internalized moral involvement, symbolically expressed in the taking and renewal of religious vows. Just as society has various procedures for socializing its members, the parent/child, educator/child, so the religious organization has not only a careful procedure for socializing the aspiring nun in the values and norms of the religious life but also a careful selection procedure which only chooses 'suitable' candidates. Once the nun is in the convent there are various disciplinary and social measures which persuade her to keep to the behaviour pattern dictated by the Rule, Customs Book and Constitutions of her congregation. The hierarchy of officials issue directives and the subordinate nun looks to them as an expression of her commitment. There is no real feeling of alienation as, for example, between a prisoner and warder, or hope for gain as between teacher and pupil or executive and worker. The commitment of the subordinates is shared by their superiors in the religious congregation. Superiors are drawn from and even return to the ordinary membership. Superiors have to be ever-watchful that they are setting a good example and that they have communicated their dedication and understanding to the sisters in their charge.

In answer to the question of how girls become nuns, there is the process of selection by the congregations and the desire to enter the religious life expressed as 'vocation' by Catholic girls. Of all the sisters I interviewed the great majority had been brought up in a Roman Catholic family, attended a Roman Catholic school, and in the case of further education, studied at a Roman Catholic college. Over half the sisters in the teaching congregation had come from Ireland. Half of those came from families of between seven and twelve children. These girls were neither the eldest nor the youngest because they would be expected to remain at home and look after the family. The local priest always discouraged a girl with ageing parents from taking up a religious vocation; she would be told that she served God by nursing her sick relatives. Selection followed the dictates of the Rule. In the teaching congregation the original Rule of 1891 forbade entry to those over twenty-five, bastards, widows or anyone who had taken the habit in another Institute. In 1932 these regulations were relaxed and it was legally possible to take in widows or women over thirty, but in other respects even greater care was taken. In trying to assess whether girls had a 'true' vocation they took character references from local priests, schoolteachers and 'respected' friends. They tried to make sure that the girl was not involved in debts, lawsuits or similar doubtful affairs. The rule stated: 'Aspirants must have a good reputation, belong to a respectable family and be free from any notable bodily infirmity.' The girls had to bring a baptismal and confirmation certificate (their proof of Church membership), a certificate of good health and, of course, a dowry.

All sisters entering the teaching congregation were expected to bring a dowry, although dispensation was granted in special cases. A trained teacher, for example, could offer her training in lieu of a dowry. Dowries were invested by the congregation but there were regulations in Canon Law prohibiting the use of dowries in house purchase or the discharge of debts before the death of the religious. It was an obvious safeguard. Canon Law attempts to protect both the girls and the congregations they join from exploitation. The congregations literally cannot afford to take on free-loaders and bizarre personalities if they are to fulfil their apostolic work in the world. When they take on a new member they promise to give that person shelter for life, clothes, food and a purpose for living. Today there are no more dowries and the congregations rely for financial viability on donations, investments and the untaxed income of their worker-nuns. The six-month postulancy was paid for by the girl's parents, though now they may only make a contribution towards the expense. In either case the congregation cannot claim compensation if she decides to leave, and the girl signs a declaration to say that she will undertake any task assigned to her during that period, without payment. In the teaching congregation, lay nuns were always the exception; they entered without dowry and at the convent's expense, and, in doing so, they accepted that they would spend their life doing menial work. As late as the nineteenth century, wealthy women had entered the convent with their maids, and in the 1930s this was still offered as an explanation for the lay-sister status. The Franciscan congregation never had this status though they did accept dowries. They tended to look for general good character and religious enthusiasm rather than specific training in their aspirants. Indeed, to be 'unmarried' in the Franciscan sense was taken to mean not married to profession, good works or hobbies as well as in the strict matrimonial sense: 'Religious should at all times be bound by nothing in order to be free for God.' (*The Life and Rule of St Francis*). The ideal Franciscan would be the type of person who would stretch out her hand first, take a humble path through life and have the strength to sustain in her lifetime all the demands of the Franciscan Rule.

In the nineteenth century girls leaving for the convent, particularly those destined to be lay sisters, were in an equivalent position to those leaving for service as maids or governesses. Sister Patrick, described her departure for the convent; friends and neighbours gathered to give her a send-off and presented her with gifts and good wishes. Then, 'before I left home my mother got my clothes ready, just the black dress for the postulancy and some underwear, but we called it a trousseau. There were plain linen shifts, cotton stockings and lace-up shoes. But you never had your own clothes once you'd professed. All the clothes were kept in the linen room and handed out by the linen lady, and the shoes were cleaned at night and then put in the corridor in order of size. They were all the same, no left and right to choose from, you never wore the same shoes two days running unless you had very unusual sized feet!' The absence of personal clothing, the sharing of shoes were just the first indications of the degree of self-abasement expected in the convent.

Sister Patrick was also struck by the rank-order and the class-division of the convent she joined. It was like the big country houses of the time where, for example, at morning prayers the gentry would sit and the servants stood at the back in order of seniority. Even in the servants' hall, under-servants were not allowed to speak in the presence of upper-servants. Flora Thompson gives a delightful description of a young girl leaving her village, Candleford, for the first time in her life. This girl could as easily have been bound for a convent as a manor house. 'When a place was found, the girl set out along on what was usually her first train journey, with her yellow tin trunk tied up with thick cord, her bunch of flowers and brown paper parcel bursting with left-overs. . . . What the girl, bound for a strange and distant part of the country to live a new strange life among strangers, felt when the train moved off can only be imagined.'[5] Such a girl went to a big house where the upper servants were her real mistress. She would share a large attic with two or three other maids. Her clothes would be dictated by her position in the household. She would have no time off and certainly no boyfriends; they were left at home. The young postulant also shared a dormitory and had all her time apportioned, but she was aware of joining an élite group; she may have had to leave boyfriends behind but she had the promise of becoming a 'bride of Christ'.

In Victorian England girls who entered the convent may have had a better deal and more freedom than their married sisters or governesses. A nun, by her poverty vow, renounced the 'independent use' of her property, its revenues and administration but retained the actual ownership of the property. She could dispose of it by will or deed of gift to whosoever she wished. The dowry and even the trousseau brought into the congregation were held by the congregation until death or in the event of the nun leaving they would be given back to her. A woman entering 'Holy Matrimony' actually had to hand over all goods, money and estates to her husband. Not only that, but any chattels and property which she acquired during her marriage passed at once to her husband and he could immediately treat them as his own. When the Anglicans began to establish sisterhoods and when the Catholics re-established convents in England they were quick to counter criticisms by pointing out that nuns had more rights over property despite their poverty vows than married women. It was not until the Act of 1882 that married women were eventually given the legal entitlement to hold property.[6] Women who made improvident marriages were in real danger of a destitute old age. At least the nun was guaranteed a roof and food and clothing until death. In a world where women belonged first to their fathers and then to their husbands who could beat them, take all freedom of action from them and claim all their property, it is not surprising that the convent was sometimes found to be a happy escape. The problem for the religious congregations, especially those like the teaching congregation with a very specific brief to fulfil, was how to change with the times. Married women did benefit from changes in the law, from social changes which gave them greater freedom, but the nuns did not keep pace. The customs of the nineteenth century were appropriate to those times but quite inappropriate to the 1960s.

Becoming a nun was not, therefore, just a matter of deciding that the convent was the place for you and going in. The religious congregations were careful to choose girls who had stable personalities and who would succeed in religious life. The girls had to choose the most suitable congregation and to be sure that they had sufficient 'vocation' to sustain a life of dedication to Christian principles—a dedication which would demand more of them than of their lay sisters. Sister Matilda, a contemporary of Sister Patrick, spoke for many of her kind when she explained, 'Every Catholic girl thinks about becoming a nun. But one day at school one of the nuns came up to me and asked if I had ever thought of it; she said she thought I had a vocation. I didn't really think anything of it for a while. But it was a thought within me that gradually came out. This thought kept coming back. I prayed a lot about it. I prayed I would make a decision. In a way I didn't know that much about nuns then. All I knew was that they were good people and they prayed. That is the impression you get, even when you are in a convent school all your life. What worried me was that I used to think, well, I'm not always good, and I don't always pray, so how can I be a nun?' Sister Matilda said that it was about two years later than she eventually decided to enter the convent, and then it seemed to her that the decision was made almost by chance. A monk from a monastery near her home sent a message to her mother saying, 'Mind you bring the girls to Mass tomorrow because there are these peculiar nuns coming.' She went to Mass, met the nuns, who were peculiar only in their dress and their friendliness, and immediately made up her mind to join them. When she told her parents they were delighted. It was always a matter of great pride for a family to have a son in the priesthood or a daughter a nun.

The only nuns who told me about family opposition were those whose families felt that they would not make a 'good nun'. They feared that the girls would not stay the course and leave the convent, which would disgrace the family. This link between family and Church provided much of the early socialization for the religious life. In her book *Nuns* Marcelle Bernstein gives us a delightful poem which expresses a father's pride in his daughter and his own hopes for heavenly rewards:

> Sure my daughter has been vested
> And my joy I cannot hide,
> For I've watched her from the cradle
> With a father's honest pride.
>
> Since to err is only human
> There's a whole lot on the slate
> That I'll have to make account for
> When I reach the golden gate.
>
> But then I'm not a-worrying
> About the deeds I've done,
> I'll just whisper to St Peter:
> 'I'm the daddy of a nun'.[7]

This emphasis on the positive value of the religious life in the up-bringing of young Catholic girls cannot be stressed too much. Certainly before the Second World War when entrants tended to be drawn from large, presumably traditional and authoritarian families, it was a natural and happy choice for a religious girl.

The choice was frequently mitigated by a sense of alienation from the outside world. Sister John, a thirty-year-old Franciscan, told me that it was not until she was in her early twenties that she began seriously to consider entering the convent. She was Irish, one of seven children. She had led a happy Catholic childhood and was a very gay person with lots of boyfriends. She went to work in the colonial office in Tanzania, or Tanganyika, as it was then. She found herself appalled by the permissive life and un-Christian attitudes of the Europeans there and determined to dedicate herself to the religious life, to bear witness to Christianity in the world. As a mature adult she expressed a degree of alienation from the outside world in her positive commitment to join the convent. She had been educated in schools run by Dominican sisters and found them altogether too stiff, too enclosed. She said that they had hidden behind the front door when they opened it so that they could not see out, which she found ridiculous. She visited several convents belonging to different orders before she decided to approach the Franciscans for a postulancy. She said that she was attracted by their open, friendly manners and by the work of the Saint and his followers.

Sometimes it is the 'glamour' of the religious life which attracts young girls. The clothing ceremony was frequently mentioned as the first occasion when becoming a nun had a strong appeal. The girls dressed as brides in white wedding dresses and then accepted their simple nun's habit from the bishop in full ceremonial dress. The nuns said, 'The Lord touches in many ways. The office and the singing are tremendously touching, so is the spirit of joyfulness, the theme of happiness.' The use of 'touches' and 'touching' here evokes the literal meaning of the religious life, the physical response to prayer and closeness to God, and the sense of being chosen. A Novice Mistress tried to explain this: 'Everyone questions, what am I doing in life, what do I want to do? The difference between a Christian or a religious and someone else is that she asks herself, what does God want of me? Of itself, the religious life may not be very attractive to a girl, but if it is God's will, then the ultimate good is to do God's will. We freely chose God, just as a wife freely chooses her husband, so we know that God wants us to be a religious, we know that that is our vocation.' Vocation in this sense can only grow out of the initial socialization in Christian religion which took place throughout the girl's childhood, at home and at school. It confirms the girl in her opinion that she is doing the 'right' thing in her life and gives the Superiors some idea of the degree of religious commitment she possesses.

Some of the sisters interviewed had used the mechanism of prayer to help them decide whether to enter the convent. One of them described how, as a sixteen-year-old, she had made a novena, a nine-day prayer, to St Thérèse of Lisieux, to whom she had a special devotion. On the eighth day of the novena she went to the door to let in a visiting sister from another order. In her hand this sister had a bunch of roses—the symbol of St Thérèse. St Thérèse is reported to have said, 'When I die let fall a shower of roses', meaning a shower of blessings. The girls had an old Irish saying, if you get a rose you get your request. Somehow folk belief combined with Christian mysticism and the young girl took it as a sign that she should join the visitor's congregation. Such reliance on the mystical resources of their religion was not uncommon and it confirmed a decision which would affect the rest of their lives. Signs such as this give divine sanction to decisions already half-taken. Really it is a psychological process of reinforcing an adopted position; it is encouraged by the Church and has a long pedigree in Christian tradition.

Alternatively some sisters made a calculated choice when they entered the convent. Some looked at alternatives to the religious life, others took a more pragmatic view of the religious life itself. Sister Barbara, a Superior in the teaching congregation, entered the convent just as the Second World War broke out. She said that everyone was making their effort for their country, her friends were joining the armed services or nursing auxiliaries, so she made her contribution and joined the convent. Another admitted that she wanted to teach, but not slum children; she wanted to teach middle-class children in a country or suburban environment. The Franciscan congregation claimed to eliminate such candidates and would look very hard for more 'religious' reasons for admission, but the teaching congregation was committed to the education of middle-class girls, and if a fully trained teacher offered herself she would be accepted.

After the Second World War the attitude of young sisters and the congregations towards vocation changed. The breakdown of family life, the increase of smaller families even among Catholics, greater opportunities for women outside marriage, all affected the degree of initial socialization and the numbers of recruits the religious congregations could expect. The Franciscans continued high levels of recruitment with the opportunity for considerable choice among applicants; approximately one in six was accepted. But the teaching congregation faced competition from other pragmatic substitutes such as teaching, nursing, social work, and while they were never short of recruits they did accept fewer than in the halcyon days of the 1930s. The success of the Franciscans, though a nursing congregation, can be attributed to the 'charismatic' pull of St Francis and the continuing impact of the Franciscan ideology. In the 1960s in particular this ideological bias towards peace, poverty and the individual, complemented the commune movement which spread from America through Europe. The congregations remain ever-watchful—in fact so intense is the search for the right type of personality that Superiors resort to psychological testing. A good nun, they say, is someone who could have been married and would have made a good wife. She needs to have a well-developed sense of responsibility, self-awareness and knowledge of her sexual needs. The slightest doubt about a postulant or a novice will be taken very seriously and they may even suggest that a girl goes out into the world for a year or so and re-applies rather than take in someone unsuitable. The Franciscans go out to schools and youth clubs around the country, showing a film of the convent and the work of missionary sisters. They have a guest house where they entertain prospective entrants. But it is with the postulancy that the real training for religious life begins. The aims of the postulancy and its place in the socialization process have changed in the last ten years. Up to Vatican II it had remained virtually the same for hundreds of years.

Socialization through postulancy and Novitiate is, like the selection procedure, a two-way process. The Superiors, the élites of the congregation, direct new entrants through a long Novitiate which trains and conditions the girls into the ways of religious life. The postulancy is a testing time, a gentle trial in which the entrant learns about the congregation and they can learn something about her. It is her first experience of the world 'inside' the convent. For the congregation it is a testing time when the boundary between it and the world outside has to give in order to allow a new member access. With the Novitiate the boundaries of inside/outside are re-emphasized in a series of dramatic rituals of which the clothing ceremony is the first, followed by profession of vows and the final profession. It is a process of indoctrination using alienative and positive mechanisms to ensure the commitment of the nun. Once a decision is made to enter—the word itself is appropriate to the moment of leaving the secular world and joining the convent—the girl prepares herself to leave a world she has known and enter an unknown, silent world, full of constraints and demands which involve her full attention to be understood.

When a girl enters the convent she leaves behind her clothes, her name, her legal rights and her freedom of action. In the traditional convent a heavy door shuts out noise and bustle, the windows are just high enough to be over the head, inside there is silence, muted colours and restricted movement. It might be ten years before final commitment is reached—years of soul-searching and self-analysis. Sister Patrick is now seventy; she has been a nun for fifty-five years. For the first forty years she lived in a religious enclosure complete in every detail. She said: 'I came straight from school to the convent. I never went outside the door, not for nine years. When I did go out, it was to move to another convent. I will never forget the feeling, the day I went outside the door. T'was a most queer feeling, going off and seeing people, seeing shop windows—I've never forgotten that sensation, it was most queer.' Not to go out for nine years! Some did not go out for twenty years or more. In Sister Patrick's day the postulancy was six months for a lay sister and three months for a choir sister. They usually entered as postulants in September and took their 'clothes' as a novice at Eastertime. Sister Patrick said that all she remembered of her postulancy was serving dinners and cleaning! Generally all postulants were given menial jobs. The majority of the teaching nuns admitted to some feeling of shock on leaving their families and entering the convent. They said it was only the knowledge that they were doing 'God's will' that made them persist. They seemed to feel the split between inside/outside worlds more keenly than those entering the Franciscan congregation.

In the Franciscan congregation the right to admit postulants and to refuse unsuitable candidates is reserved for the Mother General, unlike the teaching congregation where the General Council or its representatives took this decision. The involvement of the Mother General both formally and informally reaffirmed her personal leadership and established a relationship between her and each individual in the congregation from the outset. In the 1927 Rule the postulancy was set at six months though special cases were allowed a further six. Postulants lived in the Novitiate and tried to live within the discipline of the community, but the Franciscans attempted to minimize the shock of entry. St Francis himself said that recruits should always be received kindly. They arranged to admit them on a day when the whole community had recreation. (This really only meant that they were allowed to talk at mealtimes.) On a feast-day there might be a sing-song in the evening which was both cheerful and gave the postulants a chance to meet other members of the community. Normally they would have nothing to do with the nuns; all their contact was with the Mistress of Postulants. This was enshrined in Canon Law and served to protect postulants from persuasion by the professed sisters—possibly it was also designed to protect the professed nuns from the influence of virtual outsiders. The Mistress of Postulants described a typical initiation as not having changed since the 1930s.

The girls arrive at the convent with their families, if they lived reasonably close. Most girls would have already visited the guest house, met some of the sisters and familiarized themselves with the congregation. But some, from the Far East or India, would be in not only a strange place but also a strange country and climate. On arrival they are ushered into one of the parlours to have tea. The parlours are large comfortable rooms where outsiders can be received and given the hospitality of the convent. Tea is that quintessential middle-class meal of cucumber sandwiches, small cakes with icing and decorations, biscuits and dainty napkins. Visitors sit balancing a cup in one hand and a plate on the knee trying to make sensible conversation between mouthfuls. Parents are left in the parlour, a room decorated informally and strikingly lacking in religious trappings, while their daughters go to change their clothes. The girls send their measurements beforehand and the nuns make up dresses ready for them. They come back to their parents wearing a uniform blue dress with a small white collar, a small veil with a white band to hold it on over the hair and a little cape for going out. It is an emotional moment for parents and one which is made more meaningful by a visit to the chapel, a bright, light building with evocative paintings on the walls, where the girls pray before the altar. They probably pray in gratitude for coming to the convent, make an invocation to St Francis and add an Our Father and a Hail Mary. It is a moment when family and Church unite in the dedication of their children. The family party moves on to a welcome from the Mother General. The moment comes for the girls to say goodbye. It is a hard moment for parents who are losing daughters who have been helpful and cheerful at home, but they are usually happy for them. Once the parents have gone, the girls unpack and those who travelled alone write home. The Mistress of Postulants explained that she generally has to encourage them to do this because they are bewildered and a little lost in their strange surroundings.

In the Franciscan convent, initiation into full community life is gradual. The postulants are allowed to have a long sleep in the mornings of the first week, then they start getting up with the others at 5.30 a.m. Postulants spend their months occupied in learning about the religious state, which includes learning mental prayer, the Divine Office and something of the family spirit of the Franciscans with their general rules on politeness and religious decorum. Every three months a report is written on their conduct, for the Rule states that it is the Mistress's duty to 'know whether they are docile and of good character, if they show good disposition to the practice of humility, obedience, self-denial and the other virtues, whether they are suitable to the work and capable of acquiring sufficient knowledge in order to fulfil those tasks which later on would be assigned to them'. Occasionally girls who are not going to succeed leave in the first week, though more often they leave after a few months; but those who remain become more convinced of their 'calling' and prepare themselves for their first great ceremony—the clothing.

The Rule makes certain safeguards against exploitation either by or of the girls who enter postulancy. A fixed agreement to pay costs must be made by the parent or guardian, or the congregation agrees to pay the girl's costs. They cannot claim compensation if she decides to leave after a few months. Likewise the girl signs a declaration to say that she willingly performs without payment, any duties assigned to her by her superiors. About two months before the girl is due to take the habit and enter the Novitiate the Local Ordinary is informed and thirty days before the clothing he questions the girl to make sure that she has not been forced into the convent and that she knows what she is doing. (Only last year the press was full of horror stories about young Asian girls being sold into Catholic convents in Rome.) The Church attempts to protect its own reputation and its young by this 'examen'. Eight days before the clothing the postulants make a religious Retreat and a general confession of their life before coming to the convent. This is another aspect of the alienation process in which the entrant cleanses herself of her past.

Until the changes in the 1950s and 1960s the clothing ceremony was the dramatic ceremony of initiation, a veritable *rite de passage* in which the young girl took the habit of the congregation, cut her hair and received her religious name. A film of the Franciscan clothing ceremony shows an elaborate ritual, with all the participants dressed in rich robes or wedding dresses. The postulants approach the altar, long hair flowing over their shoulders, faces hidden under the traditional white gauze veil, a coronet of white flowers on their heads. The head is bared at the altar and the officiating priest cuts a few pieces of hair. He places the habit over the postulant's head and dresses her in the ceinture, scapular and veil. He calls her by her religious name and hands her a candle, breviary and crucifix. The choir is full of nuns singing, the altar crowded with officials of Church and congregation. The clothing of a novice is an occasion when the congregation's dependence on the wider Church is recognized, when parents watch their daughters from a distance, when the girl is incorporated into the closed community of the convent. But for the postulant, it is only an initial step into the religious life; the barriers are not yet all down, she can still leave without dishonour and she is not under the full compulsion of the Rule.

The Franciscan sisters I interviewed spoke of the emotional impact of the clothing ceremony. The night before the postulants had been merry young girls, putting their hair in curlers, giggling, preening their wedding dresses. On the day, their hair was shorn, they took the simple religious habit and a new name. The clothing marks serious intention; the real training is about to begin and a moral commitment to the ideals of the congregation is understood. In the 1960s this attitude changed in order to put more emphasis on the Novitiate as a time of trial, and the taking of first profession of vows became the more important ceremony. The name given to a girl included the prefix Sister Mary and the suffix was always a Patron Saint or a Mystery. In the Franciscan congregation the names commemorated devotion to the Virgin Mary and the hierarchy of saints. The clothing ceremony was equally important in the traditional teaching congregation. They too dressed as brides and took a religious name at the altar although it did not include Mary. The girl put up her own choice of names, and usually two or three devolved on a favourite saint or even a favourite sister, teacher or friend. One nun took the name of Ita, not because it meant in chains, but because she knew a very nice nun by that name. Sisters still used their baptismal names for legal documents or transactions outside the convent life.

The teaching sisters did speak of a sense of loss on entering the convent—not simply the loss of friends and family, but of talents, all the things given up to enter the convent. Ironically, it was the Franciscan message which dictated that you give up everything to follow God and St Francis; yet it made full use of all available talents, the stress was ideological rather than pragmatic. It was reflected in the 'ultimated' commitment of Franciscan sisters which required less of the alienating procedures such as the 'talent-stripping' used in the teaching congregation, where the loss of talent was considerable in denying musicians music, artists artistic expression, even in some cases potential teachers the opportunity to teach. Sisters had to undertake any task the Superiors demanded and these would be tasks for the good of the congregation, not necessarily for the good of the individual. One sister had been a professional singer and pianist before she entered. Once in the convent, she gave up her music—she no longer sang, never touched a piano. Now after fifty years she regrets her years of silence and wonders why her gifts were not used; she could have given some of her music to the children in the schools, but she was a lay sister and as such had no contact of that kind with the children. Another sister had been a master-tailor's assistant for years. She knew the intricacies of embroidery, appliqué, lace-making, crochet, yet she was in her seventies before she was able to return to the finer side of needlework. Sewing was not neglected in the convent; making small items was a common occupation in recreation hour, but there was a severe loss of talent to daily drudgery; the laundry and the kitchen were the domain of the lay sister. This self-sacrifice was not required of the Franciscan sisters. Their founder had brought light and music to the convent life throughout the congregation. Girls with artistic leanings brought their brushes with them, they employed their art for the congregation, their talents were mobilized in God's name. Musicians gave their music. Every opportunity was sought and taken to make use of individual contributions. It was not until the reforms of the 1960s that the teaching congregation could similarly use the talents it had shifted.

The experience of a novice in the Franciscan congregation was rather different from that of a novice in the teaching congregation despite a formal similarity in the legal requirements of the Church. The differences reflected the contrasts in aims and ideology between the congregations and the demands made by the organizations on their members. The Franciscan Novitiate was in the Mother House in England. Until the late 1950s the teaching congregation had a Novitiate in England but as the Mother House was on the Continent all their novices spent one year of their novitiate in the Mother House. Novices in both congregations are separated from the rest of the sisters; no communication is allowed with them. The justification for this is that the novices will not be unduly influenced by professed sisters, but it is obviously a discretionary measure. The novices are kept informed and guarded by a trusted official of the bureaucratic élite—the Novice Mistress. She alone controls the flow of information to and from novices. The separation is required by Canon Law which also stipulates that the Novitiate should last two to three years of which one year is 'canonical', to be devoted to uninterrupted study of the religious life. If a girl was absent for more than thirty consecutive days during this year it was invalidated and she would not be allowed to take her vows. The Franciscans used the canonical year to teach their girls the Christian ethics of medicine, surgery and midwifery. Their Rule states that 'they must be taught to see in things pertaining to Motherhood, the work of God, Infinite Purity, and to dispel all the sordid ideas that the world has associated with this beautiful gift of God.' Again this has to be seen as a protective device to shield the congregation from the possible 'impurity' of their work in the world by arming their sisters with a more demanding moral code than that of the world outside.

The Novice Mistress should see that her charges devote themselves to 'the study of the Rule and Constitutions and to the pious meditations and assiduous prayer, to understudy all that is implied by the vows and virtues, to suitable exercises for the complete extirpation of the seeds of vice, the controls of the emotions and the acquisition of virtues'. The aim is to train the mind of the novice. The sisters today use the same programme of self-formation laid down in the life and Rule of St Francis. It provides a training for the inner man. It recommends periods of quiet, meditations, recollections, times when a nun can surrender herself to God, in which God can enter, reform and recover his religious sisters. Meditation and quiet periods feature throughout the nun's life, a constant redefinition of her commitment. The Novice Mistress teaches her charges the life of St Francis and his followers. She teaches the Franciscan spirit of humility, self-renunciation and poverty. She explains the meaning of the religious vows, helps them to pray, urges them to practise self-denial, to curb their own will and leave themselves open to God's grace. The Novitiate is a highly concentrated training session in which the novices internalize the values of the community. They are given the poorest clothing to wear and are employed in the humblest tasks. They try, within the bounds of health, to mortify their bodies by fasting and abstinence. A novice is always free to leave—or be dismissed.

In the teaching congregation the preparation of novices was less spiritual, more rough and ready. The novices were still employed in the unproductive units of the convent, in housework, gardening and cleaning schoolrooms. The separation from the professed sisters was absolute with the Novitiate House which was either a separate building in the grounds of the Mother House or in a different location altogether. Novices found their year on the Continent unnerving, the travelling strange, the Novitiate rigid and uncompromising. The novices wore a long black dress, a small white veil and a pleated apron—indicative of the amount of housework they did! A few found the clothes irksome and heavy but all found the silence and lack of freedom the hardest to bear. My impression was that these novices gritted their teeth and went through their Novitiate with one aim—to take profession and become 'real nuns'. Even the Novice Mistress said that she had no real preparation for her task. She was sent to the Novitiate, so she got on with it. In the old days, she said, it was simple; you made your sacrifice to God and you submitted yourself for His examination through the medium of your Superiors. This description of her initiation by a postulant of 1923 spells it out: 'the postulant kneels at the foot of the Altar and the voice of the Church, rising grave and majestic, interrogates her: "My daughter, what do you ask?" "I ask to be allowed to dwell in this house of God for all the rest of my life." "You must know that in order to be received into this pious Institute you must be resolved to renounce the world and yourself, to bear your cross daily, and to consecrate yourself to the service of the Church, according to the Constitutions". If the postulant has the courage to do this she replies in the affirmative and the ceremony closes with the celebration of the Holy Mass.'

The three-year Novitiate ends with the first profession of vows which marks the first stage into full incorporation into the community. (After a further five years in the convent the vows are pledged again and full membership is attained.) Before they make their first profession the novices make a retreat and a will, disposing of any property they might possess. In the ceremony of first profession the Franciscan sisters arrive at the altar in their white habits and veils. There they are given the blue veil of the congregation over which is placed a coronet of white flowers; a silver ring is slipped over their finger and a medallion round their neck. They are 'brides of Christ'. The Franciscan Mother General told me that this ceremony recalled the love of consecrated virgins for their God. It was like the love of men and women, she said; just as husband and wife express their love through sexual intercourse, so the nun expresses her love of God through virginity. The loss of opportunity in the world is replaced by the opportunity for love and marriage within the convent. The ideals of the outside world are turned to the congregation's advantage. (Without questioning the psychological effects of this, it is obvious that it is yet another mechanism in the organizational control of member commitment, yet another insurance that compliance will be positive.) At the end of five years the sisters take their perpetual vows. Three months before this they go on a retreat and subject themselves to special acts of humility and self-renunciation. At perpetual profession they are given a plain gold ring. The marriage is complete. To leave the convent now would mean excommunication and social ostracism, unless dispensation was granted from the Vatican for some very special circumstance. The vows are renewed annually by the congregation in an annual retreat and individuals are encouraged to make a special act of devotion to renew vows during the year. The vows, therefore, remain central to a control of lifestyle and are a constant reminder of the nun's commitment to her congregation. In normative organizations discipline is more likely to centre on verbal appeals or symbolic deprivations than on expulsion or coercion. There is also a degree of work satisfaction, an inbuilt code of ethics not present in other types of organization. The vows are the pivot on which all these controls operate in a religious organization. The ceremony of profession is but the formal statement of informal, highly internalized norms.

The very meaning of the vows changed in the teaching congregation as it underwent radical change in the 1960s and developed in the early twentieth century. But the Franciscans kept a basic formula throughout. In the nineteenth century the teaching congregation saw the chastity vow in terms of preservation and defence—preservation of the untouched purity of virginity, and defence against bad influence and the evil of the world. It was appropriate to the dualism of the Victorian world and the founder. The first Mother General said to her sisters: 'we have no hair-cloth . . . or severe fasts . . . instead we have the subjugation of the senses, the spur of sacrifice, retreat, the avoidance of evil, and in general all that may preserve the angelic purity of our consecration.' The articles of the Rule state that 'by the vow of chastity the sisters oblige themselves to keep pure and chaste for Jesus Christ their body and their hearts.' (Article 124. 1891) The nuns observe the perfect chastity of consecrated virgins and give all their love to God. If they break the vow, they commit sacrilege; the power of excommunication will cut them off from a life eternal. The vow extends to every look, word and action that they make. Thomas Merton writes about 'that deep spirit of faith which enables us always to rise above the flesh and its storms in order to mediate on the incorruptible beauty of the world'.[8] St Augustine had defined virginity as: 'in carne corruptibili incorruptionis perpetua meditatio' (in corruptible flesh, perpetual mediation of what is incorruptible). Virginity is not just the renunciation of sex, it is a striving for a purity which is other-worldly. It is a quality which confers on the holder the membership of a religious élite, high status rewarded in the life hereafter.

The chastity vow is not a negative force. The key to why a woman is prepared to give away her fertility and sexuality lies in the premise that she does not in fact give it away or renounce it, she saves it. The Franciscan Superior General wrote in 1955 on the value of menopause, the moment when years of possible childbearing are over. 'For the faithful sister the day has now come when our Lord graciously ratifies the sacrifice she made to him long years ago, for the potential fruit of her womb. The womb very shortly will cease to be capable of bearing fruit, and the faithful virgin now has the great job of completing her offering of years ago. Our Lord is asked lovingly to accept both the fruit and the tree. For her this is the great and glorious noonday of her life—the consummation of her sacrifice . . . relying on the strength of our blessed Lord, she renews and renders more fruitful still her spiritual motherhood.' Chastity is integral to the theology of religious life; it recalls the womanhood of the Virgin Mary and the birth of Christ. The founder wrote to his sisters, 'This womanhood, patterned on Mary's, is to be accepted as it is, with all its true feminine characteristics and used to bring us to full and fruitful union with our Divine Lord.'

When the nuns talked to me about chastity they did not refer to relations with the opposite sex, they referred mostly to relations with their own sex, to their own sensuality and sexuality. Indeed, the constraints of the chastity vow were felt most strongly within the community itself. Particular friendships between sisters were actively discouraged. One old sister told me, 'You were either separated or sent away from that house if you had a particular friend—break your heart you know—but it was like that, you just had to make the sacrifice. If you sat next to the same person at table twice running you were moved round; if you were seen to be friendly with one other sister then one of you would be moved from the house.' After the Second World War the severity of these interpretations was lessened and sisters were even allowed to walk around the garden arm in arm! Chastity did not only refer to relationships with others, it referred to the nun herself, to her body. Article 213 of the teachers' Rule says, 'The sisters will cherish this angelic virtue with peculiar affection so that it may pervade every look, word and action, and that they may always give great edification by their whole deportment.' In Victorian times this meant restricting the movements of the body to outrageous standards of decorum. 'Modesty of the eyes' meant, quite literally, not looking straight at another person, guarding speech, only reading suitable texts.

To help keep the promise of this vow the nuns 'examine their conscience' every day and practise humility and mortification. The discipline is still regarded as a useful instrument of penance, and mortification is essential to religious chastity, though it is used far less today than in previous generations. The discipline is a short whip of thonged leather which is used for self-flagellation. It seems a surprising item to be included in the nun's equipment but it has a long history in Christianity and was a common item in Victorian England. The restrictions on bodily movement, on sensory perception which came to the nuns in the Rule were only slightly more rigorous than those of their secular sisters until the 1930s and 1940s. The Victorian and Edwardian middle classes were swamped with books on etiquette, manuals for the correct upbringing of girls and boys which were prudish in the extreme. No lengths would be spared to gain the correct effect. Correspondents to *The Englishwoman's Domestic Magazine*, 1868, debated the efficacy of beating your daughters: 'Nothing like leather,' they said, 'cut a strap into strips, let your governess tie your daughter down upon the ottoman after evening prayers, the strap thus cut may be depended upon to inflict acute suffering, you then make her kiss the rod and let her go.'[9] In the same magazine a clergyman offered to thrash a little girl, 'for the good of her soul because she had sinned against God and her mother'. Self-flagellation is less surprising in this context. There were safeguards against its use; writers even then were aware of the pleasure in pain.

One Catholic writer says, 'As temptations against chastity are immediately concerned with the sense of touch, there is a tendency not only to counteract and neutralize pleasure through self-inflicted pain, but also to believe that we are more secure in this virtue the more savagely we attack the body.'[10] But Superiors were urged to be alert to the over-use of the discipline; it should not be used so hard as to break the skin and should only be used on the upper leg. The seriousness with which it was employed varied with different personalities. Some sisters told me they found it difficult to remember, others that they used it regularly twice a week. Monica Baldwin describes it as part of 'the painful and monotonous job of putting to death one's natural inclinations' so that 'the supernatural life of grace might take complete possession of one's soul'.[11] It is all too easy to fall into the trap of cultural relativism when looking at practices such as the discipline which seem exotic, even erotic or pornographic today. Mortification of the senses and penance for sins have to be seen in the context in which they occur. It is a context built over centuries of Christianity, and, in the case of these congregations, the more specific time of the founder in each case. In the nineteenth century human sexuality, particularly female sexuality, was ill-understood especially by the middle classes who demanded virgin brides and faithful wives. If Kinsey *et al.* are right and female sexuality is essentially a learned response, then the nuns in Victorian times were not missing much. Their married sisters suffered as much from sexual ignorance and repression as they did, without even the value of consecrated virginity to support them. A pessimistic view of sexuality in the twentieth century offers a bleak picture of inhibition and unfulfilled desire, the neuroses of housewives on valium locked into the expectations of marriage and family. Those nuns who understand their sexuality and come to terms with it may be more fortunate than their married sisters today or a century ago.

The legal requirements of the poverty vow have already been discussed. Once professed, anything acquired or earned by a sister immediately became congregation property and the money was placed in a common fund. Food, clothing, furniture were all kept in common, even personal garments were kept in a communal cupboard. Sisters were never allowed money for their own purposes; if they had the use of any objects, such as books for teaching, they were to 'detach' their minds and hearts from them. Above all they should take care of the things they use. It is fair to say that in the teaching congregation poverty meant thrift. Habits were mended until they could no longer be patched and darned. Pigs were kept in the convent grounds to eat up scraps, and chickens were kept to provide eggs cheaply. Ordinary daily food was plain to the point of insufficiency. Many attributed this attitude to poverty to a bourgeois revival of Jansenist practices in France in the late nineteenth century.[12] The more rigorous Jansenists considered carelessness a sin and asceticism a sacrifice to God. One of the lay sisters tried to describe what happened when she was given a present. 'I was given two most gorgeous nightdresses and when I entered they were taken from me . . . about four or five years later I saw somebody else wearing them and—oh, it cost me an awful lot—I didn't say anything because you weren't allowed to, but it broke my heart.' At Christmastime a big box was put out for any presents the sisters might be given, which were recirculated round the community or given away to poor people. The dependency of sisters on the congregation and the personal deprivations of the poverty vow supported their commitment to the organization. But even Cannon Law had to change when in the radical 1960s sisters of the teaching congregation carried their own money, wore their own clothes and took on board a whole new set of theories about holy poverty.

Obedience is the most obviously controlling of all the vows, for by this vow the sisters are bound to respect their Superiors and obey all their arrangements and commands. Arrangements are, in Canon Law, the orders given to the whole community. Commands are given to an individual sister and are further divided into express commands which have to be obeyed without question and formal precepts which are only used by the Superior General and are required in writing with the witness of two signatures. Sisters are bound by the Rule to perform any penances imposed for faults even if they are not guilty of the fault accused. It seems hard, but they said that they had committed themselves to serve God and therefore they should suffer any injustice in his name. In the language of the convent exterior signs of obedience should be shown in such things as attending promptly to the convent bells. Every point in the set pattern of the convent day, from rising in the morning to going to bed at night, is marked by a bell. In the minds of the sisters I spoke to it was the petty rules and restrictions which made the most impression: not to leave a tap running, not to hurry, not to talk during a silence. Monica Baldwin, in her now famous book, *I Leap over the Wall*,[13] says that it was these petty aspects of the obedience vow which prompted her to leave the convent. Sister Luke of *The Nun's Story* also cites obedience as her greatest problem in the religious life. But obedience for the teaching sisters, at least until 1965, meant kissing the floor each night to remind themselves that in God's terms they were of dust—just nothing.

The Franciscan Rule book relates the vows to their counterparts in the seven deadly sins, thus: avarice is overcome by poverty; ambition by obedience; gluttony by chastity; and man becomes entirely free and detached from things contrary to God. Poverty for a Franciscan means generosity and sharing; it means rejoicing in the good fortune of others, not being envious, not being conceited. St Francis wrote: 'that servant of God lives really without possessions, who become neither angered nor irritated over anyone.' St Francis's teaching refers more to personality factors and to social acts than to the necessities of daily living. In this he anticipates the post-Vatican II attitudes to poverty. Similarly the Franciscans took obedience to have an all-embracing meaning. Obedience meant being a willing servant to God and service to others. Chastity too was interpreted in a wide-ranging context. Chastity, said St Francis, is utter simplicity and love of all. It was only after the 1960s that the Franciscan congregation returned to this original interpretation. Previously it described chastity as the sincere love of God which required simplicity and prudence, therefore the body must be curbed, caresses and earthly affections spurned, and solace sought in the bridegroom, Christ.

The Franciscan Novice Mistress explained her vows in terms of social history, although in practice the Franciscan congregation was not tied in this respect to the same extent as the teaching congregation. In Victorian and Edwardian times parents laid down clear precepts for their children, and their lives were arranged with very little dialogue. In religious life the Superior was very like the parent; she said, do this, do that, and she was obeyed. But in the early history of the Church the Superiors were much closer to the brethren. St Francis in particular regarded all his followers as equal brothers. More than this, he felt that all human beings were selfish and one could never be quite sure that one was doing a thing for the will of God or for oneself, even when it came to the most charitable acts. What St Francis had to teach was that everything came from 'the hands of God; he loves each individual person personally and infinitely. He is not going to allow anything to happen to that individual that is not for that individual's greater good even if it is pain and suffering.' The chastity vow is therefore a total consecretation of all the nun's capacity to love; every action she does is for the love of God. It is a good example of the total and all-embracing nature of the Franciscan's vows. They cannot be mechanical, they have to make a huge act of faith and give all of themselves to the organization. Once they have done that they accept all that happens to them willingly and unquestioningly. It is an attitude which puts them above the pressures of the outside world. While obedience in the teaching congregation was a reflection of family and society in the late Victorian era, obedience in the Franciscan congregation was legitimated by the early Church and the seraphic saint: powerful sources which were not liable to change over time.

So what does happen when you do not obey the rules in a convent? Obviously the range of sanctions varies with the nature of the offence and the rank of the offender. In the convent a relatively minor offence by a Superior is regarded with horror. It is the responsibility of Superiors to set a good example, and any transgression against the Rule would be treated with the threat of instant dismissal from office and possibly life-long denial of office. Verbal cautions are considered quite sufficient for all but the most intransigent cases. Deprivation and censure are virtually unheard of, they are so serious. If a Superior breaks her religious vows then she would have committed a sin and be liable to retribution in heaven, so the whole onus of her religion would come to bear on her before the social mechanism of removal from office, or, at worst, expulsion from the order would be enforced. Her own conscience is her greatest constraint. She must be able to see for herself the difference between necessary and unnecessary items and actions. It should not be necessary for the Superior General, for example, to point out that her office had too many comforts (an offence against poverty), or that her sisters had too much liberty (an offence against chastity). But the Superior General or a member of the general council do try to visit every convent at least every six months to ensure that standards are being kept.

The lower the rank the less onerous the sanctions on misbehaviour. A postulant does not even commit a sin if she breaks a religious vow. She has not yet professed her vows. But she would be cautioned and might even be discouraged from staying in the congregation. She may suffer some symbolic deprivation like fasting for three days or genuflecting in chapel. A novice would be treated more harshly. She would be expected to understand the vows and while she could still leave the congregation without excommunication she would be disgraced among family and friends if she left for breaking a rule. The younger fully professed sisters would be under considerable pressure. To break vows is seen as losing soul. Small misdemeanours would be censured in the presence of the whole community. Faults committed must be confessed and the nun's punishment would be to mortify herself by remaining silent in recreation time or flagellating in the presence of the assembled sisters at a 'Chapter of Faults'. Even interior faults like bad thoughts have to be confessed; rivalry, jealousy, envy, are all punished. To be caught in a misdemeanour or to confess it would bring the same sanction. The emphasis is on individual responsibility. The religious congregation is truly the 'limiting case of normative compliance'.[14]

The commitment of members is won by a series of indoctrinating and alienating procedures. But even in the hardest times the nuns describe their lives as happy. Even a young girl who entered the convent in 1931 having never cleaned a house or made a cup of tea could say, 'It was a hard life. There was the cleaning, great long corridors and huge high rooms, the scrubbing of the stone floors. But it was happy. You never thought of anything else and you felt it was your trade—you were looking after yourself and you were doing it for God.' She said that when they polished the floors they used to set up a rhythm of work, one with soapy water and then two following with clear water! All working along the corridor with huge hobs and if one got out of step they all ended in a terrible muddle. Sister Anne recalled that in morning prayer, if they were late they had to prostrate themselves in the middle of the aisle for the litany of the saints. Some mornings novices would be lying nose to tail along the length of the chapel, all giggling or doing their best not to. These were after all the wise virgins who went in with the bridegroom to the marriage feast. Their renunciation of the world was of positive value to them.

CHAPTER FIVE

Daily Bread:
Routines for Living

Everyone of us organizes our daily lives around a regular pattern of activities—eating, dressing, defecating, working, relaxing—all tending to happen in routines. Some have cocoa at 10 o'clock every night, others put their clothes for the next day over a chair the night before, others always rise at 6.30 a.m.; we feel put out or nervous if our habits are disrupted. The institutions of our society take these patterns and encapsulate them in even more rigorous routines; in hospital the meals arrive with immaculate precision; the queues outside banks before opening time, the emptying of pubs at closing time, represent a routinization of work and leisure. In the 'total institutions' of Erving Goffman's analysis, daily scheduling is a prerequisite: 'all phases of the day's activities are tightly scheduled, with one activity leading at a prearranged time into the next, the whole sequence of activities being imposed from above by a system of explicit formal rulings and a body of officials.'[1] The result of this common regulation of daily life, whoever it is applied to, remains the same—the restriction of individual freedoms and emphasis on the individual's dependence on the group. The processes of socialization, the vows, the normative force of vocation, were underpinned by this daily scheduling in the convent. The early missionary years in the teaching congregation gave way to years of consolidation, conservatism and a switch in emphasis from the individual to the group.

In the 1930s the teaching congregation revised its religious Rule. The new Rule was more like a legal document, even less of a memorandum for life than the 1891 Rule. It was instrumental in stultifying the development of the Institute which had no option but to follow its precepts. Unlike the Franciscan congregation which was able to expand and reorganize when required, the teaching congregation remained static from 1940 to 1960. For the Franciscans expansion was achieved through a variety of specific goals, new apostolates, new missions. This variety was not open to the teaching congregation because they had been instituted for the education of middle-class girls of the Catholic faith and this remained their sole aim until 1958. Both congregations shared the daily scheduling of their day, week, month, year, and the Franciscans follow these schedules virtually unaltered today. One of the alterations to the 1932 Rule was an amendment to the stated aim of the teaching congregation; it was for the 'sanctification of its members' rather than for 'individual perfection'. The trend towards the 'élite consecrated group' was not only a result of the development of the congregation but also a reflection of the times, a product of the prevailing social conditions in the first quarter of the twentieth century and the position of a largely middle-class institution in that society.[2]

The First World War had little effect on the Institute though sisters remember tales of heroic deeds, of saving the Blessed Sacrament from the enemy by smuggling it out of the convent garden in the Netherlands. Those who lived in England recalled the appalling food, the sour black bread and lack of potatoes. Some remembered working in factories and on farms only to be ousted from positions of responsibility when the men returned. The First World War was undeniably important in implementing women's rights, but the nuns were untouched by the laws going through Parliament. The position of married women was greatly improved but the social climate was still against women moving out of the home. A large proportion of Catholic professional women were religious sisters; they had opportunities which, had they married, they would lose. Even in the late 1930s attempts were made to debar women from the professions, and local education authorities were within their rights when they dismissed women teachers who married. Hilary Newitt commented, 'In Great Britain the authorities appear to regard celibacy as a necessary qualification for professional work by women.'[3] There was still a huge surplus of women. A. J. P. Taylor writes that women's emancipation was purely theoretical up to the Second World War, that in all equivalent jobs they were paid less and were still dependent. In the Post Office, for example, women were paid £3 10s and men £5 1s 6d for the same job. Taylor calculates that only about 5 per cent of households had a resident domestic between the wars.[4] Yet the religious congregation continued to organize itself as though the servant class were a reality. Less than half the teaching congregation's personnel were actually involved in teaching; the rest provided domestic help. It was partly a function of the middle-class orientation of the Institute. Without exception the convents were situated in middle-class areas, in suburban green-belts or prosperous seaside towns. The convent buildings were large, the grounds extensive, the chapels well-endowed and heavily ornamented. Each convent accommodated between twenty and thirty sisters and all but one included boarding facilities for up to 200 girls. Both the girls and the novices had to come from 'nice' families!

Only a very small proportion of the population could afford to pay for their daughters' education. In 1937, 5 per cent of the adult population owned 79 per cent of the wealth, the top 1 per cent owned 56 per cent.[5] The position has changed little today. It is understandable that these teaching nuns, in their isolation, seem to have known nothing of the depression, of the dole queues, of hunger and slums. Writers like J. B. Priestley claimed that people living in the south of England had no idea of conditions in the north, but the nuns did not know that such distress existed. When the nuns today recall the 1930s they do not attribute their lack of food or entertainment to the economic depression; they say it was part of their religious life to mortify their bodies by fast and to praise their Lord by feasts. This is confirmed by historians who say that the crisis and depression of the 1930s barely affected consumption in the upper classes; there was no visible turn to austerity.[6] The girls the nuns taught came from homes with servants, with an interest in education and the identifiable manners of the middle class, Catholic homes little affected by radical thought. In 1930 a Papal Encyclical on Christian Marriage had this to say about the place of the married women: 'The divine institution of matrimony was not instituted or restored by man but by God and hence these laws cannot be subject to any human decrees . . . the order of love which includes both the primacy of the husband with regard to the wife and children, the ready subjection of the wife and her willing obedience . . . It is recognized that certain false teachers assert that husband and wife should have equal rights. They do not scruple to do away with the honourable and trusting obedience which the woman owes the man.'[7] In many respects the nun still enjoyed a kind of autonomy, yet she is a paradox, at once the eternal feminine, demurely carrying out humble tasks, obedient and loving, yet free from the male domination of husband, father or guardian.

The Pope was not the only authority to emphasize a secondary and obedient place for women in the ordering of society. The 1930s was after all the time when Europe came under the thrall of totalitarian ideologies from the right wing of politics. Hitler himself made a pronouncement on the position of women: 'The world of man is the state, the world of man is his struggle, his self-dedication to the community, and thus we may say that the world of woman is a smaller one, her world is her husband, her family, her children, and her house . . . we do not believe it to be right for women to penetrate into the world of man, into his special sphere, on the contrary, we feel that it is natural for these worlds to remain separated.'[8] Catholics are understandably defensive about the relationship of their Church to the fascist movements of the 1930s and 1940s. They had fought a revolution in Spain, sending in troops to fight with the fascist cause for the kingship of Christ. The nuns I questioned either refused to answer or denied any political involvements of left- or right-wing persuasions. The rigorous lifestyle, the exact scheduling of the day, the demands of religious obedience should be seen as part of the contemporary political climate. William Sargant, whose life-work was the study of indoctrination, wrote in 1957, 'The techniques of political and religious indoctrination are often so similar that in primitive communities, or in more civilized theocratic states such as the ancient Jewish, they are actually identical. . . . Yet the more obvious similarities are often ignored because either the religious approach (as in Western Europe and the United States today) or the political (as in Eastern Europe and China) is accorded official respect at the other's expense.'[9] Sargant was concerned with the ability of political parties or religious groups suddenly to change the affiliations of an individual. I am concerned with the ability of such groups to hold the commitment of members. An official Nazi pamphlet of 1934 spoke to the women of Germany: 'The leitmotif then is motherhood, and closely following come the ideas of sacrifice and service.' Sacrifice and service are highly charged words belonging to centuries of the Christian ethic, the touchstones of the religious life.

Tight scheduling of daily activities is a feature of all organizations which require a total commitment from members. The life of the religious sister can be compared to the life of a member of a kibbutz or a labour camp; the organizations may have very different ideologies and aims but they need committed members to fulfil those goals. Time is used to structure daylight hours; there is no such thing as free time. Each day was taken as a group exercise in group activity. In the German labour camps in the 1930s—perhaps an extreme example, but none the less applicable to any form of intensive indoctrination—any time not working was spent in group recreation or games. Hilary Newitt describes the day: 'Absolute obedience to the camp leader is demanded. Accommodation is extremely simple . . . they sleep in bunks, with straw mattresses ranged in double tiers, 20 to a room. In summer they are woken at 5.30 and do half-an-hour early sport, then they dress and make beds; at 6.45 the flag is hoisted; 7 a.m. breakfast. Practical work follows from 7.30 to 3 p.m. with a break of half-an-hour for a meal. From 3 to 4.30 rest on their beds. After tea come 1½ hours of instruction. At 6.30 supper, and later, singing, music, games—or maybe more discussion, whilst clothes are mended, socks knitted. The flag is taken down, and at 9.30 "good-night".'[10]

Compare this day to the daily life of a sister in the teaching con-

gregation, a daily life unchanged from 1891 to 1960, a day so regular
that it could be set down in a book and its patterns followed all over
the world wherever there was a nun from this order. Each morning
the sisters were woken in their dormitories by a rising bell at 5.30 a.m.
The Superior intoned in a low voice, 'My child, give me thy heart,'
and the nuns replied together, 'My Lord and my God, for thee I rise.
Praise be Jesus, Mary and Joseph.' Then they made the sign of the
cross and a kiss for the image of Jesus crucified. They took their
habits from the hook beside their beds and dressed quickly while the
Superior continued to chant the clothing prayer in a slow, distinct
voice, the sisters repeating her words in an undertone, 'Clothe me, O
Lord, with the new man, adorn me with the gifts of Thy holy love,
purify my mind and my heart. Help me to mortify the evil inclinations
of my corrupt nature and to govern in accordance with Thy designs
and Thy holy will, my senses, my imagination, my mind and my heart.
Amen.' The clothing prayer began the day as it was to continue, in
mortifying the body, in purifying the mind. The sisters speak
emotionally of these times as years when they were empty, filled with
a nothingness and ready to serve their God. It was a vision of a
Holy Love which infused their day and, if the prayers make them
sound depressing and negative, the nuns themselves had a reputation
among outsiders for jollity and inner contentment.

Fifteen minutes were allowed for dressing and then the sisters went
to chapel reciting the Salve Regina as they went. It ends with the
Superior saying, 'Make me worthy to praise Thee, O Holy Virgin,'
and the sisters replying, 'Give me strength against thine enemies.'
Then the Superior completed the prayer, 'Blessed be God in his
Saints,' and the sisters replied, 'He is Holy in all his works.' The
sisters entered the chapel, prostrated themselves before the altar and
took up their positions, the youngest nearest the altar, the Superior
farthest away. All the time they were to be thinking about their own
nothingness and the infinite greatness of God. Lay sisters stayed at
the very back of the chapel. All prayers were repeated after the
Superior in a set pattern using prayer books.[11] Then the morning
prayers began, and these too followed a set pattern. They consisted of
an act of thanksgiving, a prayer to the Blessed Virgin, to guardian
angels and to Patron Saints, an offering of all actions performed
during the day, an intention of gaining all the indulgences that could
be gained, and a Litany. Intentions and indulgences were also set
prayers; for example, On Sundays they said, 'Let us offer all our
actions in honour of the Blessed Trinity, and to obtain the propagation and preservation of the Catholic faith.' This prayer would be
repeated every Sunday throughout the life of the nun. It could get
very boring. As Sister Patrick said, 'It was very monotonous just

working from morning till night and very little prayer life—you just went to chapel for so long and you came out and that was it!'

After morning prayers the sisters had half-an-hour for meditation. This was a routine meditation on a topic set by the Superior and included set prayers. It ended with an examen. The examen was another set prayer looking forward to the day ahead to see if there would be any moments in it which would require special care or effort, and a prayer for help in overcoming it. It was like insurance cover which admits to the possibility of an accident. If a sister had to go out of enclosure, into the visitors' parlour for example, then she would say a brief prayer putting herself under the special guidance of the Virgin Mary. It was both precautionary and protective and re-affirmed the nun's dependence on spiritual help against secular temptations. At the close of these prayers the convent priest or a priest from the nearby parish would come to the convent chapel to take Mass. This was the one time each day when the monotony of the nun's life was lit with candles, with incense, with a direct experience of the supernatural efficacy of sacraments which fed her soul and gave her a vision of eternity. Compared to the Mass—all other works and entertainments were secondary. The nuns attended Mass daily but took communion only once a week—in a well-regulated, mechanized life this drama, sacrificial and magical, reaffirmed all the positive values of religion for the nun.

In an article on the importance of belief in the persistence of social systems Shils stresses the very positive substantive content of many traditional beliefs.[12] One cannot overemphasize the nun's belief in the inherent 'goodness' of her way of life, of the value of the *gemeinschaft* and the virtue of authority. The nuns of the teaching order had a magical belief in the efficacy of the Eucharist and in the performance of rituals. Traditional beliefs, Shils confirms, tend to be stereotypical and magical; they are characterized by God-fearing and prescribed ceremonial and ritual performance particularly in relation to the immediate group, emphasizing obligations and attachments to that group. The nuns saw God as an awesome father-figure; the importance of group obligations took precedence over the individual at all times. Thus the expression of even the most magical elements of their religion further socialized and resocialized the nuns in their commitment to the religious organization. The adherence to tradition led to an unquestioning acceptance of a mode of living and thinking in which prayer life, apostolate and organization ossified over the years, until in 1960 the teaching nuns found themselves encapsulated in a way of life which the rest of the world had discarded. It left them stranded and unable to fulfil the goals of their organization. Eventually the time came for change, but until then the way of life persisted unaltered.

D

Immediately after Mass, which fed the spirit, the sisters went to breakfast. It consisted of bread and a cup of tea. Some sisters would be restricted to water as a mortification, a self-imposed restriction which often led to a degree of physical debilitation and illness. Some talk was allowed at breakfast so that the business of the day could be arranged, but it was not idle chatter. All other meals were silent, with one sister making an appropriate reading from the founder's writings or the Rule. Sister Patrick made this unequivocal statement on the routine, drudgery and silence of a nun's day. 'We got up and went to chapel and made our meditation. Then we came out for about half-an-hour's work, buttering bread or dusting classrooms or something. Then a bell rang for Mass, always a bell, then we came out and there was breakfast and breakfast was silent. Then everybody went about their work, whatever it was, either in the kitchen or around the house —that was our life. Then a bell rang and you went to chapel to examine your conscience for the morning. Then you came out and had dinner. Silence for dinner, there used to be a reading at the beginning. After dinner we went to the recreation room or into the garden for half-an-hour, then a bell rang and you went back to your duties. Usually we had all the vegetables and potatoes and bread and butter to do for the boarders. Then there was tea, we could talk then. After tea we went to the chapel for a visit. A spiritual reading or something, then you came out and did some more work. Then we had supper, after supper we had another half an hour's recreation and then night-prayers together. Everybody together, then we were gone to bed—no talk—that was what they call the grand silence. Or some people call it the great silence; it's a mortal sin to speak in it, you just had to make signs or write a little note to people and that lasted from nine o'clock until breakfast the next morning. That's every ordinary day!'

The silence was frequently mentioned as the hardest aspect of daily life. Sister Mary George said, 'Even if you met your own sister in the corridor and you wanted to speak to her you couldn't. If it was something really important then you had to begin by saying "Ave maria" and she said "gratia plena". You could never speak without permission or you had to ask a penance for it, it was terribly strict. Especially regarding the priest or the children, you should never speak to them.' On Sundays and fast-days talking was not allowed at any time on any condition. Silence was seen as an instrument of the chastity vow and extended to manners as well as to speech. The nuns had to take care to shut doors quietly, to walk steadily and quietly without hurrying. This imposed silence was an aid to recollection. Recollection is one of those words which imply far more to the religious than to the laity, just as the religious life demands far more of the religious sister than of her secular brethren. The Rule said, 'Recollection is a virtue by which we quietly apply our minds to God and thus keep our senses, our imagination, our thoughts and the affections of our hearts under the control of reason, and facilitate that continual detachment so indispensable to us for the constant fulfilment of our duties in conformity with the designs of Providence.' Silence was the regulation for the control and repression of the senses. Sign language was not allowed by the Rule, but sisters who lived in the 1930s say that they did develop a sign language for most situations. They laugh when they tell you about times when it went wrong, like the Mother Superior signing for her spectacles and a junior nun going to see who was at the convent door.

The sisters were in disagreement as to whether silence was a mortification or not. A theologian would tell us that mortification 'is concerned with the prudent organization of the human person (the higher and lower faculties of the soul and the bodily senses) in its struggle against evil inclinations.'[13] But the sisters saw mortifications as self-imposed punishments for some act of wrongdoing, conscious or unconscious, against God. They distinguished it from penance which was for punishment when some exterior rule had been broken. Any wrongdoing against God, they told me, was punishable in the 'next world' by the 'torments of purgatory or worst of all hell'. These torments could be expiated by penance and to escape God's punishments you could inflict punishment on yourself, just as God's Son Jesus Christ practised mortification and penance by being born humanly in a stable and dying on a cross. This explanation must be taken as valid for the nuns whether it conforms to Church doctrine or verges on the heretical. It was the nuns' explanation for their life and belief. Silence was a protection against the evils of the world, against the temptation of gossip and time-wasting.

Silence separated one nun from her sister, enclosure separated the group from the outside world. Enclosure is defined by Canon Law, and a Papal representative regularly checks the convents in his diocese for breaches of the law which are punishable by excommunication. Enclosure was therefore a very serious matter which extended to the physical spaces of the sisters' living quarters, the meeting rooms, dormitories, refectory, cells and infirmary. In the boarding schools, no person of the opposite sex is allowed in without permission from the Superior. But enclosure did not refer just to physical space; it covered all communications. Conversations with visitors were not allowed. Choir sisters only left a convent to move to another; it could be twenty years before they would see the world outside their convent. Letters were opened and read by the Superior. Letters written by sisters were handed to the Superior before being sent. Sisters were allowed to send and receive letters from certain sources without this interference; these included the Holy See, Papal legate and other high officials of the Church and congregation. It was a safeguard—one of the very few—on personal liberty. In the traditional convent there were no newspapers, books or radios. The whole point of enclosure was to retain the sisters in a purity untainted by contact with the outside world. If by some unhappy chance a sister did learn about a world event or some local news she was forbidden to talk to her fellow sisters about it and only in exceptional circumstances should she tell her Superior who would then decide whether or not to make it generally known in the convent.

The sisters were warned of the dangers of the visitors' parlour. The Rule says: 'the parlour is the door by which the spirit of the world enters. It is through the parlour that laxity steals into the most fervent communities. . . . Who can tell the harm that a Religious, who likes to have intercourse with seculars, does to her soul! . . . she forsakes the pure delights of the interior life for a passing gratification. She loses peace of soul, liberty of mind, the joy of a good conscience. . . . when you leave the parlour, try to forget all that you have heard there; let everything be effaced from your memory. May God preserve you from introducing into the Convent pestilential principles which would infect the pure and holy atmosphere in which your sisters live.' Outsiders were 'polluting'; sisters placed themselves under the protection of the Virgin Mary before they opened a door or entered a parlour. No sister ever took food or drink with a stranger, not even the convent priest. There was no escape from enclosure, no annual trips, no holidays. Only the lay sisters who did the marketing from the back-door had an easier relationship with the outside world, but they were one step behind the choir nun; they could be located at the back of the chapel.

Most of the nuns' day was occupied in work, the choir sisters teaching the children from the school, the lay sisters doing housework and preparing meals. But they were expected to find the time to go to the chapel and visit the Blessed Sacrament during the afternoon. After morning Mass the priest would leave consecrated bread in a tabernacle on the altar. The tabernacle then became the earthly throne of God and the visiting nuns had a very real feeling for his presence there. They knelt before it, reciting prayers and reading on a subject prepared by their Superior. It was a visit in which the sister reminded herself of God's love and strengthened her resolve to continue his work on earth. The choir sisters also had to recite the little Office of the Virgin Mary and three times a day they said the Angelus and the Regina Coeli. Every day was a struggle for spiritual welfare. Every day they went to the chapel to examine their consciences, once in the morning, once at noon and again in the evening. It was a struggle carried out in a ritualized prayer life punctuated with devotional prayers, standardized, uniform. Sisters living in the 1930s had a strong sense of their own élitism and of the evil in the world outside. They lived in a tension between their exterior and interior lives which placed them outside society at large yet outside the heavenly place they sought.

The day ended with night prayers. These, too, were written down in the ceremonial of the Institute. They consisted of a prayer of thanksgiving, an act of faith, hope and charity, the litany of the Blessed Virgin, an act placing themselves under the protection of the Virgin Mary, their guardian angels and patron saints, another examination of conscience and some preparation of the next day's meditation. The examination of conscience would almost certainly involve a feeling of contribution and the repetition of the Confiteor. Night prayers therefore involved personal prayers (thought even these were set) and acts, and common prayers with the whole community. By nine-thirty the sisters were undressing and going to bed. Fifteen minutes was allowed for undressing during which time the Superior said aloud, the sisters echoing her quietly, 'Deliver me, O Lord, from the old man and the inclinations of corrupt nature. Remove from my soul all the strains that sin has made. Purify me and make me agreeable to Thy sight and I shall repose in peace in the bosom of Thine infinite mercy.' When all the sisters were in bed, the narrow iron beds set in rows down the dormitory, the Superior intoned, the sisters repeating, 'Praise be Jesus, Mary and Joseph, into thy hands I commend my body and soul [here they kiss the crucifix], our holy Guardian angels watch over us.' The nuns were expected to go to sleep as quickly as possible. Sleep was the natural image of death. In death the nun would hope to be united with the God for whom she worked so hard. Sleep was a reward for a day spent working, a time for the body to rest before giving itself for yet another day.

The daily schedule of a nun in the teaching congregation before 1960 reflected the concern for boundaries, the boundaries of the organization in relation to the outside world and internally, in the class divisions and status differentiation of priest and nun, Superior and community, professed nun and novice. The function of religious ritual in boundary maintenance and the force of pollution ideas to uphold moral values and social rules is discussed in *Purity and Danger* by Mary Douglas, whose work in the explanation of danger beliefs is now well known.[14] The care devoted to enclosure, to silence and mortification, the attention given to purity and pollution in the set prayers of the daily routine reflect a concern with the maintenance of the group. Douglas says, 'The ideal order of society is guarded by dangers which threaten transgressors. . . . The whole universe is harnessed to men's attempts to force one another into good citizenship.'[15] At one time anthropologists interpreted these concerns as being instrumental in holding people to roles and moral positions. Now, danger beliefs, witchcraft and elaborate ritual are seen as having an expressive function in demarcating social groups and defining social categories.[16]

There are two officials, the Sacristan and the Portress, who typify this concern with boundary. The one stands between the congregation and the Church, the human and the divine, the other between enclosure and the outside world. In the teaching congregation lay sisters held both positions and they remained in 'charge' for many years. In the Franciscan congregation, with no distinction between lay and choir nun, the office was entrusted to responsible sisters who rarely kept them for longer than six months to a year. They were both appointed by the local Superior, that is the Mother Superior in the convent in question, and were directly responsible to her. The Portress was expected to keep her Superior informed of the comings and goings from the convent, especially if a sister was requested in the parlour. She collected all letters and parcels and took them directly to the Superior. She held the keys to the outside door and at the end of each day she locked it and handed her keys to the Superior. The concern in the traditional order to keep a check on the doorway, a check carefully monitored by the chief authority in the convent, reflects their concern with boundary maintenance. In the Franciscan congregation, where there was an overriding ideology of 'going to meet the people', the enclosure and silence was preserved but the doorway was ever-open, manned by a succession of nuns, presided over by the Superior with equal care. One of the dramatic changes in the teaching congregation was the abolition of the portress duty, the free entry and exit to and from the convent.

The Sacristan was responsible for the Church or chapel, her principal duty being to see that one lamp at least was kept constantly burning before the tabernacle. It was fed with olive oil or beeswax: to use any other oil required the permission of the Local Ordinary. The Sacristan could handle and touch the chalice, the paten, purificators, palls and corporals: but if they had been used by the priest at Mass she was not allowed to touch them until they had first been washed by a cleric in major orders. The water in which the articles and linens were washed for the first time was poured into the sacrarium or thrown on the fire. The Sacristan had charge of the key to the tabernacle and at the hour of closing the chapel each night she handed to the Superior both this key and the key to the chapel. The caution with which ritual objects including oil and cloth were treated reflects concern with the boundary between this world and the next. But it also reflects Church hierarchy; the humble nun must not contaminate articles handled by the holy priest. The centralized authority of the Church protected its monopoly on the sacraments and bound Superiors of convents, who could be powerful people in their own right, to the established hierarchy of its own institutional organization.[17] And it reflected the internal authority of the Mother Superior, who, when night closed, held the keys of both the tabernacle and the front door.

In both these congregations the local Superior was a dominant personality in the lives of the sisters under her jurisdiction, yet she had neither the power of the Benedictine abbots nor the free exercise of authority given to most leaders of small groups. Her role was to interpret and carry out to the letter the Rule and Constitutions of her congregation. She had to make sure that they were read regularly to her sisters together with any new decrees from the Vatican which might affect them. She had to ensure that all her sisters made their annual spiritual exercises, that they assisted at Mass and devoted themselves to 'mental prayer'. She had to pass on any directives from her Superior General and make sure they were carried out. Every month she sent a report to the Superior General on the moral, religious, and temporal state of the house. Every fortnight she gave her community a talk on the religious life. She could spend a certain amount of money fixed by the General Chapter of the congregation, on the house and on the personal upkeep of sisters. It was a fulltime job and made it virtually impossible for Superiors to engage themselves in the apostolic work of the congregation. One sister in the teaching congregation told me that on her first term of office as a local Superior (they were generally appointed for a term of three years) she had no idea what was expected of her and used to sit up every night studying her Canon Law books to make sure she did not make some serious mistake.

The local Superior was assisted by two other officials, the local vicar and the local bursar who were chosen from the choir nuns and a bevy of lay sisters who took positions as cooks, refectorians, linen ladies, etc. The organization at local level mirrored the organization at a 'general' level, where the Superior General was assisted by a Vicaress General, Bursar General and four councillors. It is a common form of organization in Catholic congregations and few differences were revealed between these two congregations, though such as there were were crucial. The teaching congregation had grown so large by 1900 that it was divided into provinces as well as houses. The procedures for election, dismissal, appointments and the powers of governing the sisters were all clearly specified in the Rule. The original freedoms by which, for example, an eighteen-year-old was able to take charge of a convent were over. The General Council was a permanent body looking after the affairs of the Institute but in general reliant on the Superior General for directives. Councillors lived in the Generalate house and were not allowed to do any other work. All matters discussed in council were secret. Divulgence of any information was a grave fault. A councillor had to be a model sister; she was expected to voice her opinions with moderation and humility and show no annoyance if her advice went unheeded. The Franciscans were particularly enjoined to 'uphold the authority of the Mother General and to be foremost in the example of humility, obedience and religious observance'.

Management of the congregations was by written document. Each monthly meeting of the General Council, triennial meetings of the General Chapter, which were attended by local Superiors as well, were all recorded by a Secretary General and her entries kept in the archives. All inter-departmental communications and directives from the Superior General were by written memorandum and these too were kept in the archives to form part of the tradition of government. Financial matters were attended to by the Bursar General. In the teaching congregation she was responsible for all the houses and received quarterly balance sheets on expenditure, with receipts. In the Franciscan congregation the individual houses had the juridical capacity to acquire and possess property on their own account although overall responsibility still devolved on the Bursar General. Regulations concerning property and money were stringent and, since they were required by Canon Law as well as by Rule, the local Papal representative made periodic checks on the financial viability of the congregation. Nor were they allowed to mortgage, sell, give, exchange or alienate in any way any property over a certain value without prior permission from the Vatican, the implication being that no congregation could accumulate either debts or monies without the knowledge and approval of Church hierarchy. Expansion and profitable enterprises could only be carried out with Vatican approval, which made the congregation's relationship with the local diocese a crucial one. In all houses the money used for current expenses was lodged in a Bank under the names of the local Superior and her Vicaress or Bursar. But in the Generalate there was a safe or strong chest, locked with three different keys, of which the Superior had one, the Vicaress another, and the Bursar General a third. Whenever the safe was to be opened (and all title deeds of property, cheques and shares are kept in the safe), all three had to be present. They were not allowed to lend their keys to anyone else. The controls on mis-appropriation of funds were considerable!

In the religious congregation the General Councillors and the Mother General were selected for their general ability and verve as administrators rather than through some particular qualification. The same might apply to most local Superiors and the Novice Mistress. The Mistress of Novices was chosen by the Superior General and the Council together and was elected for three years initially. She did not have a vote on the General Council though she might be called to give evidence on the Novitiate to Council members. She was always at least thirty-five years old and in perpetual vows of ten years profession. These types of qualification were required for all offices. She would also be recommended by her 'prudence, charity, piety and religious observance'. These are good examples of the qualities required for office in a religious congregation. In an ideal-typical bureaucracy all officials have specialized knowledge and specific training for office. This principle is not rigorously born out in the religious congregation. Appointment to prestigious office requires a general competence rather than specific expertise. It almost exactly parallels recruitment to the top levels of the Civil Service from Oxford-educated men, or the example of the Chinese *literati* described by Yang.[18] Yang makes a distinction between administrators and other officials. The administrators were men of general knowledge, scholar/officials with the general stock of the Confucian classics at their disposal, not the skills of a specialist. They were the backbone of the Chinese bureaucracy and were to be found in positions superior to the specialists. Certainly in the religious congregation the administrators had high status and general abilities, while other officials such as the Mistress General of the teaching congregation had to hold exceptional teaching qualifications as well as a generalized ability in administration and co-ordination. Meanwhile, lower down the administrative scale, the head of a small school, or the sister in charge of farming activities in the Franciscan congregation, would be chosen primarily for their specialist skills for which she would have received specific training.

The appointment of all officials was confirmed by the General Chapter, a meeting of senior officers, local superiors and delegates from all houses. From the 1930s to 1960s the Chapter met every six years, the Franciscans at Pentecost, the teaching congregation at a convenient time before the expiry of the office of Mother General, for the General Chapter's prime function was to elect or re-elect their leader. Election of delegates, procedural voting and election and ratification of appointments were all carried out in secret ballots with trusted scrutineers, sealed envelopes and locked ballot boxes. Tellers were appointed by relative majority and swore an oath to perform their duty faithfully and silently: 'I swear to fulfil my office faithfully and always to preserve inviolable secrecy.' After the count all voting papers were burnt. In any election canvassing of votes was forbidden, but in the case of the Franciscans the sisters were allowed to inquire about the qualities of sisters to whom they intended giving their vote; however, they were forbidden to discuss it. The emphasis on secrecy seems surprising in view of the already stringent rules for silence and enclosure. It was enjoined by Canon Law and also served to isolate one sister from another, inhibiting the formation of interest-groups and encouraging adherence to the norms and values of the organization. To break the Constitutions was sinful, to commit a sin was to lose grace; thus the pressure of religious belief was once more brought to bear. Every Chapter was preceded by attendance at Holy Communion in a Mass dedicated to the Holy Ghost—giver of Grace. As the sisters entered the Chapter, two by two, they recited the Veni Creator and took their places in order of precedence.

The election of a new Mother General was presided over by the Papal Ordinary, the representative of the Church, and it was he who would proclaim the new incumbent. Once installed, the Mother General is the absolute power and authority within the congregation. The Franciscans emphasize this power and authority; the teaching congregation mitigates it by stressing her dependence on her General Council for day-to-day decisions. In the election of the first Superior General to the teaching congregation, the founder of the order, a local bishop, directed the ceremony of installation. He asked, 'Are you sincerely resolved to act in all things according to the desire and teaching of the Catholic, Apostolic and Roman Church? Do you consent to govern the pious family of . . .'. She answered, promising to observe the rules and to protect them against any attempt at innovation. Then the Canon blessed the ring and cross, and gave them to her, together with other symbols of authority, the seal of the Institute, keys and a book of the Rule. The new Superior General then seated herself at the foot of the Altar and the nuns in turn knelt before her and promised obedience. In the case of the Franciscans the sisters knelt before the new Mother General in Chapter and kissed her hand in an act of religious homage, then they proceeded to the chapel to join the remaining members of the community in singing the *Te Deum*, a thanksgiving to God. The ceremony emphasizes, in its ritual, the importance of the external legitimation of authority, the presence of the bishop, and the commitment of all members of the organization to the authority of the Mother General.

The Franciscan Mother General retained power over all the houses and sisters in her congregation and was bound to keep that power intact by the Rule. At the same time she should not forget St Francis's injunction that Superiors should be 'servants of all the Brethren'. The

spirit of prayer and divine contemplation should be the keystone of
her office. Both Mother Generals governed through their General
Council and by visitations to the houses in their congregation. The
process of these visitations was laid down in the Rule. Each house
must be visited at least once every three years; in the Franciscan
congregation visits were more frequent. The purpose of the visit was
to establish the material and moral state of each convent. Sisters were
seen in private and were bound to give an account of any abuses which
might have crept into the life of the house or any actions which she
might consider contrary to the good of the congregation as a whole or
of any particular sister. The Rule contained an article prohibiting
Superiors from pressuring sisters, or inhibiting them in answering
the visitors' questions, or even molesting them for the answers given.
Should a Superior be found guilty of trying to intimidate her charges
she could be deposed and precluded from holding office again. Every
three years the Mother General gave her congregation a report on the
disciplinary, personal, material and economic state of the Institute
and Novitiate. She was expected to make an examen (a meditative
prayer) on the needs of the Institute every day, and was responsible to
the Church for the exact observance of the Rule and Constitutions.
All the higher offices in the congregation, but particularly that of
Superior General, carried a degree of status and privilege and social
esteem. Superiors had their own rooms, they could move about from
convent to convent, they were not subject to silence and enclosure to
the same degree as their subjects. But this was not seen as conflicting
with religious notions of humility for it was mediated by normative
role definition. All officials were to be 'foremost in the example of
obedience, humility and religious observance. It may even be that
those who have shown the greatest humility will be singled out for
office.'

The developed religious congregation has a bureaucratic organization for the management of its affairs. Weber set out the essential
principles of the process and officialdom in an ideal-typical bureaucracy. These principles included the expectation of an ordered
hierarchy of office authority, fixed official jurisdictional areas and
stated rules of office management which were conducted mainly by
written document. The management was to be a fulltime occupation
which would require specialized knowledge. The six characteristics
expected of a bureaucratic official included a sense of vocation, the
expectation of social esteem, some pecuniary compensation, career
prospects, the appointment to office by a superior and the tenure of
that office for life. In the religious congregation all lower officials
were appointed, as were those involved in the specific instrumental
goals of the organization. Other high officials were elected and re-

cruited from an élite group. But the Mother General herself appointed her Vicaress General and the second assistant and Mistress General of each house, so many officials were in fact appointed by a superior authority as in an ideal-typical bureaucracy, although some officials were elected from a select élite. Each official certainly had a fixed jurisdictional area, stipulated in the Rule book, which was of course a legal document, a set of codified rules regulating conduct and authority. For example, the Novice Mistress alone was responsible for her novices, and the Mother General was the only official who might interfere in that office, and then only in an official Visitation. Not only do the two congregations fulfil many of the principles of the ideal-typical bureaucracy, but they also exhibit other characteristics of bureaucratic administration anticipated by Weber. These include a degree of formality, the use of hierarchy and departmentalism, a remoteness between controllers and controlled, the use of written communications, codification of Rules, centralization of decision-making and possible rigidity in the face of radical innovation. With regard to the last point officials were actually forbidden to change rules in the teaching congregation, and the Franciscan Mother General was only able to initiate change by virtue of a special relationship to Papal authority which allowed her speedy ratification for any changes she might want.

All the officials had a title, and while in the teaching congregation all choir nuns were called 'Mother' and only choir nuns were eligible for management positions, in the Franciscan congregation an office-holder was called 'Mother' rather than 'sister' for the duration of her office only. The named officials formed part of an ordered hierarchy of office authority. It was a hierarchy prescribed in the Rule and acted upon at all formal and ceremonial occasions. At every mealtime an order of precedence was observed in the seating arrangements which admitted not only the office hierarchy but also differentiation by age and length of profession. Weber considers that all officials in an ideal bureaucracy choose their office by vocation. Vocation in a religious organization is part of that total commitment to organizational goals demanded of all participants. The nun reinforces the vocational nature of her choice by placing herself totally at the disposal of the organization. There is little conflict between active apostolate and the demands of office in a religious organization because the nun's whole lifestyle leads her to a total commitment to organizational goals, whatever they may be. Top officials, with excessive work-loads, do not refer to the 'heresy of work' for it is demanded of them by their Rule, whereas the over-zealous pursuit of the apostolate is something to be guarded against by the general membership. In return for this commitment the nun receives no pecuniary compensation for office but the organization keeps her, as it keeps all its members, in health and relative comfort until death.

The religious organizations broadly conform to all but two of the twelve principles characterizing bureaucratic organizations. One point of divergence is that their officials are not appointed to offices held for life. Some sociologists regard this as a key factor in bureaucratic administration and its absence could be regarded as a weakness in this analysis. Martin Albrow, for example, says that Weber, 'refused to call the elected official or the one selected by lot, a bureaucratic official'.[19] I suggest that when Weber stresses that the bureaucrat is, by his nature, an appointee he is talking about the 'ideal' bureaucrat. He was well aware that reality will present variations from his ideal type. Further, the nuns were not appointed by the legal process of the election alone. They had to have that election ratified by a superior authority, whether internal to the congregation or external by reference to Rome. To this extent, the legitimacy (in the Weberian sense) of their office depended on the approbation of superiors in just the same way as it would have had they been duly appointed. Similarly, though the term of their office was restricted to six years for most cases, once a sister had an official position she was simply moved to a similar one of roughly equivalent power and status. The only official to whom this could not apply was the Superior General, and in both congregations one sister had, in fact, held the position for more than the maximum term laid down in the Rule. Papal approval had been sought and given to an extension of service.

The principle of fixed and official jurisdictional areas, ordered by rules, that is laws or administrative regulations, is basic to 'bureaucratic authority'. Official areas are the regular activities of the organization and can be seen as official duties. Weber claims that officialdom acts in a quite specific manner.[20] In the religious congregation the discharge of duties was contained within a strictly limited Rule which set out the means by which the official could give commands and expect compliance in addition to the actual duties he should perform. The religious Rule cannot be thought of as an abstraction, a theoretical concept or a construct of the sociologist. It is a specific text which is constantly referred to by the religious sisters. It is also the key to the legitimacy of bureaucratic authority wielded by officials in its name. Michael Hill describes the Rule as 'an important nexus of authority because it regulates the internal organization of the group but it derives its legitimacy externally from the church, which plays an important part in framing the constitutional blueprint'.[21] The legal precepts derive from the Canon Law of the Church, but the distinctive characteristics of each congregation derive, as we have seen, from the personality and aims of the founder. In relation to the government of congregations the Rule refers to management as well as to authority. It is a rare case in which there is a virtually complete correspondence between sociological abstraction and the actuality of cultural context.

The checks and balances which operated on the individual in her daily routine were echoed in the governmental structure of the religious congregation. The teaching congregation developed from a small missionary community to a large bureaucracy in the years between its foundation in Victorian times to the early 1930s. I suggested that the cultural and political movements in the outside world, particularly the totalitarian movements of Europe in the 1930s, accelerated the movement towards standardization and the emphasis on control and discipline. The use of devotional prayers, of common rituals, the dictates of a Rule which was unchangeable, all ensured members' commitment to organization goals without allowing much room for individual expression. By the outbreak of the Second World War the teaching congregation was locked into a fearful conformity and uniformity which was to inhibit its further development. The Franciscan congregation escaped this situation despite the obvious similarities in organization: the formal definition of status and role of officials, the departmentalism of convent life, the secrecy of voting and decision-making precedures, the Visitations and the silence and enclosure. But the Franciscan congregation had the innovation power of charismatic authority built in to its organization and perpetuated in the Rule and Testament of St Francis. While there was no legitimation for change in the established order of the teaching congregation, the Franciscans had the possibility for change woven into the very fabric of their ordered hierarchy.

CHAPTER SIX

Freedom for Nuns

When I began my visits to the nuns in 1969, first impressions were confused by the diversity of lifestyles I found. The Franciscans appeared solidly conservative. Their lifestyle would not have seemed strange in Victorian England or even in earlier centuries. The teaching congregation exhibited a variety which included old convents where one could still find sisters in the full traditional habit keeping to old prayers and old routines, and modern convents which could hardly be distinguished from the suburban houses next door, convents where sisters rushed to and fro engaged in numerous different tasks, wearing the everyday clothes of middle-class housewives, and chattering about their holidays and their travels. There had been many changes in the outside world, not least in the Catholic Church itself, expressed in the promulgations of the Second Vatican Council in the early 1960s. The council urged congregations to change their ways, yet the Franciscans resisted the pressure to change and sustained a place in the world of the 1970s with minimal disruption to their lifestyle and organization. The teaching congregation responded with a drastic, revolutionary change in an organization which during the 1930s had become paralysed by formal rules and bureaucratic regulations. They had a number of missions in Africa but the experience of the great majority of sisters was confined to one large convent. I was interested not so much in *why* they should desire change and seek a freedom from their well-regulated, highly routinized day, but *how* they were able to break the patterns of generations. Every woman who lives her life in the expected patterns of marriage and family is familiar with the conflicts a career or a job can bring. The nuns became only too familiar with the 'heresy of work' as personal freedom conflicted with the demands of religious life.

The 1960s was a decade in which the 'alternative society' became a byword. The underground press, the 'new' theatre, the commune movements were seen as radical alternatives to the establishment in Europe and America. People—young people in particular—questioned the authority of those in power and sought new ways of living with their fellows. Their protest took the form of small groups, organized as relatively unstructured units, anti-authoritarian, non-hierarchical. The massive reorganization of the teaching congregation followed the same lines as this 'alternative society'. The nuns, the hippies and the radicals were all searching for new freedoms. Freedom is an emotive word, misused, misunderstood, having different meanings for different men. It is provocative: the religious become evangelical, the political become violent in the cause of freedom. Concordet said that the term 'revolutionary' can only be applied to revolutions whose aim is freedom.[1] The teaching congregation was founded with such a spirit. The founder encouraged a group of dedicated women to teach the Catholic catechism in defiance of the civil authorities, in the cause of religious freedom. That group had grown, developed a bureaucratic organization which ultimately encapsulated its members until they too sought to throw off the yoke of established practice. Hannah Arendt says, 'It is frequently very difficult to say where the mere desire for liberation to be free from oppression ends, and the desire for freedom as the political way of life begins.'[2] In discarding their established Rule and Constitutions the nuns were liberated; in striving for an alternative lifestyle they pursued freedom.

It was a concept of freedom which had to remain within orthodox Christian precepts, yet it owes much to modern atheist philosophers. The history of the early twentieth century had been all but lost on the nuns. The work of educationalists, philosophers and politicians influenced by Marx and Freud was prohibited. When the opportunity for change did come, it was the liberal philosophies of Russell, Bonhoeffer and Teilhard de Chardin which held the most appeal. Russell wrote, 'the humanistic conception regards a child as a gardener regards a young tree, i.e., as something with a certain intrinsic nature, which will develop into an admirable form given proper soil and air and light ...'[3] Russell inclined towards libertarian concepts of education and social organization. He believed that the principle of growth in men and women was hampered by inherited institutions. The efforts of the teaching congregation take their place in this particular twentieth-century expression of revolutionary endeavour.

The seeds of revolution are always to be found further back in time, and in this case it was the impact of the Second World War which had a profound effect on the personal life of the nuns. A lay sister, Sister Mary George, told me, 'It was during the war that things started to change for me. I suddenly had to do the cooking in one of the houses. I had had that little experience as a cook, I practically poisoned the few postulants and novices that were there. I began a new life from then. I used to help with the children at night and I felt more—well, quite a different person for having been allowed to do things.' The lay sisters were particularly vulnerable to the drudgery of religious life; their talents remained unexplored, their skills unused in the traditional teaching order. During the war these sisters found their talents reborn in the necessity of the times. The war was a watershed in the development of the Institute. It marked the death of an old order, a 'quality of life'. A social historian tells us how 'The old London teashops that preserved a little of the "muffins-under-a-silver-cover" cosiness of the Victorian era had vanished from the scene for ever.'[4] Not just the muffins but the servants who brought them to the drawing-room had disappeared. The fact that pre-1940 one talks of a servant class and post-1945 of a service industry is highly relevant. It took the teaching congregation another twenty years to eliminate their servant class, but they did eventually do it.

The war meant evacuation, night bombing, changing demands on women particularly in agriculture and industry. At the outbreak of war the nuns lived in the old traditions, in large convents, in silence and enclosure. Hierarchy embraced even the newest sisters; the youngest manned the door, the second youngest the window in the chapel. Poverty meant thrift and saving, chastity meant being friendly without having friends, obedience was a written Rule and the dictates of a Superior. There was no individual responsibility, no trust. Sister Evans, a middle-aged teacher, gives an example: 'In the relationship with the children there was no trust. If a child wanted to go down the corridor to the toilet she would be accompanied by a nun. In any movements from class to class the children would have to walk in silence, as a group, accompanied by a nun. A nun slept in every dormitory in the school. There were never any occasions when the children were unsupervised or the nuns remained alone.' Sister Evans was teaching in a school in South London when one night in October 1939 the school was destroyed by a bomb. One sister was killed, several were injured but none of the children were hurt. The whole school was evacuated. In evacuation, Sister Evans remembers, the silence and enclosure and routine had to go. In the black-out they had managed with timetable rearrangements and a faint blue bulb in the dormitories at night. But with the bombing of the school and the sudden evacuation the sisters were thrown on their own resources. Private schools had to find their own premises and Sister Evans's school was scattered about a Somerset village before they found a suitable large house.

The scale of evacuation is often forgotten. In four days 1,300,000 official evacuees were carried by rail out of London in nearly 4,000 special trains. Children were mustered in playgrounds, parents kept outside, and, following a 'marked' man carrying a placard with their name and reference number the schools made their way to the railway stations.[5] Sister Evans said that in these conditions she became 'an organized sort of person'. She had 200 children to look after in a building not designed to hold a school. Norman Longmate says, 'While the British Army was being rescued from Dunkirk, mistresses, maids and children were struggling to transform a country house into a wartime home, with classes being held in the summer house, the gunroom, a drawing-room and the corner of a huge indoor tennis court. The girls revelled in the break from routine and in the unexpected treasures their new home revealed, from the deer in the park to the bath-chair in the indoor tennis-court, which was in demand for rides in "break" '.[6] This is just how it was for Sister Evans who had epidemics of measles and chicken pox, and, of course, the rationing to cope with.

The sisters remember the war years as a period in which food was plentiful, but presumably this was a result of relaxing the stringent regulations on fasting and extravagance in the convent. One Mother Superior described helping her kitchen staff to manipulate the 'points' system in an effort to produce a reasonably balanced diet for the children. Under this system every holder of a ration book had sixteen to twenty 'points' to spend as he wished in the food shops. At first only canned meat, fish and vegetables were on points, but as the war continued item after item was added, including rice, canned fruit, condensed milk, cereals, and biscuits.[7] In some areas the schools took in civilians, soldiers and labourers to assist in the war effort. Sisters who had led sheltered lives teaching their 'relatively' quiet, middle-class girls, were brought into contact with the general populace and the ruder facts of life. For some sisters the experience left them with a burning will to work among the poor and disenchanted. They applied for the missions, or, many years later when the opportunity at last arose, they took up social work after a long career in teaching.

The excitement of breaking silence is communicated for us by Sister Mary George, the lay sister who suddenly became a cook. She says: 'Well, I felt I was beginning to be somebody, you know, you're a human being again. You can go out and talk to people and converse with them. But I felt it was worthwhile, too. Looking after all those children and cooking for them—'cos a lot of them were very down and out because they were children who had been evacuated because their parents—well, the fathers had gone to the war and their mothers had gone skewy—you know, left their husbands and gone off with other men, and left their children to us. They couldn't be bothered with them. Then in the war the great silence finished. We got permission because it was so terrible, the bombing and everything. So at first we were allowed to talk during the night and the excitement when that first happened! You used to be longing for the sun to go (laughs) so's you could talk, and then we used to be in charge of so many children during the night. When it darkened you had to bring them down to the cellars and you got to love them. You know, really love them, and help them. It was really lovely.'

During the war the sisters had to live in the present; it would have been foolish, even negligent, to have tried to keep to the letter of the Rule. They were given a taste of individual responsibility and a view of the world which provoked them to question the values of religious life as they knew it. The effect of the war on British society was profound. The historian David Thompson comments on the social effect: 'Socially the war was a mighty crucible, melting many pre-war contrasts and softening (though not always removing) old rigidities. Experience of evacuation, of mutual aid in air-raids, of great collective sacrifice and service, of stringent rationing and "equal shares", all helped to strengthen a tide of egalitarian sentiment that had been generated before war began. Common humanity began to seem more important than distinctions of wealth or birth . . .'[8] The 1930s had been a time of inertia, of resistence to change, of depression and repression. In 1945, Thompson says, 'The national mood was in many ways the opposite to the mood of 1918. Then there had been a prevailing desire to get back to the good old days . . . now the pre-war mould of the 1930s seemed so insecure and blameworthy that there was little nostalgia for the past . . . uppermost in their minds was the desire for fuller social justice, a lessening of class differences and greater security and peace. The most important cultural and intellectual phenonemon of the years after 1945 was the upheaval (an extensive abandonment) of traditional values, and the quest for new values felt to be more appropriate to life in a rapidly changing materialistic and scientific civilization.'[9]

But after the war the old routines were taken up again in the convent. In the face of deep changes in the social structure of England the sisters returned to their old way of life. The return to the Rule, return to full religious obligations, led the nuns into a way of life which was, if anything, even more strict and conformist than it had been before the war. Many had the feeling that life had been better before, that the food had been of a better quality, the feasts more energetically welcomed. They could have been correct. During the 1950s many sisters caught T.B., an illness exacerbated by poor diet and insufficient rest. More than half the sisters were not employed as teachers, they were still menials or subsidiaries. They all took their religious obligations very hard; mortification of the senses was rigorously practised. Sometimes, after getting up at 4.45 to begin prayer, followed by a full morning's work, a sister would exist on water alone until midday. Others went all day on bread and water and became weak and prone to illness. The Superior General of the congregation during this time was later judged to be incompetent; many areas under her jurisdiction ran into difficulties, debts were incurred, recruitment was low. Yet two new missions were opened in Africa, both attached to schools, and a large training college was staffed by sisters in England. It was from these two areas that the most progressive ideas originated, but they were not to be given expression until a new Mother General was elected.

The post-war years were years of development and change in the outside world. There was the building of the Welfare State, the development of new towns and the redevelopment of urban areas, changes in the occupational structure of work, the increase of white collar employees, a change in family size which affected Catholic families as well, changes in the laws of marriage to make it more of a partnership of equals. But to the teaching congregation these were as nothing compared to changes in the English educational system. The nuns could not remain impervious to changes which seemed to make their services redundant and threatened the financial viability of their congregation. Convent schools could take advantage of state aid, but they had to pass inspection to qualify. In 1902 the cost of a school place in an all-age school was calculated at £4 or £5, by the late 1930s the cost of a junior school place was £50 and a senior school place £100. In the 1960s that cost had risen to £500.[10] In their efforts to provide an adequate alternative to state education the convent schools took on a huge financial burden. In the pre-war situation they had not taken advantage of state aid, they had wanted to remain true to their founder as Catholic teachers in Catholic schools for Catholic children.

After the Second World War the Butler Education Act of 1944 came almost as a threat to the denominational schools. The Act, compromise as it was, made possible the development of a national system of State Education. The old elementary schools were to be replaced by primary and secondary schools in which an agreed syllabus was compulsory. The Act wanted 'to extend public control as is necessary . . . to ensure the effective and economical organization and development of both primary and secondary education'.[11] The Act gave denominational schools two options. They could apply for a 50 per cent grant towards the cost of alterations and improvements, but not towards the building of a new school; in return the state retained rights on the appointment and dismissal of teachers and on religious instruction. Or, and this applied mainly in single-school areas, the schools were to be handed over and used as council schools; in return, the local authorities would undertake the entire financial responsibility, the denomination being entitled to use the premises on Sundays and on weekdays when they were not being used for educational purposes. They were allowed one period per day for religious instruction and would have no control over teaching staff.

Catholics were horrified by this development: 'Take the buildings, take everything you want, but every teacher must be a Catholic and the child must have his education in a Catholic atmosphere.'[12] The teaching congregation took advantage of the Catholic determination to educate in Catholic schools and remained outside the state system, determined to remain independent. However, by the mid-1950s the effort to maintain standards and buildings and keep fees at the level the average middle-class parent could afford became too much, and they were forced to accept state aid and state control in several of their schools. Then they found that the demands of a modern curriculum were beyond the capacity of some of their teachers; they were no longer able to fill in with unqualified staff, and secular staff infiltrated the closed world of the convent boarding-school. The convent schools had to face Her Majesty's Inspectors if they were to receive recognition and financial assistance.

One very able teacher told me what happened to her. She was very young, just two years out of training college, when she was sent to the north of England to take over a prep school. She said, 'I had been Froebel-trained, but I had never taught juniors let alone infants. To make matters worse, in two terms the H.M.I. were going to come and examine the school working and look at its standards and decide whether or not to give it ministry recognition. Recognition was essential if we were to keep pupils in competition with other Catholic and non-Catholic schools in the neighbourhood. So in two terms I had to decide on the best methods of infant teaching and put them into practice. The inspectors came, took three days looking over the school and we got our recognition. But it was very worrying.' Sister Magdalene took over a local education authority school fifteen years after in 1968. She was an exceptional person and a very good organizer but she was typical of the new breed of nun in the teaching congregation. Her ideas, her Froebel training, her attitudes to herself and the children were in conflict with the ideals perpetrated in the religious congregation to which she belonged. In the 1950s the founder's teachings on the education of children were still read and given official approval in the Institute. The founder said that a child was a wild creature to be tamed and fitted for society; 'Born incomplete we must help them to perfect themselves, because they are born partially developed, we must help them to put themselves in tune, because they are born discordant'. Froebel took an opposite view, that a child is born complete and good and it is up to us to keep it that way. 'The Child's nature being what its Creator intended it to be, that is, in its essence good ... what we have to do is merely to help its normal growth.'[13]

Froebel's effect on English education was slow in coming but when it did come it was profound. In 1875 the Froebel Society was founded to propagate his principles but it did not succeed on a wide scale until after the Second World War. The educationalist Blackie makes a guess as to why this was: 'The war was a disaster for education as for every other liberal growth, but it was not an unmitigated disaster. Education and bombing broke up the schools but they forced all teachers into a new relationship with the children, jerked everybody out of their ruts and made all sorts of improvisations and makeshifts necessary. Teachers who had taught the same stuff in the same city classroom for fifteen years found themselves in the fens, or the hills, or the farmlands, the only link with the children's background, and they simply had to re-think what they were doing.'[14] By the late 1950s the teaching congregation was not only taking in teachers with a Froebel or Montessori teacher's training behind them, but other entrants who had been recipients of that education. They found themselves in conflict with some of the basic values of their Institute.

In the face of a changing world the organization of the teaching congregation became more rigid, its personnel expressing that 'fearful overconformity'[15] to rules as a justification in itself. In 1962 Cardinal Suenens' book, *The Nun in the World* was published. This highly influential man wrote of 'the contrived and artificial nature of certain customs in religious houses—a sort of "house etiquette", a stilted, stereotyped behaviour. It has been said of certain congregations of nuns that they are the last strongholds of the very studied manners of the middle-class women of the nineteenth century. People would like to see more natural and straightforward reactions.'[16] This was certainly true of the teaching congregation. In 1958, when most middle-class women were facing up the lack of servants and were buying machines to do the housework, the nuns were still divided into two classes, each distinguished from the other by dress, privilege and task. The most pious nun tended to be the one who knelt straightest in chapel. It was a process of fossilization, in which the original goals had become surplanted; instrumental values had become terminal values. The sociologist Merton explains this process: 'Adherence to the rules, originally conceived as a means, becomes transformed into an end-in-itself.... Formalism, even ritualism ensues with an unchallenged insistence upon punctilious adherence to formalized procedures.'[17] As we have seen, the conditions under which this formalism and rigidity occurred can be traced back to the new Rule in the 1930s.

One of the most crucial differences between the teaching congregation and the Franciscan congregation lay in this Rule. The Franciscans always had the Rule and Testament of St Francis alongside their own books of Rules and Customs. The Franciscan documents provided a universalistic approach to the religious life. The teaching congregation had the commentaries of their founder, the Augustinian Canon, whose writings were dry and pragmatic by comparison. Furthermore the commentaries were not in an easily digestible form and the selection of passages from them depended on officials already committed to a formalistic approach to the religious life. Their choice reinforced the instrumental and expressive goals held by the organization at that time—in this case goals which were rapidly getting further out of step with the outside world. A good example is the founder's writings on exercise and clothing; he wrote in 1817, 'One will observe that the comfortable garments of the Greeks, which did not hinder their bodies, contributed greatly in both sexes to give them those beautiful proportions which are admired in their statues. . . . Physical education mingled with suitable rest, makes a person gay, vigorous and robust which undoubtedly brings about the true perfection of the body without speaking of the advantages which the mind draws from it.'[18] He continues with suggestions for graded exercises to be done in the open throughout the year. This passage was obviously not one of those read out at mealtimes to a group of nuns swathed in heavy black fustian, faint from mortifications. Much more likely would be a passage which reads, 'Always be exact and on time, restrain oneself constantly in many things, in words, attitudes, in one's bearing, in the innumerable details of propriety and decorum, even when one is alone.'

The standardization and bureaucratization of the 1930s were accompanied by stereotypical and magical beliefs in the ritual and sacraments of the Church. God was an awesome father-figure and in the hierarchy of the convent the Superiors were obeyed unquestioningly. Traditional beliefs tend to elevate those in authority, and the effect of this when the Superior is a radical pressing for change, is that she will be able to carry a good number of her subordinates with her, simply because of the traditional acceptance that what the Superior does is right. Similarly, the stronger her authority the more chance there will be that her innovations will, in turn, replace traditional beliefs. At this point in the history of the teaching congregation a powerful leader emerged, who, by manipulating the existing order and belief systems, provoked a revolutionary situation in which all aspects of the nun's life were changed.

In 1957 a new Mother General was elected to the teaching congregation. It was not an extraordinary event; the retiring Mother General had been in office for twelve years and the Constitutions rendered her ineligible for a further term. It was an extraordinary personality who replaced her. She was born in the Netherlands, had a university education and had travelled to the missions. She had also spent much of the 1950s learning the 'new theology' at the feet of

Cardinal Suenens. She attended his lectures and noted both his criticisms of the religious life and his dynamic ideas on the apostolic life—the nun in the world. Suenens emphasized that the world the religious leaves behind on professing her vows is, in a supernatural way, the very heart of her vocation. 'She wants to go from God to God in prayer, and from God himself to God in her fellow-creatures in the apostolate.'[19] She fulfils in some way a function as a mediatrix in her role as a dedicated person praying for intercession. Later Suenens was to sit on the Vatican Council, and to work on the promulgations for religious congregations. The year of the Mother General's election was also the year of Pope John's election. Their terms of office expressed new interpretations of the Christian ethic. The head of the Church and the head of the religious congregation used the constitutional means available to them, as heads of hierocratic bureaucracies, to bring about immense changes.

The new Mother General was a strong, determined woman who was a prominent candidate for election. Consultation and 'canvassing' of votes were prohibited, but on her election her views were widely circulated. Immediately before the election, using her status as a General Councillor, she spent a lot of time travelling in England and on the Continent, visiting convents and talking to delegates. Two sisters described her to me in rather different ways. One said she was an example of a truly spiritual person. 'There is a oneness, a joy, a confidence in others ... an outward-looking person who is not afraid of the effect of what she says on others.' The other described her as 'very austere, very radical, she could never see two sides to any question. She made the decision and that was it.' She chose a method of governing which both circumvented bureaucratic procedures and yet used a tool which was part and parcel of the bureaucracy—the memorandum. Memos were sent from the Generalate to all local Superiors during her first few years in office, which changed more aspects of the nun's life than any General Chapter since their inception. The first dramatic reform was the removal of the lay sister status.

Any teaching nun, asked about the difference between life in the convent before 1960 and after it, replied in terms of the lay sister. If she was a lay sister she invariably told you how much freer she felt, how much more like a person. If she was a choir sister she talked about the difficulties of running a house without the lay sister to do all the domestic and menial tasks. In effect what happened when the Mother General abolished the lay sister was that all sisters wore the same habit, that of the choir nun. They all called each other Mother instead of making a distinction between mother and sister. This lasted a chaotic three months and then all the nuns, except Superiors in office, were called Sister. There was still some confusion in individual convents, with seventy-year-old sisters still referring to ex-choir nuns as Mother, long after the change. In the division of work the menial tasks still tended to be done by the same nuns. Deference was still shown to ex-choir nuns by ex-lay nuns. It took more than the removal of the class barrier from the Rule book to banish it from the organization altogether. Other changes met with a similar response.

Another memo from the Mother General instructed that where possible all sisters were to have their own rooms or cells. Large dormitories should be partitioned and each sister should be given a small wardrobe and a shelf for books in their cells. Previously, all the sisters' personal effects and clothes were kept in a linen room under the overall supervision of an official. Now the sisters were made responsible for the cleanliness of their own dresses and scapular, and the basic requisites for personal hygiene were kept individually. Not all sisters took advantage of the change. Some persisted in using the linen room if only to keep their summer clothes there. They felt that it was a breach of their vow of poverty to hold clothes and personal effects in their own cells. But most sisters welcomed the change; they were the ones who had found restrictions rather petty and out of date —ritualism for its own sake rather than based in the life they were leading. Meanwhile the Mother General was trying to change the habit itself. It proved to be a very difficult move and it was ten years before even minor changes in dress were possible. It was probably harder to change the habit than the place of the lay sister because the lay sisters were all much loved personalities in the convent; there was a humane element in the change which made it easy to assimilate. It was not until the spiritual exercises, the prayers and the key elements of the religious life had been changed that she was able to alter the habit.

She began her governmental changes with the institution of a provincial form of government. This immediately gave each section of the Institute a platform on which to discuss local problems. By 1962 the Generalate itself had been moved to Rome, which was considered a more suitable place for a congregation which was fast developing into a worldwide concern. The Mother General encouraged the establishment of missions and of convents in the U.S.A. Meanwhile, on 25 January 1959 the Church's 21st Ecumenical Council was convoked (Vatican II). It was to inaugurate the first major reconstitution of the Church's affairs for one hundred years. The first promulgations of the Council appeared in December 1962, the last—the ones which vitally affected religious congregations—in 1965. During that time the first really well-formulated arguments for change were heard.

When the English province held its first provincial Chapter in June 1964 the Mother General wrote to her assembled sisters, making her expectations quite clear: 'I am closely united with you, praying with you and for you, searching, in Christ, to discover the design of the Father, so that from our renewed life may burst forth, by a single movement, the response of love to the love of the Trinity, and Charity freed for the better service of men.' She continued her homily: 'Most congregations of religious women, founded in the nineteenth century, patterned the organization of their life on the monastic orders, and that without sufficient reference to the end in view, or to the contradiction existing between the monastic life and the active or mixed life . . . by definition, the monastic vocation is the call to the contemplative life, and everything in it is organized to foster contemplation. The active apostolic life requires a different structure, for it is the accomplishment in Christ of the creation and re-creation of the new man by God . . . as religious we are first and foremost women of our times, and it is as such that we are on our way to God.'

Women of our times, nuns in the world, and what were they doing? In the early 1960s they had begun the teaching of catechetics to children and adults, with the encouragement of a few parish priests, not in the convents but in the homes of the people they taught. They had taken in one or two trained nurses and, in 1963, the first sister was sent for training in a hospital. They asked for an alteration to the Rule, requesting that the special aim should simply stand as 'devotion without limit to Jesus Christ, his Church and all our Brethren'. The proposed amendment caused great controversy. Some sisters felt that to extend the scope of the Institute without limit was to diffuse its aims and weaken its effectiveness. But it was passed and justified by reference to the founder. His lace school, they said, was only a means to reach souls. If he were alive today he would establish contact with souls by means other than education alone. The affect of the amendment was profound. Not only did it alter the 'material base' of the organization, but the demands of diffuse goals pursued outside the framework of the enclosed convent were to have far-reaching effects on the organization of daily life.

The widened aims also attracted more recruits and there was a burst of recruitment between 1959 and 1964, until one-fifth of their number was under temporary profession. New styles of apostolate required new styles of training which in turn contributed to the changing beliefs of the sisters and eventually changed the emphasis of their vows. An English Novitiate was established. The novices' habit was revised and made simpler; a long black skirt, white blouse and black cardigan, and a small black mantilla on the head. In their canonical year novices were sent for courses in Divinity to a local theological college—it happened to be one of the most progressive colleges in the country. They were also sent to the local college of further education to do courses in a variety of subjects, including taking the chair at a public meeting, leading and taking part in discussions, first-aid and home nursing, health education. But these courses were still slotted into a day of silence with the old-style prayer routines. It was to be another four years before these were swept away. Professed sisters too were encouraged to move outside the convent. Teachers took a year's leave to follow courses in religious studies, missionaries took language courses, ex-lay sisters took courses in home economy and dress-making. The individual was emerging again. The Mother Superior of a house of young sisters said, 'In religious life people can be used as objects, and women can be dominated by other women; there can be a tremendous lack of integrity if each person's rights are not considered as their own individual rights. I know that when one enters one gives up those rights, at least to a certain extent. Some Superiors don't understand at all . . .' The era when nuns entered the order and were allotted their tasks would seem to be drawing to a close. Now an individual's talents and capabilities were to be assessed and put to good use through well-organized training schemes. Nuns were to be active, fulfilled women contributing all their talents to religious life.

To achieve these sweeping changes the Rule would have to be rewritten and the religious vows themselves would have to take on a new meaning. But the sisters were not ready, they were still parochial. The new Mother Provincial urged them not to hide behind outdated observances and customs, only to do what was essential to the Church of the 1960s. They set up a working committee on the vows, but the Chapter itself was disappointing for the progressives. Sisters were too concerned with the minutiae of life. Were the visitors' parlours too luxurious? Should they use vans or brakes instead of cars for community transport? Hours were spent discussing food. Higher standards of nutrition brought complaints from some sisters that food had become too elaborate and from others that it was not cooked properly —cuisine became an issue in some convents! The whole notion of feast-days came under attack from reformers who wanted a more spiritual celebration to take the place of actual parties. But it was individual poverty rather than community poverty which brought the greatest problems.

The sisters were now going out of the convent, to college, to schools, to hospitals, whether they were engaged in social work or just shopping for the community. Every item of the nun's clothing and the tools of her trade were scrutinized under traditional concepts of poverty. In the past, all small personal items, like mending materials, writing paper, items for personal hygiene, were held in common, and a system of 'permissions' used. A general permission was granted by the local Superior for things like soap, sanitary towels, cough mixture, toothpaste, and the sister just had to renew this request every month or so. Now they did not have to ask permission; it was up to the individual to use her own judgement on the necessity of each article. She was less dependent on her Superior but more responsible to herself and to the new normative values which were inculcated in every member by the reforming élite.

The barriers between the convent and the outside world were steadily eroded. By the end of the 1950s convents began to own cameras, radios, televisions and cars. This ownership and usage of luxury items increased and caused some concern. Communications media penetrated the convents, and the nuns also began to travel. It began with 'holidays'. In the traditional convent the idea of holidays for nuns was laughable. But the Mother General introduced holidays for both the physical and psychological well-being of her sisters. They were allowed to visit their natal families and send them a small gift at Christmas. Travel became the norm rather than the exception. Sisters were given money to pay for fares and petrol. A two-week holiday was arranged for every sister in a seaside home; during this period they were given the free use of a small sum of pocket money. In 1960 it was five shillings, not riches but a very real adjustment for a nun who had not handled money for twenty years or more. The days when a nun could virtually disappear behind the convent walls were over. And the effect of the increased freedoms and contacts with the outside world had a profound effect on the interpretation of the chastity vow.

Greater contact with the outside world could mean greater tempta-tion, so sisters were prepared even more carefully for assaults on their chastity. The Mother Provincial was most practical. 'Ignorance', she said, 'can be no safeguard for innocence. Our young nuns need to understand that it is their love that they have given to Our Lord, and they should not regard this vow as a negation.' In the nineteenth century chastity was a defence against the evils of the world; now the sisters were urged to observe Christian celibacy so that 'in complete detachment from earthly ties they may belong wholly to give their time and interest to all, in selfless charity, and will unite together in a community of love which will reflect the love of God to the world around them'. This was radical thinking in a congregation which was still sufficiently enclosed to worry about the social rather than the psychological aspects of the vows. Instruction on the physical as well as the spiritual side of matrimony was given to novices, so that they would realize just what it was they would have to give up. Courses in the facts of life included lesbianism and masturbation in their curriculum but they did not alleviate the self-consciousness of the majority of sisters. Deportment, courtesy and religious enclosure, the operating medium of the chastity vow, were also put under review.

Sisters were anxious to eliminate restrictions on body movement—such as walking with hands under the scapular—which were inappropriate to their new freedoms. Because of their enclosure they were self-conscious of their community and of the world looking in at them. The barriers with the outside world were not yet broken down. The doorways were still guarded by a portress who had to be told when the sisters left the convent and when they would be back. In the street or when travelling on public transport they were told to behave in a 'religious' manner: always to wear gloves and cover all books or light reading matter in plain paper to avoid giving a bad example to seculars. Young nuns were told to offer their seat to standing passengers and to avoid entering a carriage full of men. The instructions were a mixture of middle-class manners, concern for 'good breeding and politeness' which the founder had been asking for a century before. Within the convent the sisters were expected to acknowledge their Superior by opening doors for her and standing when she entered a room. This deference was not accorded to her replacement, the 'sister-in-charge', when the office of Superior was finally disbanded in 1970. The committee included a whole section on 'table-manners' in its recommendations. They suggested for example that a full place setting could be used and that this would not be considered a breach of the poverty vow as it had been in the past. Their concerns were not trivial; they wanted to bring the nun's manners up to the standard of educated people outside the convent. Other rank distinctions were discouraged and some show of affection was allowed between older and younger sisters with the proviso that it should not include loud laughter or 'vulgar' behaviour or the use of nicknames. It created some misunderstandings; younger sisters were accused of lack of respect for their elders. This was a reflection between those who accepted change and those who did not. The Mother General had wanted her nuns to transform their lives and become 'women of our times' but the majority of her sisters were ill-prepared for such a transformation. The opportunity for revolutionary ideals to be discussed in General Chapter was frittered away in considerations about whether an extra half-hour in bed was permissible, or how to ensure that each sister had a spare set of shoe-laces.

The major changes, like the abolition of the lay sister status, had been accomplished by direct memorandum from the top. The smaller changes took place gradually out of a concern for rationalization. Every little change was noticed. Nothing had changed for so long. Change is cumulative. Religious routines are so well-integrated in the past that to change one aspect had a ripple effect on numerous others. No sooner had sisters been granted permission to visit aged parents than they were asking to stay overnight with them. Having stayed one night, why not stay two or three, or spend the two weeks' annual holiday with them? Parish work involved many sisters who felt it was a logical move onward from their work with children. Once they became involved with the sick or the poor of the parish they found further demands on their time and solicitude: a young couple never able to get out together—the nuns wanted to babysit for them; an old person waiting to go to hospital in the middle of the night—a nun could sit with them until they were comfortable. It would not have caused difficulties in an order primarily concerned with social work, but this congregation was new in the field and their Rule was written for a teaching apostolate. Sisters who attended theological college asked for good literature on the scriptures and current periodicals to be included in their house libraries. Every sister was now encouraged to use the library and such writings had an immediate effect in broadening the nuns' outlook and giving them more reason to question their acceptance of things as they were. A lay sister explained how she never read books or gave the Old Testament a thought during her early years as a religious. 'I'm more educated now, you see. We've got the lectorate. We never had anything like that before and you can do reading—you can choose your own book to read, you can go to the library and choose it. Before you were just handed your book each month, any ordinary kind of meditation book with all things written down. We never had a bible either—it sounds terrible doesn't it! I've got my own bible now.'

By the end of 1964 the days of the week had been freed from special devotions, the number of feast-days were drastically reduced. Sisters were made personally responsible for meditation or mental prayer as it was now called. Then the morning rising bell was dropped. For the first time in the congregation's history the nuns did not rise as a body and go to chapel together. They were responsible for themselves and were expected to arrive in chapel without the prompting of a morning bell. The nuns had been shown the way of freedom but they did not take it up without anxieties, problems and ambiguities. The changes the Mother General had initiated in her memos had been taken up but they had not been carried further. The majority of the sisters were cautious and deliberative, but they had not reckoned for the revolutionary dynamism of the Mother General and the radicals, nor for the far-reaching proposals of the Vatican Council. The Mother General urged her sisters to action: 'It is by action, Eucharistic action, that Our Lord Jesus Christ wished to offer Himself to the Father for men, so long as there will be need "to save that which is lost". He has asked us to pledge ourselves with Him to this action. Let us not fail Him! The future in this matter depends upon our openness to the designs of God and your openness to our times, which is the same thing, if you do not want to throw aside the work of salvation for which the father sent His son to assume human nature. . . . Under pain of not being faithful to our origins, we must go back to our primary care—by that I mean, search—not accepting things as they are done and which have gone on for years as tradition, under pretext of fidelity; this is false. Search! Question the times in which we live. Go to the heart of the present-day vital problems. Respond to the expectation of God and of the men today, for that is the deciding point of our action and there is none other . . . together you must find the truthful answer; not sentimentality, imagination or illusion.' It was with this Churchillian oratory that the real revolution began.

CHAPTER SEVEN

Revolution in the Convent

Sister Anne, a thirty-year-old school teacher, said that the traditional religious life was 'worked out frightfully logically, like a wall with every brick in place, and if you removed some of those bricks, you broke up the logic'. In giving her sisters freedom from enclosure, from old-fashioned notions of piety, from outdated manners and customs, the Mother General had removed some of those bricks. It left the nuns in a state of confusion. Then the first promulgations of the Vatican Council were announced and all religious orders and congregations were offered a three-year experimental period free from the full jurisdiction of Canon Law. This was the opportunity the radicals had been hoping for. It enabled a fundamental restructuring of the governmental organization of the Institute. The confusion which the adoption of new apostolates had created threatened the economic viability and material base of the Institute. The effect of the new questioning attitudes of the sisters provoked a crisis in their commitment to organizational demands. Finally the value of the religious ethic itself was questioned by progressive Catholics and the very plausibility of their religious beliefs was put in question. Just why the teaching congregation underwent a radical restructuring and the Franciscans did not has been the constant theme of this book. The explanation lies in the fundamental relationships of society, in the relationship between social structure and belief system, in the basic decision-making processes and authority structures, in the processes by which society or organization gains the compliance of its members.

The single most crucial factor which enabled the radicals to push through change in the teaching congregation was the collapse of their instrumental goals. The changing demands of education not only devalued an apostolate which was dedicated to the education of a sectional interest in society, but the provision of adequate state education starved the convent schools of money just as costs were rising astronomically. But why did the Franciscans, who were largely in private hospitals, not suffer a similar crisis? The goals of an organization have an intimate relationship with other factors such as communication networks, consensus on various matters, and compliance (that relationship between controllers and controlled). In most organizations goals are images of a future state which may or may not be brought about. In the case of religious congregations the goals are stated aims in the formal Rule and the more abstract aims of religion, which may or may not be included in the Rule or other formal statements. Religious organizations pursue cultural goals. Their business is the preservation of symbolic objects and the reinforcement of commitment to such objects; economic goals are secondary. There were certain crucial differences both in the cultural and economic goals of the two congregations.

Teaching and nursing are both professional tasks but they demand rather different resources, and in the changing world of the National Health Service and State Education in England these resources were not so readily available. They also demand a rather different commitment from practitioners.[1] All the time the private hospital was a real alternative to state hospitals the Franciscans felt no need to open up new goals. When the need arose they were able to respond because private medicine did not absorb all their resources of manpower and finance, and because all their members were committed to general aims rather than a specific goal. In the case of the teaching congregation, once boarding education for middle-class girls was no longer in demand, their sole economic goal was in jeopardy. Further, only half their members were involved in teaching and when the schools went so did the cohesion and stability of the organizational structure. In the teaching congregation a refectorian or a cook held that position for life; in the Franciscan congregation such positions were rotated. Even the Mother General had been seen washing the paintwork in the chapel. Officials were seen as part of the fraternity. In the teaching congregation there was a marked difference not only between officials and the rest but between choir nuns and lay sisters. Social divisions were expressed in rituals like finding a footstool for a Superior at recreation time, or always standing back in doorways when a choir nun went past. In both congregations officials in charge of expressive activities, the 'spiritual' welfare of the nuns, took precedence over those in charge of means. Local Superiors would be the head of a hospital or the headmistress of a school. This compares with the Jesuit head of spiritual matters who is superior to the Father Minister, head of temporal and exterior discipline. In the Franciscan congregation the Mother General kept control over all expressive communication. Her directives would be read to the sisters at mealtimes or recreation time when they were assembled together. In the teaching congregation she delegated this responsibility to a certain extent and this too was ultimately to affect the stability of the

E

organization. After the Second World War there was less agreement on performance obligations and more dissatisfaction with organizational goals in the teaching congregation. They drew recruits whose own education was in conflict with the Institute's educational aims. But the Franciscans depended on 'ultimate' values which were expressed in the unique Franciscan ideology.

In religious congregations commitment to ideology rather than to authority can lead to extreme conservatism. In a comparison of the Benedictine and the Jesuit orders, Volmer has described how the decentralized authority structure of the Benedictine order is subordinate to ideology and the whole is deeply conservative, whereas in the Jesuit order authority is centralized in a Superior General whose authority is not only 'unconditional' but legitimated by direct mandate from God. Ideology is subordinate to authority and the organization is capable of unlimited expansion and innovation.[2] In the Franciscan case authority is centralized and maintained by the charismatic authority of St Francis. Franciscan ideology itself is of such a kind that innovation and expansion are available through its very spirituality.

The Franciscans emphasize the 'inner will' of their members. There was always less emphasis on devotional prayers, more emphasis on capturing the 'spirit' of the movement. Charisma itself has been defined as an extraordinary quality of a person, which revolutionizes men from within. Charisma is 'the ability of an actor to exercise diffuse and intense influence over the normative orientations of other actors.'[3] Political and religious leaders have charisma because they exert influence on the normative orientation of their followers.[4] Both St Francis and the Mother Foundress of the Franciscan congregation had these qualities, but can they really continue to be of use in these organizations? Is there reason to suppose that charisma can be built in to the compliance relationship and the authority structure of these organizations? Weber claims that people could 'develop' charismatic qualities in top positions in an organization. He distinguishes between initial charismatic claims and the routinization of charisma such as occurs in charisma of office. Etzioni goes further and postulates that charisma can develop in a large number of offices through an organization, its distribution related to different forms of compliance.[5] In the Roman Catholic Church, for example, charismatics fill all 'line' positions in the organization because the priesthood requires both office and personal charisma. In the medical profession charisma is limited to one or two 'ranks', that is if one can say that every doctor has a certain charisma for his patients! In the religious congregation charismatics are invariably concerned with long-term goals related to overall meanings.[6] In the case of the teaching congregation the

Mother General and her officials were concerned to fulfil and protect the Rule and Constitutions; she had little actual involvement with the main body of her congregation. In ordinary times her authority had no charismatic basis and she was only concerned with decisions about means. In contrast, the Franciscan Mother General kept in close personal contact with all her sisters. She and other high officials were chosen for qualities of leadership as much as for their training and experience. Not only was she responsible for the moral involvement of her sisters in their organization, but she could make decisions about ends—decisions to introduce a new apostolate for example—and she could innovate at the level of the expressive performance of ritual and religion. The Franciscans initiated new pilgrimages and celebrated feast-days in ethnic costume while the teaching congregation remained locked in a routine expression of their religious involvement. In an organization like the Franciscan congregation there is a spread of charismatic elements throughout, but especially in goal-orientation. The fact that there was an almost exact fit between the action boundaries and the normative boundaries of the collectivity works towards a greater acceptance of innovation from *all* members. And the new recruits to the Franciscan congregation took vows which relied more on charismatic elements, the early Church and St Francis. The move back to the early Church formalized in the promulgations of the Vatican Council brought no conflict for these sisters.

Charismatic domination can prove dysfunctional both for the organization in which it occurs and for the 'good' of society. In sociological terms charisma has no 'value' but in social action we may perceive otherwise. The Nazi party is a classic example of a fusion between charismatic domination and totalitarian bureaucratization which overran all humanitarian controls. It is a particular combination which enables decisions to be implemented at such a speed that they are accepted enthusiastically or as *faits accomplis*.[7] The Church had always been aware of the volatile nature of the Franciscan message. The canonization of St Francis, the production of 'official' biographies and ceremonial remembrances at his shrine, all served to contain the schismatic tendencies of his organization within Church control. Organizations which incorporate charismatic office also have mechanisms which keep out deviants. They set requirements which keep out unsuitable candidates and ensure the absolute loyalty of office-holders by education and pre-socialization and devices such as accelerated promotion.

The new Superior General of the Franciscan congregation had been a chosen successor for many years. She had practical experience as Vicaress General and her position as Novice Mistress had given her an intimation of those who would, in time, vote her into office. She was also very young. Charisma is a highly innovative mechanism both in decision-making and in the compliance structure of an organization. Properly controlled it can enable an organization to survive without radical upheavals, and to adapt without trauma to almost any situation. The teaching congregation was virtually charisma-free until a leader emerged with those qualities of personal magnetism which are associated with charismatic domination. It is interesting that the Mother General elected in 1957 followed a leader with very low charisma. Since charisma is authority perceived by followers, this implies that her authority was legitimated by legal and traditional sources rather than by a personalized relationship with her nuns. Etzioni comments that personal charisma may develop in office; he uses the example of Queen Victoria, who had little charisma during the first years of her reign when the monarchy was fairly unpopular; it was only under the influence of Disraeli that she became both popular and influential and the monarchy strengthened.[8] The teacher's Mother General was already well known before she took office, and more appropriate examples are Churchill who followed Baldwin, or Roosevelt who followed Harding. In both cases men with high charisma followed men with low charisma. But one has to be very careful in attributing every strong leader with charismatic authority.

The anthropologist Peter Worsley criticizes the Weberian concept of charisma. He claims that only individuals in certain social positions will be acceptable as revolutionary leaders, and that their authority is therefore derived from the indigenous order.[9] Weber's use of charisma is, he says, irrational. Worsley does raise a problem here, for obviously charisma cannot be utilized as a residual concept which mops up the cases which cannot be explained any other way. Weber is using charisma in a 'value-free' sense. When he writes about its irrationality he only means that it operates in areas not covered by his other ideal-types of authority, the rational-legal and the traditional, though it may be found in conjunction with them. The election of the new Franciscan Mother General brought her authority into the rational-legal and the traditional structure of legitimation. The question arises: would she have been able to initiate the radical change of her organization without some charismatic legitimation for her authority? That question cannot be answered without first establishing whether she used the position of Mother General to push through change or whether the changes in the 1960s in the teaching congregation were the result of very deliberate moves by a sectional interest group to gain power for their ideas.

There is an analogy between the revolutionary model of political sociology and the situation in the teaching congregation. Theoretically, what happened to the nuns in the 1960s could happen in any similar organization. Power changed hands and the structure of the organization was profoundly altered to accommodate the change. The end-product was a form of devolution in which a centralized government was democratized. In the political model, the preconditions of revolutions include a central government, competing interest groups and revolutionary intellectuals. These were all present in the teaching congregation, though I would not like to take the analogy too far because the lay sisters can hardly be described as an oppressed group. They accepted their role in the spirit of their religious beliefs; it was only in relation to the outside world that they could be described as a class of underprivileged 'menial' workers. The revolutionary intellectuals were certainly present.

In the 1920s and 1930s the Roman Catholic Church had been rocked by a great liturgical movement which began in the great monasteries in the nineteenth century. The teaching congregation, with its attachment to devotional prayers and the routines prescribed in the Rule, remained oblivious to the changes in the wider Church. English Catholics had anyway been left behind—possibly, as Latourette suggested, because 'to follow the service by the use of a missal smacked of Protestantism and partly because the majority of the faithful were of Irish ancestry and the Irish were inclined to be subjective and individualistic and not to have the sense of a worshipping congregation essential to the (liturgical) movement.'[10] The liturgical movement encouraged the revival of Gregorian music, Bible study and a more thorough participation of the laity in the life of the Church. This was expressed in the conduct of the Mass and in a fundamental principle that Christianity was not a doctrine but life, and that both priesthood and laity were as one, united as the mystical body of Christ. During the 1950s a small group of sisters attended theological college. The more intellectual ones, including the Mother General elected by the teaching congregation in 1957, went to Louvain, where even more progressive ideas discouraged the use of the rosary, Stations of the Cross, private meditation and the confession of venial sins. These were all central to the religious routines in the teaching order. Further, the progressives attended Mass where the priest faced his congregation and said the Mass in an audible voice in the vernacular, the congregation joining in the responses. Everyone present had a part to play. Meanwhile, the majority of the sisters in England were telling their rosary in private prayer while the priest stood with his back to them mumbling in a strange language. The numbers of the revolutionary intellectuals were swelled by a small group of missionary sisters, a brave group who had experienced at first hand the sharing of God in humanity and who recognized only too clearly the stilted nineteenth-century manners of the English convents when they came home.

The preconditions for revolution were present; the small group pressing for change grew yearly with the influx of new recruits to the congregation. Once their socialization was complete and they became full members their influence was felt in every convent. Then a leader emerged who was elected to the highest office in the knowledge that she was dedicated to renewal. Was she a charismatic? Or, more properly, to what extent was her authority legitimated by charismatic rather than by legal or traditional sources? The political sociologist Zollschan suggests that 'the occasion for charismatic leadership varies in strength inversely with the level of formalization and the means of organization available to the interest group.'[11] Clearly the interest group, that is the group pressing for change, were not formalized, nor did they have a ready means of organization, existing as they did in relative isolation in a bureaucracy whose operation restricted consultation at every level. Remember that the sisters were still restricted by silence, by enclosure, by geographical distance, and there were virtually no mechanisms for them to overcome these blocks on communication. Zollschan also argues that whether a charismatic leader will actually appear is dependent on two variables, the prevalence and valency of infantile needs for a 'strong father' and the availability of a 'value-giver' who can supply the *mot juste* for the change. These variables are highly debatable.

Charismatic leadership is not a psychological mechanism. Although an intense personal relationship distinguishes charismatic from other forms of authority, it is the legitimate exercise of that authority which must be considered rather than the psyche of individuals. But it is undeniable that in the traditional convent there was, built into the compliance relationship, a degree of dependency which inhibited a mature expression of differences and led to immature behaviour. It was one of the key justifications for change. The sisters should not continue to spend a lifetime in a child-like relationship with their Superiors and with their God—the awesome Father! As to the availability of a 'value-giver', the writings of the founder are a traditional source of legitimation for change in religious orders. Michael Hill has shown how the numerous changes in the Benedictine order were achieved by a 'revolution by tradition'. Each change was legitimated by an appeal to the 'pristine tradition' of the Rule rather than by the inspiration of exceptional personnel.[12] In the case of the teaching sisters, reference was made back to the Founder and his writings were quoted in support of the changes made. But, as we have seen, the 'spirit' of his commentaries belonged to a different century and to a different ideology. They did not in any way constitute the 'value-giver'. Nor was there any search for a 'pristine' message in his works. The radical movement which provoked so much change in the 1960s was not a revolution by tradition in this sense.

To some extent 'tradition' did play a part in validating and making acceptable the changes, and 'traditional' methods were employed to bring them about. The Mother General did not have the same impact on all her sisters. Many, even the majority, accepted changes because they had to 'obey' in the traditional context of their obedience vow, not from any personal motivation towards the new Mother General and her ideas. Others, a small group initially, already committed to new ideologies, formed a classic 'disciple' group around her and fanned out into other areas carrying the 'word' with them. These 'disciples' were committed to their leader by personal loyalty and shared values. There was, therefore, an element of charismatic authority in her leadership. The 'disciples' tended to be drawn from the more mobile, highly educated section of the organization and many held positions at the top of the bureaucracy, in the General Council for example. Others were young radicals, newly professed in the religious life, who sought a new lifestyle. It was noticeable that the minor officials, sisters in the middle years of their life, were the most resistant to change; they were, of course, the ones who would benefit the least. They had spent many years in the old system, the fruits of which would be delivered to them in due course. With the radical changes, those fruits were to be redistributed in such a way that they would never enjoy them. They would have to work hard again at a different set of values and organizational goals, whose rewards were more diffuse and less recognizable. The Mother General of the teaching congregation did carry some charismatic authority, but more important was her position at the top of the bureaucratic hierarchy. One of the features of bureaucratic organizations is a tendency to stifle initiative at the lower echelons. All decisions are made at the top and a vicious circle develops in which a failure of communication between top and bottom of the organization isolates the top and renders it impervious to changing needs at its base.[13] Failure of communication is sometimes due to rigidity of task definitions and roles, task arrangements and the human relations network of the organization. Certainly the teaching congregation, at this stage in its development, had ossified task, role and even belief system. What happens when change is instigated at the top of such an organization is that the whole unit is affected *en bloc*. This is precisely what happened in the teaching congregation.

In the period of initial change, from 1958 to 1965, the Franciscans had retained their traditional organization virtually intact. When

Vatican II urged religious congregations to look at themselves and consider whether what they were doing and how they were doing it really had a place in the twentieth century, they were able to answer with a thriving community, adaptable and successful. They found no need to make radical alterations. Theirs too, was a bureaucratic organization, but one without the rigidity and ossification of the teaching order. In his book *The Dynamics of Bureaucracy*[14] Peter Blau found that a key feature of change in bureaucracies lay in changes in their goals. The Franciscans, in the period immediately preceding Vatican II, were achieving their goals and creating new ones. Peter Blau insists that change is such a recurrent phenomenon that bureaucratic methods are instituted to deal with it. One of these methods is task differentiation; officials who have fully mastered their tasks welcome new challenges, while less competent officials object to procedural changes which might make their work more difficult. In the Franciscan congregation charismatic authority facilitated change in goals and structure, while the teaching congregation, with an addiction to formal rules, paralysed innovative behaviour in both the individual and the institution. Even bureaucratic methods failed to modify goals, and the officials could never be satisfied with their achievements, as it was such a struggle for them even to get the job done. As Blau says, officials who feel insecure are most unlikely to press for change. The minor officials in the teaching congregation tended to be the most conservative, they were the ones with the least qualifications. As one local bursar put it, shrugging her shoulders at the enormity of her task and the paucity of her own knowledge of book-keeping, 'God uses the weakest instrument to do his work.'

It was not until October 1965 that the first of the promulgations of Vatican II which closely affected religious was published.[15] It was *Perfectae Caritatis* which not only set in motion the work of renewal but put no limit on that work. It left religious with full responsibility for shaping their own *aggiornamento*, and suggested means of achieving it. The means would be an extraordinary General Chapter, called after the advice of experts had been solicited and the views of all members of the congregation had been sought. These views could be gathered by questionnaire, committee, discussion and study groups. Before the General Chapter was called the religious would have a three-year period of experimentation to put new ideas into practice. The main aim of the Chapter would be to revise the Rule and Constitutions. The Council suggested that an ideal Rule would be one in which spiritual principles and legal provisions were well-balanced, and which included statements from the founder and the gospels. The Franciscan Rule was already like this, but the teaching congregation had a Rule which looked like a legal code. They would obviously have to make many alterations to comply with the wishes of Vatican II. The Council also recommended that the Custom Book should be revised. This never had as much force as the Rule but it was often regarded as equally important by the nuns. They were urged to omit 'formalism'. Suenens' influence was in evidence here, for he preached against formalism which meant 'external forms where the internal content is meaningless or irrelevant'. An example was given of an order where breakfast cups had to be lifted with two hands, a mannerism enshrined in the Custom Book. On investigation it was found that the custom originated in a French Mother House where morning coffee was drunk from bowls. Both the Franciscans and the teaching congregation found outdated customs which they erased from practice. Using cups without saucers was one of them; it was considered to belong to an outmoded interpretation of poverty.

The recommendations of the Council, whether for the role of prayer life in the apostolate, alterations in the liturgy, or Rules and Customs Books, remained recommendations. The essence of these decrees was that they formulated a mood for the religious life. The order and congregations themselves were left to follow it up as they saw fit. In particular the Council clarified the difference between contemplative and active congregations. The basis of the monastic tradition had been that the monastery is the house of God. When a person enters he enters to perform the *opus dei* and he remains a member of the community until he dies. The traditional training of a monk was centred on making him a full and useful member of a community, accepting without protest the letter and spirit of the Rule and the directives of the abbot. In contrast the Ignatian training for an apostolic life emphasized personal involvement and a relationship with Christ. The Jesuits were modelled on the Apostles, who began their life in a tight-knit community and then moved out to carry their message about the world. Ignatian spiritual exercises emphasize the basic experience of meeting God personally in an increasing spiritual simplicity and poverty. The personality of the individual was deeply respected. In the past women's congregations had tended to take a monastic form of training and then graft on an active apostolic vocation. This would not do, the Council said. An active apostolate in the modern world demanded a recognition of individual contribution; there could be no general looking back on past precepts or towards a higher authority for day-to-day decisions. Obviously, the Franciscans were already in step with this kind of thinking, but the teaching congregation were not, and would have to adapt.

The Council's recommendations for prayer life followed lines already taken by progressives in the 1960s and already practised by many priests and religious. For example, it recommended the recitation of Divine Office as well as the Little Office so that everyone could share more fully in the liturgical life of the Church. The Little Office had originally been introduced into congregations of women religious whose members had neither the time nor the education to recite the Divine Office in Latin. General reforms and the use of the vernacular brought it within reach of everyone. Interestingly, the Franciscans had always recited the Divine Office and they actually continued to recite it in Latin once a week. As to the rest of the daily prayers, the Council suggested that all manuals of prayers and ceremonies should be revised and many of the hourly prayers could be dropped. But they recommended the retention of Lauds and Vespers, possibly Compline to end the day and devotional exercises like the rosary and the Stations of the Cross, providing they were performed correctly. Similarly, they did say that while traditional ascetic practices which involved the self-infliction of bodily pain had come under fire from psychologists and clerics alike, some penance and mortification was necessary in the religious life. It is no surprise to find that the two congregations interpreted these recommendations very differently.

The teaching congregation retained only the bare bones of the day, but they made an effort to improve their singing. They brought in a friendly Benedictine sister who taught them some chants. They cast aside their rosaries and ceased to say the Stations of the Cross. The Franciscans also sang Lauds and Vespers but they expected any sister whose working hours permitted, to keep the minor Hours of Terce, Sext and None, as well. They kept Matins at a time suited to each individual house and Compline was sung as a night prayer. They also kept their rosaries in their habits and continued to say the Stations of the Cross when they wished. The Franciscan day therefore continued to have a structure of prayers which patterned each day identically throughout the organization.

In general, the recommendations on prayer life and the vows emphasized the importance of the individual's personality and initiative. Moreover, the communities in which these individuals lived should be 'fraternal', a community whose cohesion depended on the 'recognition of the Word of God', not a rigorous uniformity. The Franciscans kept their daily routines, but they also had a common ideology which played a powerful part in gaining the compliance of members to organizational goals and gave their religious life a colourful spirituality. The shared timetable was not the most important factor for the Franciscans. In encouraging a more egalitarian community, the Council suggested that all sisters should have the power to vote and that at least two-thirds of the members of any General Chapter should be freely elected. Even the Superiors might stand for election, or the whole community might elect a group of persons to share the executive power of Superior. In any case, all major issues should be decided by the vote of the majority of the elected group, the Superior simply being in charge of execution. This would obviously widen the executive power base without making it either inefficient or autocratic. Lastly the Council suggested some form of judicial power in each institute, to protect not only the rights of the individual but also those of the Church, Institute and Superior, a form of board of arbitration made up of trusted, independent and wise people. In this way any serious anomaly of power or discipline could be referred to independent arbitrators, and changes in the government of the congregations would not threaten the authority of the Church. Whether the government of the Institute was exercised in a more corporate or a more personal way, its power was still granted by the Church and any changes would, ultimately, have to be ratified by Mother Church.

The Franciscans did introduce regional government in 1968, but it was still old-style government with the Mother General effectively choosing all the officials. Similarly, while more elected delegates were sent to the General Chapter, they still only accounted for one in every fifteen sisters and were outnumbered in the voting system of the Chapter. The responsibilities and powers of local Superiors remained the same as before. The Mother General remained the supreme internal authority, but she shared the executive functions of her office with her General Council, including some responsibility for individual sisters such as the dismissal and reception of postulants and the appointment of sisters to General Office. General Councillors became more important and their numbers increased under the post-Vatican II reorganization. But the framework of the congregation, a bureaucratic framework with a titular autocratic head, remained the same. They even justified the retention of the title 'Mother' for all senior officials with the explanation that all families have a mother; it is a title which expresses love and warmth. They tended to keep the dependency relationships, the traditional modes of thought which go with the 'family spirit'. They did not take up the challenge to 'fraternalize' their convents, believing in a rather different form of 'fraternity' given to them by St Francis. They retained silence, penance, routine, bells, the habit, and a degree of compulsion—all those aspects of religious life which had been swept aside by the teaching congregation, or were finally discarded in 1968. They earned their reputation as the 'most conservative of nuns'.

The three years' experimentation between 1965 and 1968 saw changes which affected every aspect of life in the teaching congregation. The nuns were catapulted into the twentieth century, and into a radical expression of their religious life. The dramatic changes began with a change in the religious habit. The face was exposed. Instead of the montenere, badeau, certet and gimpe the sisters wore a short veil hanging to just below the shoulder blades, attached to a head-band which covered the hair. I shall consider the symbolic implications of this in a later chapter, but it can be imagined how even such a small change felt to a nun who had spent most of her life in the enclosed habit. For the first time in maybe thirty years, she could move her chin without restraint. She could feel the wind on the back of her neck. She had to grow her hair. Sister Matilda, who had been a teacher for forty years, liked the old habit but made the change. She said that her worst moment was facing the children. The children liked the enclosed habit, it had a sense of mystery about it. She said, 'The children have all sorts of funny notions about nuns. In the old boarding school I was looking after the children with a qualified nurse. One night, one of the children woke up with a fright and went to the nurse instead of coming to me. I was surprised and wanted to find out why. "We didn't like to see." "See what?" "See you in bed," the child said. Well, it turned out that the children were constantly talking about what a nun was like under her habit and it frightened this child to see me in my nightie.' With this episode in mind, Sister Matilda wondered what the children's reaction would be to seeing her in everyday clothes. But when that change came it was much easier, she said. After a few months of wearing very thick stockings and very long skirts she adjusted and now says, 'I love clothes'. And she seemed quite at ease in a smart suit.

In 1967 the first move towards creating smaller communities in the teaching congregation was made. They sold the largest of their convents and divided the community between two smaller houses. Then, later in the year, the first house of less than ten sisters was established. It was the first to be so small since the congregation had established itself in England. The sisters who went to live in the small convents celebrated new forms of the Mass and demanded new concepts of community. Nowhere this was more obvious than in the newly formed House of Studies in London. The style of this convent was radically different from any previous foundation in the order. It echoed a general movement towards London and away from Oxford and the provinces, and a move towards the new theological centre of Catholic learning and the centre of professional training.[16] It was an urban house, a London terraced house with peeling stucco and a damp basement. It was in an area of London with a high immigrant population and a twilight housing problem. The house itself was sparsely furnished and large parts remained unpainted until the sisters themselves had the time and spare cash to do the decorating. The basement was let off to an old man on a controlled tenancy. Most of the furniture was purchased second-hand. The chapel was a small upstairs room with no specific decorations. A small wooden table served as an altar and chairs stood about in random order. The only concession to style were two green panels painted on the wall behind the altar table. Each sister had her own front door key. Mealtimes were informal and visitors frequent. The house was a constant flux of visiting sisters, who often stayed the night in transit to another convent. Sisters from different parts of the world exchanged information and impressions of the culture and politics of the secular world, providing a strong contrast with the old enclosed convents of previous years.

By 1968 there were numbers of sisters on courses in various parts of Britain and Europe. There were five in Rome, three in Paris, many in London, all engaged in religious studies. There were five different sisters at five different British universities pursuing first degrees in a variety of subjects. The universities included London, Dublin, Cardiff, Glasgow, Keele, Manchester, and now even Open University courses are taken. There were a number of sisters in teacher training college, eight in nursing training, one in catering at Leeds and a sister following a course in philosophy and scriptural theology in Fribourg, Switzerland. Accommodation was a problem. Rooms were rented in hostels and small communities were set up either in rented properties or in conjunction with an existing convent. The material base of the organization was changing, and would be altered further once all those in training took up their profession. At the same time the Institute still owned four large schools in England and a number of missions. Instead of one specific goal, it now had, willy-nilly, a series of diverse goals to maintain and only a very experimental framework with which to achieve those goals. A key factor in equipping the sisters to cope with the new 'open' life in the smaller convents was formation—a new word for Novitiate. Formation would be the fundamental process on which depended the commitment and value orientation of members to organizational goals.

Formation was envisaged as a never-ending process but one which had particular relevance to those who had not yet taken final vows. Novitiate, Novice Mistress and novices were replaced by a team of trained nuns, selected candidates and a number of suitable communities for those candidates to live in. Finding suitable communities was the worst headache. To succeed the communities had to be 'a true, living, fraternal community', one which was open, where co-responsibility was lived out. But such communities tended to be lived in by busy nuns who were out for most of the day, and the young trainees were employed in housework and left on their own. Several were lost either to secular life or to other congregations. Not all experiments were successful and the lack of recruits was to have a drastic effect on the viability of the congregation. Unlike the Franciscans the teaching congregation were all the time rejecting the notion of the family as the model for community. The title 'mother' was deleted, Superiors became 'sisters-in-charge' and their authority referred to as co-responsibility. In this they followed Suenens, who said that the old mother/daughter relationships of the convent must be replaced by individual contribution to responsibility for the whole community. As in the sacrament of baptism, they said, lending a theological gloss to social reforms, the person of Christ is recalled in the baptized. 'It is no longer the religious who obeys; it is Christ in him who obeys the will of the Father for the salvation of the world'. And they quoted Suenens who said: 'If the relationships are to be real, the obedience of an adult must be adult obedience. Passivity and confirmism are not synonyms for obedience. All that smacks of maternalism or paternalism on the one hand, or its echo, childishness, on the other, must be pitilessly cut out. Thus the way will lie open for the co-responsibility so necessary within religious communities.'[17] Co-responsibility at a local level was soon followed with the suggestion of co-responsibility at all levels of government. At the Chapter in Rome in 1969, one sister suggested that all roles should be suppressed for a year as an experiment—a suggestion which was not taken up for its sheer impracticality, but which indicated the mood of reform.

Authority became the key issue in the Chapters of 1968 and 1969. In order to make the open communities work there had to be a real alternative to the old hierarchy. Even the progressives admitted that there were great difficulties. They suggested sensitivity sessions, group dynamics, workshops to build up person-to-person relationships and equip individuals to cope with the egalitarian society. As in the wave of T-groups and sensitivity sessions which swept America in the late 1960s, the nuns sought help in understanding their own psychology as a way to come to terms with a society which was abandoning old forms. They considered the idea of 'subsidiarity'. A Superior can only take responsibility when a person or group can no longer make a decision of their own accord. The point at which the authority can step in raises the question of the 'common good'. One sister explained, 'If I see something that is good for myself, but not for my family, I do what is best for my family. If I see something that is good for my family, but not for my country, I do what is best for my country . . .' The sisters were undecided about how this would work and agreed that they needed a year to work out the principles of subsidiarity and co-responsibility in practice.

In 1970 a solution was agreed upon in which the 'logic' of hierarchy was replaced by the 'logic' of co-responsibility. This was a cellular structure in which individual houses held a fair degree of autonomy and the whole was co-ordinated at local, provincial and general levels by elected officials. There were always some who wanted to retain the old structures and by this arrangement, they hoped, everyone would be happy. Uniformity is not necessary, the sisters were told, 'for it is impossible to find unity at the level of ideas. Consider the monastic community at Taize where members of sixty-five Christian and non-Christian sects live in deep communion. If they were to begin to discuss at a doctrinal level, this life of communion would be impossible. Shouldn't we simply be ourselves? In whose name are we gathered together? What is the Institute for us? We must try to live the gospel together, accepting that each one should live it differently.' The new structure of government enabled a diversity of forms at a local level without threatening the viability of the Institute.

At the end of 1970 a new Mother General was elected. The retiring Mother General was the last of her line. The changes she had initiated implied that no successor would be in a position to push through a revolution as she had. It was in the very nature of the traditional hierarchical system of government that the Mother General and her council had powers at their command which could revolutionize the system. They had destroyed the very system on which that power was based. Now their successors would always have to seek the approval of every sister in the Institute before implementing change. Government in the teaching order was now co-ordination. Authority was individual responsibility. Corporate responsibility did not eliminate leadership but reduced the powers of the leader, replacing the function of legislator with the function of co-ordinator. If a decision did have to be made by the leader alone, then it was justified on theocratic lines. The principle of subsidiarity worked on all levels; thus an individual was to take the maximum responsibility of which she was capable. Equally the local group must take its responsibility as fully as possible and the provincial government must respect this. At each level the higher group, as co-ordinator, has to balance the needs of the individual, or the local or provincial good, against the needs of the local diocesan, regional or universal Church. The structure was not rule by the majority, but agreement at all levels on the common good, tempered where necessary by a decision from the co-ordinator.

The change was not from bureaucratic hierarchy to democracy, though egalitarianism had been an initial impetus. A democratic organization has been defined as 'an organization established to ascertain the common objectives among men on the basis of the will of the majority or their representatives, and the organizing principle is the freedom of dissent necessary for the majority opinions to form.'[18] In the teaching congregation a body of elected officials, the co-ordinators, made decisions at various levels for the common good. This is neither bureaucracy nor democracy, since the officials are not appointed and their decisions are not based on a choice between alternatives, but rather on what *they* decide is good for the majority. The implementation of their decisions is up to officials at a lower or higher level, not in the hierarchical sense but in terms of local units. The autonomy of provinces was such that the Mother General and her Council were little more than a bond between them. All officials were now elected to their positions for periods of up to three years. In one sense the General Council was redundant, but in another sense their task was more vital for it gave the congregation a unity and identity, a task increasingly difficult as the provinces and their work became more diversified. Not only the provincial co-ordinators, but local units and individual sisters were encouraged to examine their position and decide whether the work they were doing could be done by another agency; if so they should give it up and move to another area with a specific need. Sisters were especially to remember that 'they were called to witness to the Risen Christ in the area in which they live.' They rented properties rather than buying them, and took an active part in the life of the parish. They shared their convents with other religious, even forming mixed communities of brothers, sisters and priests from different congregations. They continued to experiment, to question their roles, their apostolate, and their lifestyles. Each local community had the possibility of implementing change where they felt need. The possibility of radical transformations from above had been removed, but an element of change had been built into the fabric of the organization.

Change was legitimated by 'charism'—not the charisma of Weber, but a theological concept—a grace. 'Charism', the sisters told me, was 'listening to the spirit which moves'. It could be distinguished from grace and other benefits from the Holy Spirit by a property of detachment. A sister with 'charism' could pass it on to the community and to the Church, while grace remained within a person. A truly free individual would, the sisters said, be free to follow the Spirit constantly. She would move in the 'provisional' and offer her gift for the use of the Church. Individual decisions were all seen to devolve from the movement of the Holy Spirit within the individual; one should be careful therefore of attributing the changes in this congregation to a general process of secularization. There had been a shift in the symbolic and religious interpretation of organizational patterns and forms of lifestyle, but not an erosion of the religious element in favour of secular forms. This is to use a rather narrow definition of secularization. In this century when religion takes a decreasing role in the lives of so many, it is important not to talk of secularization in a value-loaded sense. It has meant many different things in the history of the Church, from heralding a world under the domination of Satan, to a specific legal term referring to the transfer of land to civil control.[19] Secularization can simply mean a decline in religion, a loss of social significance by religious thinking, practice and institutions.[20] It can be applied to 'practice' but great care has to be exercised when applying it to thinking. It must not be used in such a way that it implies there was a time when a 'real' religious spirit existed, compared to now, when that spirit is diffuse and weakened, for that is neither how the actors see it nor how religious institutions today respond. Old forms of religious thinking and belief may have lost validity, even plausibility, but the participants of a religious institution still underpin their social lives with religion and lend their religion social significance.

The sisters did see themselves turning from 'other-worldly' to 'this-worldly' orientations. They read and quoted Harvey Cox[21] who saw secularization as 'the liberation of man from religious and metaphysical tutelage, the turning of his attention away from other worlds and towards this one'. He takes his source from the Bible, where the three different elements of secularization—the disenchantment with nature, desacralization of politics, and deconsecration of values—are to be found, Cox asserts, in the description of the Creation, in the Exodus and in the Sinai covenant—especially in its prohibition of idols. The teaching sisters threw out their religious pictures and statuary. The new theology led them to find God in humanity, in this world. Cox is careful to distinguish secularization—a term glowing with the promise of never-ending change in religious groups, from secularism—the closed ideology opposed to the freedom of thought that secularization produces. Cox's whole notion of the secular city is based on the idea that secularization is positive, that it has an excellent pedigree, and that it is 'this-worldly' in orientation. Theological justification for the radical changes in the teaching congregation always came from the Bible rather than the founder's writings, and the changes were very much the result of opening the convents to the full impact of the secular world. In giving their children to the state education system Catholics had recognized a certain 'disengagement of society from religion'. But, as Michael Hill has pointed out, this is differentiation rather than disengagement[22] for while the children go to state schools they still go to denominational schools by choice and receive additional daily religious instruction either in school or by supplementary classes in catechetics. The sisters did not abandon teaching; they went into the state schools or specialized in the teaching of religion and catechetics.

Secularization has another implication which involves the notion that the world is gradually deprived of its moral character. In the most restricted sense this means that magical beliefs and practices are gradually eliminated and the world becomes disenchanted. Magic is generally defined as the performance of ritual acts whose efficacy is unquestioningly believed by both actors and audience—the use of Holy Water, for example. Certainly the teaching congregation did try to eliminate many magical practices in this sense. It cannot be seen as a 'sign of the times', for the Franciscans retained all their traditional magical interpretations of the Mass even though they had an apostolic work firmly located in this world. In the teaching congregation the reinterpretation of the Mass and the values attributed to the Eucharist brought it into a symbol system allied to this world, to secular orientations, rather than to magical or proto-magical devices. Right at the beginning of the changes in 1958 the Mother General had talked to her sisters of 'horizontalism', the bringing down of God and spreading him out. He was to be a member of the small group, not seated on the topmost pinnacle of an ecclesiastical hierarchy. The Franciscans, in retaining the magic of their world, retained it within a value-system and an ideology which were virtually impermeable to the influence of Vatican II. The Franciscan ideology in particular included a notion of brotherhood, a spirituality and an emphasis on nature, which constituted a world-picture. It gave the Franciscans something which outsiders did not have and gave them a focus for integration and for change within their organization. It also isolated them from the rest of society, an isolation reinforced by physical enclosure and silence. The Franciscans remained 'in habit' but this did not mean that they remained resistant to change. The teaching congregation broke down the barriers, laid themselves open to the secular society and, lacking the ideological integrity of the Franciscans, they were forced to accept more and more changes on utilitarian, secular criteria —as in the move to rented accommodation. If we think of the teaching congregation as making a change from sacred to secular, it is a change from a 'closed' system of rationality resistant to change, to an 'open' system of rationality where alternatives are accepted more willingly. Seen in this operational context secularization is a less useful concept than would appear.

I see the response of the teaching congregation to the promulgations of Vatican II as a conceptual revolution in the Kuhnian sense. John Moore has made a very helpful analysis of the priesthood, in which he uses Kuhn's paradigms to explain the changes brought about by Vatican II.[23] Kuhn uses the term paradigm to stand for 'the entire constellation of beliefs, values, techniques, and so on, shared by the members of a given community'.[24] He also uses it to describe one element in the constellation, 'the concrete puzzle-solutions which, employed as models or examples, can replace explicit rules as a basic for the solution of the remaining puzzles of normal science'. Kuhn argues for revolutionary breakthroughs in the progress of science— breakthroughs which can be marked by a change in the paradigm in favour of another. Such desertions occur when anomalies appear in the paradigm, when theory and fact are irreconcilable. It provokes a crisis situation which is handled either by the old paradigm or by a newly emerged one, with all the battles for acceptance which that implies. The Franciscan response to Vatican II took place within the old paradigm which was well able to cope with the crisis situation of the 1960s—crisis in the form of deep introspective questioning. But the old paradigm did not withstand the criticism of the teaching sisters. It had to be replaced. Moore describes the preconciliar paradigm as a Tridentine paradigm, a defensive, totally integrated, holistic theology, where each person had a clearly defined role and corresponding behaviour pattern. The Council of Trent gave the Roman Catholic Church a 'closed' rationality. It had to claim to be the true Church founded by Christ, with a monopoly of truth and the means of salvation in answer to the damning criticisms of the Reformation. Salvation was achieved through the ministry of its priests who received their spiritual powers directly from above, transmitted by Christ. The priests were seen as *alter Christi*. Priests were different from ordinary men; their role has a sacred character and their lives should differ in quality from that of ordinary men in the Tridentine Church.

The nuns too have this quality of exceptionality. They exemplify the virtues of obedience, docility and loyalty. The nun's life bears witness to her dedication to God in a way which ordinary people cannot hope to imitate. Such exceptional qualities, as I have shown, demand rigorous socialization. The priests went to seminaries where, from a younger age than the nuns, they were submitted to socialization and indoctrination equipping them for a yet higher and more sacred office in the Church. The priests were the mediators in the communications between God and his people on earth, for it was in their consecretation of the Eucharist that the Church held its monopoly on truth. When Vatican II redefined the priest's role and the interpretation of the Eucharist, it shattered the Tridentine paradigm. The priest could no longer claim a different, superior position to the laity. After Vatican II all people in the Church were *alter Christi*. The emphasis on participation, on co-responsibility, implied that the priest should be open and responsive to the views of the laity, not held up as an exemplification of certain values. He now had to show that he was of service to the community, hence the worker priests. It is not enough for him just to perform an expressive function in the Church, he has to perform instrumental acts within the context of the laity. At the same time the Eucharist ceases to be the moment of communication with God and takes on the function of an everyday meal, on which people on earth survive. In the teaching congregation, the breakdown of the 'closed' convent system resulted in the Tridentine paradigm being replaced, in the case of the progressives at least, by the post-Vatican II paradigm. With the acceptance of the new paradigm the work of the congregation, its development and even its recruitment were resumed and it thrived again after the years of turmoil.

The teaching congregation did lose a number of its professed sisters between 1969 and 1973. It also had to cease recruitment for three years until in 1974 a small Novitiate was opened. But now requests for dispensations have ceased and numbers have stabilized. The congregation is now composed of a number of separate units, loosely confederated in provinces and under the overall co-ordination of a Mother Superior. A huge number of secondary goals occupy the organization. By the 1970s there were a plurality of forms; in some convents sisters had managed to continue with the old paradigm, in others the boundaries between the convent and the outside world were so diffuse as to be scarcely discernible. One sister explained it as the difference between adaptation and renewal. Adaptation was possible through obedience, following the rule of the Superior and altering your way of life without really changing your beliefs, so that the co-ordinator was treated and respected in just the same way as the Superior had been. Some sisters refused to discard the old monastic habit; they were allowed to keep it if they wished. But they would also go back to using the linen room (two old convents remained in 1970) and they used the *prie-Dieu* in chapel, even trying to maintain the old rank order—with gaps! Here, at the grass-roots level, the battle for the acceptance of the new paradigm was waged, a battle confused by the pluralism of the congregation. Those aspects of the old paradigm, commitment, compliance, responsibility and authority, now had to be privatized in the individual. If they did not succeed in this, the congregation would not survive the intense competitiveness of ideas and the plurality of forms which it arrived at by 1970. The complexity of life-worlds, the 'peculiarly individuated'[25] nature of modern identity constitutes a threat to the very plausibility of religious definitions of reality.

CHAPTER EIGHT

Sacrifice or Feast:
The Sacred in Everyday Life

We must accept, if we are to understand the nuns, the reality of their belief in the power of the supernatural. When Evans-Pritchard wrote *Nuer Religion* in the 1950s, he felt the need to justify Nuer belief and the Nuer God and to prove that they could not be reduced to or explained away by the social order. Belief in the Nuer God was, he said, interior, something not even the most persistent investigator could hope to understand.[1] Thirty years later, I feel the need to make a similar statement about the nun's beliefs. Old-fashioned distinctions between the world religions and primitive religion are often still falsely applied. Primitive peoples, it is said, believe in magic; they are superstitious; they spend a lot of time and energy in elaborate rituals. The civilized world is more sophisticated; beliefs have a traditional validation; theologians schooled in doctrine, dogma and divinity provide an intellectual status. The nun's belief in her God is not something which can be explained away by an anthropologist. She has a belief in a 'supra-empirical reality' with which she shares the temporal world. The religious organization is primarily instituted to celebrate an awareness of, and obligation to, a God. The language used, the rituals, symbols, and even daily organization express this function. I would agree with Durkheim and his followers that religion is something eminently social, with the proviso that to restrict religious belief to the function of maintaining and expressing social forms is to misunderstand the fundamental process of that belief. It is essential to recognize a dialectical relationship between the believer, his beliefs and his social life. Like the compliance between superior and subordinate, the compliance between society and its religious representations is open to change, speculation and manipulation. To study the nuns is to study a human group which emphasizes the part played by religious actions, the sacred and the magical in the ordering of their social lives.

The beliefs of the laity have always been recognized as belonging to a different order from those of the clergy in the Catholic Church. But that was more an expression of hierarchy than of an understanding for the beliefs of ordinary people. Keith Thomas writes about the medieval Church: 'For ordinary men, what stood out was the magical notion that the mere pronounciation of words in a ritual manner could effect a change in the character of material objects.'[2] Not just for the medieval Church. Sister Ignatius told me about a wonderful old priest who used to be so overcome by the act of consecrating the hosts at Mass that he could hardly proceed. She said, 'As he got older he began to think of the tremendous power he had, changing all that bread into the body of Christ. He used to say the Mass in Latin, Hoc est enim Corpus meum. He used to say oc-oc-o-occe- and he couldn't go on. He used to shake with the tremendous thing he was doing. We used to be in the chapel for hours with him, waiting for him to go on!'

The sisters would deny that their beliefs are magical; they would say they are mystical. Magic is a word loaded with false judgements in our present Western society. Scepticism has reduced magic to something laughable, fit for conjurers, but it is, like religion, something to be believed in. When I asked another sister about the power and efficacy of holy water, she replied, 'It's symbolical really, to show that you are cleansed of original sin.' A little later she described a baptism she had just attended and the reality of her belief was revealed. 'It was an awful cold day in March, and the baby was about three months old. The father wasn't a Catholic and they poured this water, cold water on the baby and the baby was asleep when the water touched his head and of course he began to scream. So the priest went on pouring the water and said, "I baptize thee" and took the baby out. The father got straight up and got a towel to mop the water up. I jumped up and said, "Stop that, that's good, leave it on, that's good, it's baptismal water. You can't rub that off." I got the impulse to stop the man doing it.' That baptismal water was both precious and efficacious. The nun's belief in its power and potency was no different from the superstition of Keith Thomas's medieval man who used it on numerous occasions to ward off evil spirits and bad luck. The nun told me that pouring the cold water on the baby's head cleansed it from original sin. 'There is this story about babies, that before they are baptized the devil's got power over them. If they see anyone like a nun, or someone related to God, then they shriek in their presence.'

Baptism is the only sacrament which the nun herself could bestow. If a baby was in danger of dying, or even in some cases was a Protestant baby or one not likely to get a 'proper' baptism, it could be baptized by a nun or a 'good Catholic' who would simply sprinkle water and say the words, 'I baptize thee'. But this was, I was told, exceptional, for all the sacraments relied on the power of the priest to make them efficacious. The sacraments were the most potent expression of the Church's connection with the supernatural. Sister Ita expresses her sense of awe and mystery at the chain of authority which goes back to St Peter. 'The priest gets those two fingers consecrated when he is ordained so that he can turn the bread and wine into the body and blood of Christ. He gets the power to do these things which is the greatest power on earth really. The first time he can do it is when the bishop consecrates him, and only the bishop can do that. The bishop holds his hand and he does it together with the bishop. And they hold it together, and they say "This is my body", and when they say it together that bread is no longer bread, it's just the form of bread, it's the body and blood of Christ. If the priest were not there then that bread would not change into the body of Christ. It would be just a symbol, if the priest were not there. It's a tremendous power, isn't it?'

If you wonder how someone living today in the sophisticated age of science can believe that bread is not bread, then you can be answered by Sister Ita herself. A small boy asked her, 'If God is in the bread I receive, how is he in the bread of all the other people as well?' She replied, 'That's the mystery. Of course God can come to everybody at the same time because he is everywhere. He can be with everybody intimately at the same time. It's a mystery, you see.' The mystery is the rationale for the leap from unbelief or disbelief to belief. It is not for us to question the inherent ambiguities and paradoxes of religious belief. While sisters would answer very logically for their beliefs and qualify them by describing them as symbolic or analogous, the very language they used to express them and the emotion which accompanied that expression confirmed the underlying reality. The reality of the priest's power, the reality of the spirit of God in grace, the reality of transubstantiation were shared by all the sisters; some could answer for a world-picture which included angels, devils, heaven and hell. Periodically children are asked to describe God and they often answer that he is an old grey man with a beard. Adults laugh indulgently, but would they so easily laugh if 'he' was a 'she'? Sister Mary Thérèse tried to explain to me the reality of her world. As a child religion had been used as a weapon against bad behaviour. All her efforts to dispel dark fears had been in vain. She said, 'Occasionally when I am very wicked I get very frightened. I was taught, Hell, purgatory, Heaven and you're not likely to get to Heaven because you're not likely to be that good—so at best you'll have a long time in purgatory and at worst you'll go to Hell. I don't like it. But I can't get away from it. Actually I try to go around being happy. We all know that we feel much happier if we have helped so-and-so rather than told him to shut up. So if you go around pursuing this aim, you won't be wicked, you'll be good and end up in Heaven.

I don't think of it in terms of I'm going to be good to get into Heaven, but it's what will happen if I am good.'

The picture was very confused, but in general it included a very real Hell, a place the opposite of Heaven, where demons and unrepentant sinners lived, while Purgatory was a place where you expiated all the sins you had committed on earth. One of the older sisters told me, 'If a person dies with the priest's absolution, her sins are forgiven, but for every sin you commit you must expiate it. If you die without that debt being paid back to God you must expiate your sins in the next life. Then you have a short time in Purgatory. But it's something terrible. There was a story about someone offered a choice of suffering misery for four years or Purgatory for half-an-hour, and she was dying, and said, "Purgatory", and after a few minutes she said, "Oh! you said only half-an-hour and I've been here years". Her suffering was so great.' The clearest description of Purgatory was of somewhere without duration, a process which you went through when you were dying. But if you lived your life well and in true humility then you had nothing to fear, death was a happy hour. Heaven is universally a place 'up there' and the nuns were no exception in locating it above. As Sister Ita said, 'Nobody has seen an angel, but an angel does come down from Heaven to earth with messages; that's their job. The angel in order to fly down has to have wings. It can be in the shape of a man, or in the shape of anything else, but one showed itself to Our Lady the Mother of God, and that was a messenger from on high. Well, I suppose you don't really know where Heaven is, but because Christ went up it must be up.' So angels have wings because they have to get from up there to down here. Hell is still further down and somewhere to be afraid of.

In the process of the changes in lifestyle and governmental structure, the beliefs of the teaching sisters also changed. The progressive sisters had rejected the idea of Heaven and Hell. Theirs was a more friendly world-picture which did not include such fearsome places. But they did not give up the old beliefs without a struggle. A young artist, Sister Anne, explains her feelings about dropping the Stations of the Cross, a devotion discouraged by Vatican II. She said, 'I made a movement, a stepping stone, a very traumatic one, when I decided to stop saying the Stations of the Cross for the Holy Souls. There is this idea that there are souls on earth and saints in Heaven and in between are the souls of the dead who have not yet been admitted to Heaven. It is up to those on earth to intercede with the saints, through prayer, to plead with God to let them in. So you can see how traumatic it was to decide not to pray for them, not to help them, because one might be condemning them to Purgatory for ever.' Keith Thomas says that the official Church has always complained about the laity's resort to magical practices and beliefs. Sister Anne has shown how no amount of explanations from theologians will ease her discomfort about those lost souls. As she said, 'Christianity wouldn't admit to being superstitious because it's such a highly developed religion, but it doesn't alter the fact that the people's response to it is superstitious rather than religious.' Sister Hilda, a middle-aged teacher, admitted to being most confused by all the questioning of beliefs in the 1960s. She said that she still believed in praying for the dead because they may be in Purgatory. But then, if Purgatory is a process you go through when you're dying, why pray for them when they are dead? 'Is Purgatory just when you're at your last gasp? You've got all the theologians saying they are not dead until their soul leaves their body—but what happens in between?' Her solution was to pray for the Holy Souls when she remembered just to show she still cared for them! By 1970 the plurality of social forms in the teaching congregation was matched by a plurality of religious beliefs: some sisters had given up praying for the souls; others believed that souls must have the prayers of the living to ease their path to Heaven; some believed that people had an innate goodness which found them a place in Heaven regardless; others rejected the whole traditional schema and determinedly lived their life on earth as if it were their only salvation.

The plurality of forms and beliefs in the teaching congregation was impossible all the time the sisters lived within a 'closed' system of beliefs. A nun entering the teaching congregation in, say, 1925 was thoroughly indoctrinated by the group. Not only was her acceptance of the Rules and Customs of the organization unconditional but she was also asked to accept a parcel of religious beliefs and magical rites to which she was expected to adhere unquestioningly. Fifty years later that closed system had been blown apart. The world-picture which included Heaven and Hell and all the rites which supported it had been shattered—but how? Just as the organizational controls are accepted by the individual as he becomes a group member, so, too, he becomes part of the 'plausibility' of the collective representations or 'world-picture' of that group. Those sociologists who regard stability as a cultural imperative, like Durkheim, and later Peter Berger, say that individuals in society construct meaningful worlds for themselves —a *nomos* in Berger's terminology—to protect themselves against chaos.[3] A fundamental dialectic process between externalization, objectivation and internalization allows for the possibility of change in the picture. You may not accept this view of man. You may, like John O'Neill, accuse Berger of 'social Machiavellianism'. Berger's *nomos*, says O'Neill, allows for 'the permanent possibility of organizational sabotage, daydream, and the ecstasy of negative thinking which reduces every social given to a possibility only'.[4] So much depends on your own subjective stance. O'Neill's criticism is as much an expression of his own anarchic nature as of Berger's conservatism. I should say it is more accurate to assume that the social world constitutes a *nomos* both subjectively and objectively, and it is when, for some reason, this coherence breaks down, that change can be expected. Once the socially established *nomos* is internalized it merges with other fundamental meanings for man. One of these includes man's striving for an ultimate meaning for life, what Berger calls the *cosmos*. Religion is the 'human enterprise by which a sacred cosmos is established'.[5] Religion, which appeals to some ultimate reality, becomes a key source in the legitimation of the social world. For example, every religious believes that death is crucial in understanding the meaning of life. The ultimate reality for a religious lies in death itself, for that is what restores her to her God. Death is a key feature in the nun's religious life; she reminds herself constantly of the death of man and celebrates his life with God.

The second Superior General of the teaching congregation had summed up the successful religious life in 1870 with the words, 'Nothing disturbs the peace which our religious enjoy. Their life is freed from care, their last moments from anxiety. Their existence becomes a cloudless day, of which death is the evening, and the morrow eternal light.' In the traditional convent one day each month was given to the preparation for death. Death was treated with special rituals, prayers and good intentions. The death of a sister was an occasion for extra Masses and extra prayers. But every week, on Mondays, the Mass was dedicated to the sisters' own deceased parents, pupils, benefactors and fellow nuns, while a list of the deceased was kept in the sacristy and the community room of every convent. Death was also a time to remember the congregation's ties with the wider Church as the priest came to give the last sacraments and, if possible, be with the sister in her last hour. In the larger convents older sisters tended to have a morbid fascination with death, especially sudden deaths or deaths of children. As to deaths in their convents they describe it, without exception, as a happy release. No regret was shown for the pain and suffering which they truly believed people went through on death. The conversation of older sisters was sprinkled with phrases such as 'Merciful heavens', 'It's God's will', or when referring to a death, 'God rest her soul'. On death the nun is laid out in her habit, with her vows and her crucifix in her hands. Every nun visits her to pay her last respects. A plot is set aside in the local cemetery and the graves are visited if it is within convenient walking distance. In 1970 I was present at the death of a sister in a convent which had not reconciled all its members to the 'new theology'. Within half-an-hour of the fatal fall which led to this ninety-year-old sister's death prayers of supplication were being offered in the local parish church and in the convent chapel. The priest was called even before the doctor and travelled in the ambulance with her as he administered an 'anointing of the sick'. All the sisters from the community attended the Mass that evening and took communion even though some of them had been experiencing difficulties in reconciling their beliefs in the Eucharist at that time and had not taken communion for some weeks. In the crisis intellectual differences were forgotten and the traditional rituals were accepted by even the most sceptical. But in calmer times the rejection of the after-life, the repudiation of Purgatory and Hell by some of the sisters, had to affect the theology of Christ's death as dramatized in the Eucharistic Mass.

'Religion legitimates social institutions by bestowing upon them an ultimately valid ontological status, that is, by locating them within a sacred and cosmic frame of reference.'[6] Thus the father/priest reiterates for his audience at Mass the actions of his sacred prototype, God the Father. Specific social roles become representations of larger complexes of objectivated meanings. But this is not to assume that it is the sole function of religion nor is it necessarily a causal relationship. Peter Berger and Michael Hill see religion in some cases as an independent variable, in others a dependent variable in social change. As *cosmos* and *nomos* must share a degree of congruency or plausibility to be meaningful, when that plausibility is challenged 'the result might either be the redefinition of the religious belief system (in which case religion would be the dependent variable) or it might be an attempt to adapt the social environment so that it became congruent with the belief system (in which case society would be the dependent variable)'.[7] When the teaching order first bought ordinary houses for their sisters they used them like a custom-built convent, with a parlour for visitors and a tradesman's entrance at the back. When the full theological impact of Vatican II was felt, even the traditional convent lost some of its boundaries and became more like a home with visitors welcome in every quarter.

Tridentine Catholicism relied heavily on the 'closed' nature of its belief system and on discrete social groups for its plausibility. The plurality of roles and lifestyles in the modern teaching congregation not only threatened the function of religion as an overarching 'canopy of symbols' but constituted a threat to the very plausibility of religious definitions of reality. The breakdown of any area of ritual or belief was bound to have repercussions. For example, the use of the vernacular in religious services broke the boundary between priest and people and began the general movement towards the laity. In the increasing confusion as traditional beliefs were assaulted from within the Church and by changes in the secular world, the nuns turned to a more direct approach to their God—they took a 'hot-line to Heaven' and talked to God directly and without intermediaries. It was the individual's answer to competing plausibility structures. It can also be the small groups' answer. God became a small-group member when validation could not be achieved through traditional means. Mary Douglas explains this phenomenon with a firm Durkheimian analysis in which the idea of God is constituted from the idea of society. Alienation from society will imply the desacralizing of God's image. 'And from that the idea of God, dethroned from the centres of power, will be set up again in the small interpersonal group which is alienated.'[8] This interpretation fits the case of the teaching congregation very well. The sisters, having broken the hierarchical relationships of their religious life, took to their hearts a personal God, one who was a friend, who would be with them all the time. But the Franciscans also had a friendly God and they did not live in small groups but in large enclosed convents where they retained all the features of the old paradigm which placed God out of reach. The Franciscans, whether in a large convent or out in the mission field (where it is true their numbers were few), pursued all the ritual of the Catholic Church to reach a God who was none the less personal and reachable by them at any hour, in any place. It had been one of the striking features of the Franciscan order since its inception and is explained by the importance of charisma. The personal appeal of St Francis, the charismatic leader, entailed a plausibility structure which acknowledged the charismatic legitimation of his authority and the religious representation of that in the *cosmos* with the idea of a personal God. As it turned out, there was no clash between this cosmology and the new theology propounded by Vatican II. There was no reason for the Franciscans to make radical alternations to their belief system. There was no crisis in credibility between the plurality of their specific instrumental goals and the universal nature of their expressive goals and value orientations.

The Franciscans kept the rituals and beliefs which the teaching congregation dropped; sometimes they made small modifications, the rosary for example being kept in the pocket instead of hanging from the belt. The rosary consists of reciting the 'Our Father' fifteen times, the 'Gloria' fifteen times and 'Hail Mary' one hundred and fifty times. Repetitious and mechanical possibly, but the nun who said her rosary every morning was reminded of the full mystery of her religious beliefs. As the recitation progresses her mind dwells in turn on the five joyful mysteries: Annunciation, Visitation, Nativity, Presentation, and the Discovery of Jesus in the Temple; on the five sorrowful mysteries: the Agony in the Garden, the Scourging of Christ, Crowning with Thorns, Christ Carrying the Cross and the

Crucifixion; and the five glorious mysteries: the Resurrection, Ascension, Descent of the Holy Ghost, Assumption of the Blessed Virgin Mary, the Coronation of Mary and the Glory of all the Saints.[9] The rosary has dropped out of favour yet the telling of it had many of the effects that the progressive nun sought. It was a technique of prayer which pacified the body and the mind, concentrating both on the mystery of the sacred. It also reaffirmed both Church and Institute in the participant's mind, as the introitus of the supernatural. It tells its adherents that God and man are factually but not basically separate, encouraging them to accept its explanation of the meaning of life. But the progressive teaching sisters, who had embraced Protestant theologians like Bonhoeffer in their quest for the meaning of life, came upon a very different view. The rosary became a historical rather than a spiritual exercise. Bonhoeffer rejected the distinction between man and God and brought them together in humanity. 'Man can serve God in and through his existence. Faith is manifest in true humanity in the service of God.'[10]

Sister Anne, the young teaching nun, tried to explain why a Lutheran theologian should be so useful in working out her theology of community. She said, 'I don't necessarily agree with all that Bonhoeffer is saying but it makes me link up, make a bridge between the older ideas and the newer ones. This is because he is so practical, because he obviously lived what he says. I admire very much the idea that in the whole of life, through all the aspects of life, we can be obedient to God as long as we give time for thought and for reflection, and give room to God to get ideas through. A biblical background gives you the same sort of thing, a background of Christ's attitudes, why he acted in certain ways with certain people, that sort of thing.' Sister Anne spent a quarter of an hour morning and night 'letting God get through' as she describes it. The rest of her day was spent in the service of the poor and the underprivileged. As she said, 'There is this argument that God and humanity are two separate entities, that you give up your time to God and you pray in the chapel and all that. There was a split between God and humanity and I fought against it. Then there is this argument that you should spend less time shut up in the chapel. You should be working, helping people out there.' Traditionally the Church had been the sole introitus to the supernatural; now in the restructured teaching congregation new forms of prayer life were being suggested to replace the frequent visits to the chapel. The General Chapter of 1969 tried to gather a consensus of opinion on what constituted an adequate prayer life for the sisters. It revealed the sharp divisions between different groups. In the English province there were four areas; the north of England and the missions represented the most extreme views, the south and the west and the

London areas the more moderate views. Each report took Vatican II as their starting-point and gave a different emphasis to the precepts found there, the most striking of which were the emphases placed by the north on the Old Testament and by the missions on the New.

The sisters of the north of England who represented the more conservative opinion in the teaching congregation wanted to retain religious silence, to retain Benediction and the Holy Hours, the rosary and other devotions. They found in the Old Testament a relationship between God and his people which should be echoed in their own relationship with God. Many of the older sisters had only just begun to read the Old Testament and they found justification for change and for retention of old practices there. The Hebrews, they said, had a marked conception of unity of being one race. They showed great spontaneity in their prayer life. Prayer was, they felt, a gift from God. Some of their older sisters were recognized as being close to God in the simplicity of their lives; they had this gift and it was borne out of silence and recollection. Even in the New Testament they found evidence of Christ at prayer all night, of public prayer, of feasts and meetings and devotions, and they found silence. The older sisters grieved for the loss of silence in their religious lives; some even stalwartly refused to speak during the day. In contrast, the missions went to the New Testament to learn all they could of Christ's personal and communal prayer life and to model their own on his. They decided that 'prayer may not be separated from daily lives because there can be no religious world apart from our genuine existence. It is very necessary to insert prayer into the real rhythm of our life with all its ups and downs.' In practical terms this meant that they recommended two communal prayer meetings a day to which outsiders would be welcome, especially pupils and staff of schools. They favoured readings from the scriptures rather than the psalms in the office and sometimes Bible vigils could replace the office altogether. 'A shortened version of the office would be more suitable as a conclusion to communal mediation or sharing,' they said. They could make no recommendations on personal prayer because they regarded it as a person-to-person relationship with God and as such it was not possible to make any formal statements about it.

The more moderate view held by London and south-west areas contained many practical suggestions both for the proper arrangements for prayer, its direction and its practical application. 'Prayer life', they said, 'must be relevant to today.' In this they followed *Perfectae Caritatis*: 'The manner of living, praying and working should be suitably adapted to the physical and psychological conditions of today's religious and also to the extent required by the nature of each community, to the needs of the apostolate, the requirements of a given culture, the social and economic circumstances everywhere.' The sisters had an existentialist view of the world in which everything had to have a meaning in relation to the present as well as to the ultimate meaning of things. Their recommendations were suited to the lives of busy sisters, who, after battling with the stresses of the world today, could retreat into solitude for spiritual renewal from time to time. Therefore they decided that time, place and method of prayer should be left to the individual. Ideally no one should be criticized for their method of prayer. Sitting in a comfortable armchair might be just as rewarding as kneeling on the cold stone floor of the church. They recommended that at least an hour each day should be devoted to prayer and two retreats of three days each would replace the monthly day of retreat. In addition an annual retreat of eight days was suggested, preferably in a special retreat centre, ideally a community house where sisters could go for a day or so to be quiet, benefiting from the withdrawal from work and the normal milieu. Each community should also have a quiet room, which might double as a chapel, where sisters could retire from the bustle of the modern convent. They quoted from the Anglican Bishop of Woolwich. In *Honest to God* he says: 'Times of withdrawal are for standing back, for consolation, for letting one's roots grow and deepen, even though we know and admit that love can be fertilized and made creative by engagements and encounters as well as by disengagements and withdrawals.'[11] The sisters recommended a period of leisure time in each day so that the retreats and recollections would take their place as more meaningful to the spiritual side of their lives.

The essence of prayer for these sisters was that it must be human prayer, arising from the human condition. Effective prayer arose from effective human relationships and an effective apostolate. Prayer, they said, was not a talking to God but an expression of a quality of life. Continual formation would assist them; reading lists, devotions and alternative methods should be suggested; the Constitutions should only state guidelines. In the case of the smaller groups of nuns, group prayer was essential, communal celebration of penance, scriptural rosary, the Mass, Bible vigils and group meditation. Group meditation in particular should be arranged informally in a spirit of openness and sincerity. Some silence was recommended, the silence which was a listening to God; a nun could gain great support from that activity. The Chapter took many of the recommendations from the moderates. Prayer would be seen as a twofold relationship with God; directly through personal prayer and indirectly with one's neighbour. There was a feeling that the sisters would need a deep faith to live in the twentieth century in the midst of man's technological advance and spiritual withdrawal. They must be given every assistance in their prayer life. They should read the scriptures daily, go to Mass and receive the Eucharist daily, for the 'bread of life' was an effective symbol of their common membership of Christ's mystical body. Their daily human contacts were encounters with God, yet periods of withdrawal for quiet would be necessary to make each aware of God's will and action.

The Chapter was addressing a congregation whose traditional prayer life had been marked out by bells and orders. Now, in 1969, there were no bells, no orders, no schedules, prayer was a matter for the individual. Whereas in the past the whole congregation moved as a body, whether the sister was in Africa, Durham or Brighton, following the same pattern at the same time day after day, now she would find wide variation wherever she went. Not only did individual convents differ but so did the individuals within those convents. Several of the older sisters still wore a rosary; they found the lack of silence very disruptive and tried to keep some silence for themselves. A degree of manipulation was taking place. If the official line was extending the boundaries to an intolerable degree then the individual adjusted them to suit herself. This conscious manipulation of belief is most likely in periods of rapid change when the competing plausibility structures offered to the participants allow for it. What one sees in the teaching congregation is a general correspondence between religion and social organization. The rituals which are the enactment of religious belief are more than just a dramatic representation of those beliefs just as they are more than a mirror reflection of social organization. Ernest Gellner has made the point that a minimum requirement of reflection is a 'one-one correspondence between the two mutually reflecting systems'.[12] Neither social organization nor belief system consists of easily separable or identifiable 'parts'. What one sees is certain specific elements of both in the form of condensed symbols or ritual action. Indeed the very fact that ritual involves action makes it more easily observable and open to analysis. For example, as the nuns file into chapel they take up positions directly representative of their social position in the convent. The rank order is prescribed in the Rule, and the differentiation of status is reaffirmed in the chapel on every community gathering. But the teaching congregation no longer went into chapel together in rank order. Sister Patrick gave me her perception of the change: 'A good nun was someone who was very controlled and stood in line and did everything right by the book. You could be an excellent nun without doing anything really thoughtful, but by mechanically following the routines. Now it's up to you and you have to be much more careful about why you're doing things and what they mean. You know, it's like crossing yourself before taking food, I think I always say a little prayer to myself before I take food or when I go into chapel, but now sometimes I deliberately do not cross myself so it doesn't become a meaningless gesture.' Sister Patrick would previously have crossed herself in the company of her community as they sat to any meal in the refectory. The fact that she can now choose not to cross herself is as much due to the disappearance of organized meals in a large refectory as it is to her own need to feel involved in such ritualized gestures.

Every ceremonial and ritual proceeding carries a load of symbols charged with meaning. Symbols, whether they are objects, acts, relationships or linguistic formations, stand ambiguously for a multiplicity of meanings. Their very flexibility ensures a measure of continuity in a changing world. In the teaching congregation, after the changes of the 1960s, the symbolic presentation of the Mass was the same; it retained its traditional form. Yet for a nun who had celebrated in less conventional forms, who had embraced 'radical theology', the interpretation of those symbols would be very different from those of a nun who had not been through a 'renewal'. The congregation could remain together and worship together while its individual members exploited the ambiguity of its ceremonial. The Mass, of all Catholic rituals, carries that 'sacred canopy' of symbols and signs which make up a world-picture, integrative, ambiguous, a daily affirmation of the nun's position in her group and her life. The sacraments are central to the Roman Catholic's relationship to his God. In the sacraments *cosmos* and *nomos* are united. Sister John spoke for all her sisters when she said, 'There is nothing more important to us than the Mass. The Mass means everything. It was the ultimate sacrifice, our lives are consecrated to him as he gave his for everyone.' Sister John was in her eighties. To her the Mass had always been the ultimate sacrifice, but for young Sister Anne, for whom the Mass was still the most important ritual of her religious life, the death of Christ was not sacrificial but political. The daily Mass reminded her of her commitment to 'God in humanity'. It was a meal rather than a drama, a feast rather than a sacrifice. Christ's death was inevitable, she said, 'because of the action he took, you know. The proof of his love for us was that he didn't play the coward and go and be a hermit. He went on preaching the kingdom and trying to lead men to a better relationship with God which made enemies among those who were high up—that's what led to his death.'[13]

The key feature of symbolism is that one thing stands for another, normally involving some relationship of concrete to abstract or particular to general.[14] The problems of how a symbol is recognized as such and the relation of symbols to cognate ideas have been tackled by philosophers through the ages. Cassirer, for example, argued that symbolic representation was an essential function of human con-

F

sciousness. He distinguished three particular functions, an expressive function as is seen in myth, an intuitive function as in language and a conceptual function as in science. The anthropologist Raymond Firth explains, 'In myth, sign and signified merge (as with Aquinas, existence and essence merge in God): in ordinary language and the world of common sense they are differentiated, producing systems of objects or substances; and in science their differentiation produces systems of relations.'[15] Other philosophers, Langer for example, take a more pragmatic view. For her, sign, symbol, denotation, signification, communication, are our stock in trade in arriving at a concept of meaning.[16] The symbol is an instrument for expression; it can be used as a simile, a metaphor, an emblem, image, allegory, myth. A symbol may be used for communication, for knowledge, for control. Clifford Geertz gives us a definition of religion which derives from Langer's notion of symbolism. He says it is 'a system of symbols which acts to establish powerful, persuasive and long-lasting moods and motivations in men by formulating conceptions of a general order of experience and clothing these conceptions with such an aura of factuality that the moods and motivations seem uniquely realistic'.[17] Geertz's definition of religion and of symbolism takes account of the ability of either to be an independent or a dependent variable in the process of change. The essence of a symbol's communicability is that it may generate as well as receive.

Broadly speaking, sociological analyses of symbolism follow two alternative lines of inquiry depending on whether they start with Durkheim or Freud. The Durkheimian is interested in groups, in abstract interpretations, in the function of symbols as expressive of solidarity or in giving some meaning to reality. The Freudian tends to concentrate on the individual's use of symbolism as a solution for pragmatic problems, in the expression of dissonance, in the use of symbols as disguises to avoid reality.[18] This distinction can be seen in those analyses which tend to equate symbol with custom (myth, ritual, social structure) and those which concentrate on the individual, symbols not usually shared with other people (like dream symbolism, hallucinations, prophetic visions). It was supposedly the God-sent purpose of St Francis's dreams which provided the impetus for his religious order and a major source of its legitimation. The distinctions are not mutually exclusive for the routinization of St Francis's dreams; their incorporation in written texts, and their passage from mouth to mouth as myth, established them as a basic component of the custom of all Franciscans through the ages.

Recent anthropological analyses of symbolism have tended to concentrate on the mysterious and ambiguous nature of symbols (Mary Douglas, Victor Turner). In both the congregations which I studied the acceptance of the mysterious nature of their faith, of their idea of God, even of popular manifestations—miracles and signs —was part and parcel of the nun's religious life. In the human imagination and comprehension symbols may embody mystery, but this must be seen as a part of the process of making sense of the world. Malinowski used to say that man resorts to magic to fill the gaps in his knowledge of the world. Raymond Firth elaborates and says, 'Men in their social existence construct and inherit the intellectual and emotional frames in which they set and attribute meaning to the details of the external world.'[19] The anthropologist does not have to unravel the mystery. It is enough for him to understand the relationship between the individual and collective symbolization and then proceed to use his insights in finding out 'for what' are the symbols. What really do they represent of the social order and the individual's place in it? The teaching congregation is an example of an organization which interpreted a single ceremony, the Mass, in a number of different ways during the 150 years of its growth. The Mass is an ideal vehicle for studying the interplay of symbols, the ritual form and the plausibility structure of belief.

The Catholic Mass is a ceremony in which bread (the host, from *hostia*, a sacrificial victim) and wine are taken before an altar, purified with incense and consecrated with solemn invocations. The priest who performs the act of consecration then drinks the wine and those 'qualified' members of the congregation eat the bread. The legitimation for the ceremony rests in the New Testament accounts of the Last Supper and every Christian group sees it as a commemorative rite, though some, in addition, see it as symbolizing Jesus Christ's sacrifice for humanity. Catholics (by the rules of their Church) have to see it as a 'divinely efficacious sacrament'.[20] At the moment of consecration the bread and the wine are mysteriously changed into the actual flesh and blood of Christ. This transubstantiation has been confirmed by the Article of Faith 1215 and re-affirmed by the Council of Trent and, indeed, by Vatican II. It is not just Christ's body substance which appears under the guise of bread and wine but his whole personality, renewing his sacrifice on the cross, hence the doctrine of the 'Real Presence'. The Council of Trent says, 'The same Christ is contained and is immolated in an unbloody manner, who, on the altar of the Cross offered Himself once in a bloody manner.'[21]

The original 1891 Rule of the teaching congregation set out the intentions for the Mass following the directives of the Council of Trent. The Eucharist, they said, had two purposes. It was 'food for our souls, and in virtue of its being a Sacrament, that it may preserve, strengthen and renew in us the life of grace; secondly, to give to the Church a perpetual Sacrifice to offer to God in thanksgiving for His benefits, in atonement for our sins, and to obtain the remedy for our weaknesses and divine assistance in all our general and particular necessities' (Constitutions 157, 1891). In Victorian times it was these two aspects, a strengthening food and a reparatory sacrifice, which were the ones to be stressed. The sacrificial aspect is the one which has been lost in future developments. Here, and right up to the 1950s, it was a direct reference to Calvary and the moment of the crucifixion, in which the Son of God was offered as a bloody victim for mankind. In the Eucharist Christ offered himself as an unbloody victim both to mankind and to the God his Father. The Eucharistic sacrifice not only stressed the human relationship between man and God, it symbolized the way in which the sisters thought of their vocation. They were offering themselves to their God and to mankind in a victim-like posture, a posture symbolized every morning by the line of nuns stretched out on the chapel floor in profound genuflection. Self-sacrifice was a virtue stressed by the founder and reiterated in the Rule, Constitutions and daily life.

In his structural analysis of the *kava* myth (a Tongan myth in which *kava* is drunk as a sacrament), Edmund Leach examines the connection between symbolic killing and sacrifice.[22] He distinguishes three types of theory about sacrifice, each of which emphasizes a different aspect, the communion, the gift, or the sacrament. In various versions of Robertson-Smith's 'communion-theory' the sacrificial victim is, at the moment of slaughter, identified with the deity. Leach says, 'The eating of the meat of the sacrifice is deemed an essential element in the rite; the congregation shares a collective guilt in participating in god murder and ritual cannibalism; this collective guilt is an "atonement"; it makes the members of the congregation aware of themselves as a collectivity that has jointly sinned yet assimilated itself to God.'[23] The Victorian nun not only identified with Christ on the cross, she had sacrificed herself for this world. Her prayers for the Holy Souls, the prayers of intercession, were made in reparation for the sins of the world. As a member of a ritual group she is keenly conscious of her position as a member of the congregation; her status is marked out by the rank order of seating. She not only witnessed but took part in a great drama. This daily drama was a highlight to an otherwise mundane and ordinary life. Huisinga makes this point, that 'ritual is in the main a matter of shows, representations, dramatic performances, imaginative actualizations of a vicarious nature.'[24] As such, a Mass is a cosmic happening which is played out within a limited time and space and thus enables the audience to participate for a little while in something 'outside' ordinary life. The element of collective guilt, backed by the 'real presence', gives the Mass a normative content which is immensely useful as an organizational principle. Leach's second general theory on the meaning of sacrifice he calls 'gift theories of sacrifice'. It involves the notion that in making a present to the deity you will get something in return. It is an explanation often given by informants, even unconsciously. The whole idea of reparation involves the notion of a favour returned, as does the sister who says that really she would hope to go to Heaven when she dies, knowing that her hope is based on a reward in return for her sacrifices and struggle for perfection on earth. But in the constellation of beliefs involved in the Eucharist this is not one which I would place very high; it has the obvious difficulties of motivation and control.

The third class of theory derives from Hubert and Mauss, the early French anthropologists. It emphasizes the sacramental aspect of sacrificial performance. In other words the Mass would have somehow to make the participants more sacred, improve their mystical condition; the sacrifice involves purification. The sisters had to be, in all conscience, free from sin when they partook of the Eucharist. One of the older sisters told me that her once-weekly communion was a source of tremendous power. She tried to explain to me, a layman, her simple belief in the soul, and in grace which was God's way of communicating with the soul. Grace could only be communicated to a worthy soul, she said, and to see if she was worthy she would search her heart for purity, comparing her efforts to observe the religious life as dictated by her Rule from one week to the next. In truth she would ask the confessor for absolution or a blessing out of devotion for she rarely had committed a sin. The blessing from a priest would anyway help keep you away from sin. Sin kills the soul. No soul, no grace, you are without help in the world and without hope for the world hereafter. But with absolution and contribution for any sins committed the soul comes alive again and you can go to communion and receive the sanctifying grace, which in turn helps keep you away from sin for another week. In this theory the Mass is a key factor in the normative control of the organization, which operates to constrain its members' actions and reard them with additional helps—graces—for the rest of the day or week.

Through all these theories there has been a persistent theme in which a victim exists as mediator between deity and donor—Christ between God and the nun. The complication to this simplistic view is that in the Catholic case they see the deity as donor. God gave his Son as victim; the mediation occurs between man and God in the person of a specially gifted man—the priest. It is only on the priest's correct performance of the consecration rite that the whole sacrificial performance is enacted. His is a position of immense power, and it is the ultimate control exercised by the Church on all its sub-units, the opening and closing of the channels of grace—excommunication, or the cutting off of the sacraments and the life-renewing grace that flows from it. I would agree then with Raymond Firth, who sees the Eucharist primarily as a statement about power and the source of power. The Catholics would assert that the inner substance of the Eucharist is power; it is sufficient for the sociologist to note that it is not only a symbol of power but a powerful weapon in authority, for those who believe in its efficacy. And in the traditional teaching congregation this efficacy was unquestioned, the sisters even believing that the closer they stood to the tabernacle (where the consecrated bread is kept) the closer they stood to Christ. Firth says, that 'assertions about the bread and wine are assertions in defence of established positions or claims to such positions, on a pragmatic social level as well as on a conceptual level'.[25] He gives as an example the Council of Trent's reaffirmation of the doctrine of transubstantiation, which it used as a bulwark against the advancing tide of Protestantism. Mary Douglas, too, had pointed out that Pope Paul's encyclical, 'Instruction on the Eucharistic Mystery', 1967, preserves it as an efficacious source of power.[26] She believes that modern man has lost the power to see the magical/mystical elements of the Eucharist: 'the mystery of the Eucharist is too dazzlingly magical for their impoverished symbolic perception.' Have they lost it, and if so, what are the symbolic referents now at work in the Eucharist?

In the traditional teaching congregation the sisters were urged to visit the Blessed Sacrament at frequent intervals during the day. They could then benefit from the grace of God and dwell on consciousness of their dependence on that grace. Novices were taught that the Mass gave a sense of solidarity and security to the community, that they must therefore always be absolutely punctual in their attendance at chapel and especially at Mass. But the progressive sisters in the 1960s did not use punctuality or the display of solidarity to express their sense of community; they used the symbolism of the Eucharist itself. There had always been a sense in which the white circle of bread, the host, had symbolized the body of the faithful. Indeed it had symbolized the body of each worshipper and its connection to that greater body. It also symbolized the cosmos, the history of the Church and many other elements.

A sister who had always celebrated the Mass before a high altar with all the traditional symbolism described the intense effect of her first experience of a 'modern' Mass. She stood in an ordinary room with a number of other religious and a priest. They gathered round a table. The Eucharistic sacrifice, the consecrated bread and wine, was laid on the table. Each participant had a part to play, not just as a member of an audience but as an actor. They read the epistle and bidding prayers. They took the communion bread and wine in their hands and fed themselves. Whereas previously they had sought the real presence in the sacrament itself, in some magical force, they now felt the real meaning of the Mass was in the communion they felt with the other participants—symbolized by the passing of the cup from hand to hand. It was, of course, the first time the sister had taken the wine as well as the bread.

This sister experienced the Mass in the same form, but in quite a different venue and social context, from the one she was used to. She had just moved out of a traditional convent into a small community in a suburban house which was experimenting with co-responsibility as a form of authority. It was one of the first communities to encourage a more mature approach to authority, to obedience and to participation through community life. The move from audience to actor in the drama of the Mass can be seen as quite logical, as can a psychological interpretation which might recognize feeding oneself instead of being fed as a sign of maturity. There is, in fact, no loss of symbolic meaning; there had been a change of direction. American sisters in the congregation had shared the enthusiasms for an alternative society which swept the country during the 1960s. They claimed to represent a 'sign' of fraternal love through the unity and chastity of their communities. They said, 'We are all one body because we are all partakers of that one bread.' The Holy Meal had been brought to the dining-table and there it was filled with symbolic meaning as it had been on the high altar. Norman O'Brown adds his own characteristic comments: 'Identification, introjection, incorporation is eating. Eating is the form of the fall. Eating is the form of sex. Eating is the form of war. Eating is the form of redemption. Communion: oral copulation. Eucharist is marriage feast, the union of the bridegroom and the bride. He gives himself to his bride with the bread. Eat your fill, lover, drink, sweethearts and drink deep. The two become one flesh, incorporate each other, by eating. The transubstantiation is the unification: is in the eating. By eating we become his body; eating makes it so.'[27]

In the modern Mass the priest as representative of the Church still holds power, particularly the power of consecration, but in sharing the wine he makes tacit recognition of his desire to share, to bring co-responsibility into the picture. In the move from the sacrificial and sacramental towards the group itself, the sisters took on a new relationship to their God and moved away from the conception of the Church as the sole introitus to the supernatural. The real presence, the progressive nun said, was experienced through people in their relationship with one another around the communion table. The progressive nun had moved out of the closed structure of her religious community and wandered in the world. She was pushing the ortho-doxy of her beliefs to the limit and she had lost the security of a stable human group. The progressive nun shared with the missionaries a sense of being on the edge of Catholicism itself. The saints, the holy men who went out into the desert, traditionally returned with 'special' qualities. Some extra-terrestrial communion was believed to have taken place 'out there'. In the eyes of the lay Catholic, the nun herself stands on the threshold of life on earth. Now the progressive acquired a further sense of liminality. Just like the ancient holy men, the pro-gressive claimed for herself an experience of the real presence in and through the people gathered round the communion table. She claims that the mystical properties of the Eucharist, still present, are now located in the participants rather than in the bread and wine. The magic still exists in the power of the priest to transubstantiate those substances, and in sharing them the lost group is reborn in the ritual sharing of the Eucharist.

The Mass represented, for the progressive sister, a celebration of the group *per se*. One sister said, 'A few years ago, the receiving of the communion was something intensely personal and when I was sick or unable to attend I would ask for it. Now I would not; I see it in a different way, apart from the individual relationship and the contact with Christ. I can see it is historically based on a meal and it's a social event.' In 1967 she had attended a concelebration of the Mass in Africa at which several priests said the Mass together. The liturgical form of the service was experimental. A big circle was formed round the table-altar in the church and they took the bread themselves and fed themselves, hand to hand, standing. There was no separate in-cantation for receiving the wine. This sister had been entertained in African families where an old clay pipe had been handed round the group. She said that she knew of other cultures where a cup was passed round, like our own ceremony of the loving cup. She believed that her response to the passing of the chalice was conditioned by this knowledge and she understood the symbolism of the group act, but she still believed in the real presence. In Africa guitars, drums and shakers were used to create more atmosphere at the Mass, while in England during the 1960s more and more experimental forms re-moved it from the confines of the chapel to ordinary rooms, and it was enlivened with singing and dancing. Even in the most traditional con-vents, the clergy were setting up tables in front of the high altar and saying the consecration facing the people instead of having their back to them. By 1970, the convents of the teaching order had as many varieties of the Mass as it had structures of convent life, until the historical chronology of social and religious change was spread over the ground for all to see.

The sisters did not come to a sudden realization of the meaning of the Mass; there was a deliberate attempt on the part of a few progressives to socialize the less adventurous. The main impetus for change came from those sisters who had attended the more radical European theological colleges—the missionaries and the very young. All the sisters were encouraged to read current periodicals and new books which might help them to an understanding of the religious life. From these they learnt of the interpretation of the Mass as a covenant. It was a progression from God's covenant with his people in the Old Testament. Like the second of Leach's theories of sacrifice it involved the notion of offering something in return for something else. The young sister who accepted the historico/political description of the death of Christ replaced the plausibility of the Calvary sacrifice with the plausibility of the covenant between man and God. The sisters who read the history of the Eucharist through the ages also formed their own impressions. One popular author was Nicholas Lash who, in a study of Eucharistic worship and theology, makes a convincing case for the concept of Eucharistic brotherhood, and demolishes Barth's man/God dichotomy.[28] For the first three centuries after Christ the Mass was an act of community, he says. The participants were directly and primarily conscious of this. Today a catachetics teacher will stress the importance of the consecrated bread to her children; the Eucharist is just like a family meal, she will say. In the early Church the use of bread was important not only because it was a staple food but also because it was a familiar substance. In the fourth and fifth centuries the use of a more sacrificial terminology crept in as the Church became more aware of its power as a mediary. But, Lash claims, the ordinary man still had a three-dimensional, concrete image of the actual assembly foremost in his mind, an image of an assembly of people taking, blessing, sharing and consuming food and drink. During the High Middle Ages, with increasing clericalization of ecclesiastical structures and an ever-widening language barrier, the ordinary man became excluded from the celebration; he became an audience only. A pre-Christian situation existed in which 'holy men' and cultic officials carried out the acts of ritual worship. Calvary took precedence over the other images, and it was set in the imagery of a temple sacrifice. Here Lash says, 'the mood is not of joy but of timorous petition.'[29] The magical overtones grew in importance. The Reformation removed a whole section of the congregation to the confines of Protestantism, where, with legitimations back to the early Church, transubstantiation was dropped altogether. The Council of Trent redefined the Catholic Mass but the separation of clergy and congregation persisted largely, Lash claims, because of the failure to vernacularize the liturgy. The great liturgical movement of the twentieth century returned to the original pastoral orientations of the Church. The Eucharist became once again the expression and source of Christian communion.

The exposition Lash gives is a very general historical impression of what took place over a much shorter time-span in the teaching congregation. A tight model like Douglas's grid/group theory has not been used in this analysis because, as an analytical tool, it is too inhibiting. The teaching congregation in the nineteenth century and its representations in the symbolism of the Mass can be described in terms of dense grid and group, just as the progressive convents can be described as loosely structured, but it does not explain the changing referents over time, nor the internal dialectic of *cosmos/nomos* in a satisfactory way. The Mass is an example of a complex of symbols which can represent a hierarchical power structure in one context and the ideological concept of universal brotherhood in another; in either case the mechanism is one which operates as a control in holding people to their compliance relationship. It is an integrative factor in the context of its operational group and it 'makes meaningful' universal values of the organization. In addition to these functionalist interpretations, the Weberian theory that religious beliefs can have some independent causal significance in the process of social change, must be given credence. Symbolic concepts are used as a framework for organizing experience and as a way of understanding the world about one. A ritual like the Mass is full of condensed symbols (symbols with a multitude of possible referents) and it is the articulation of those symbols by the perceiver which gives the sociologist his clues.

The Franciscan congregation have not basically changed their conception of the Eucharist or their perception of the religious symbols involved in the ceremony since their foundation in 1920, and quite probably this could be extended back to the first Franciscan foundation in 1221. The Franciscan sisters see the Eucharist now as they did then, as a great sacrificial banquet. The mystery of transubstantiation is not for them to understand, it is for them to believe. The rationality of this belief is unquestioned because it is accepted as an article of faith. A sceptic would remark that once this leap in the dark has taken place the Catholic is dependent on all that the Church has to offer him. The Franciscan Novice Mistress told me, 'We love God because he is love, we open up our faith in God and become the Children of God.' The connection between St Francis and Christ lies in this perfect love, they said. Just as Christ looked on the woman taken in adultery and loved her, so St Francis loved everyone he met. It was their perfect way of showing forgiveness. She made the point that as the religious vocation developed you became more, not less, dependent on God because you became more humble. The religious sister was on this earth to let people know about God's goodness and love. As such she was his instrument and nothing more. The difference in emphasis between this understanding of the religious life and that of a nun from the teaching congregation is staggering. The sacrifice witnessed in the Mass is a personification of goodness and love, those two concepts which run through the Franciscan ideology.

St Francis left his followers a great strength, an ideological *communitas* which imbued their religious life with a sense of fellowship and brotherhood, an ideology which other congregations had forgotten and were striving to attain. Ideology is always a significant variable in the organization of a group and in the complex web of associations which hold individual members. It is one of the prime integrative mechanisms especially in groups which face a number of basic operational problems, for example, distinctiveness, communication, decision-making, authority and discipline.[30] The Mass, which carried many referents to this ideology for the Franciscans, was seen as a sacrifice because it re-affirmed their own total self-offering. It was seen as a banquet because it nourished them with the 'mystical body of Christ', the bread alone. There is a complete rapport between this conception of the Eucharist and the organization of the daily life and ultimate goals of the Franciscan nun. She lives in a hierarchical organization with a charismatic leader at the top who embodies the mystical qualities of goodness and love. She devotes herself totally to the organization and goes wherever she is sent, prepared to give herself to her task wholeheartedly. Any changes in the structure of her daily life or of her beliefs are minimal and related to practical considerations rather than to a crisis in plausibility. Their only concessions to modernity are to use the vernacular in the Mass (they were one of the first congregations in England to do so), and to stand a table in front of the altar. Their present chapel, built in the 1960s, still concentrates the eye on the high altar and on the ultimate goals of the congregation.

Sacrifice or feast? The Mass could be either or both according to the articulation of symbols in the minds of the participants. It is the social referents of the symbols which change. The Mass lost none of its efficacy as a symbol of Christ when it was handled by the nuns in an ordinary room, round an ordinary table. The Mass celebrated by the group celebrates the group. The ritual form of the Mass, taking place in the community room, expresses community rather than the hierarchical relationship between priest, church and congregation. The contrast between the perception of the Mass in the two congregations illustrates once again the persistence of tradition in the Franciscans and the need for radical innovation in the teaching congregation. The persistence of religious beliefs, rituals and symbols in the Franciscan congregation is a feature of their resistance to current theology and the directives of the Church. This was made possible by the special relationship between the Franciscan order and the Church which began when the Pope first granted St Francis permission to base an order on his own charisma and radical vision. In an article on tradition the sociologist Shils says, 'Tradition-seeking persons exhibit a combination of resistance to currently prevailing and authoritatively recommended beliefs, and an intense and active sensitivity to elements of the sacred contained in monuments or documents or texts which have come down from the past . . . Tradition-searching has a marked tendency towards being ideological.'[31] The Franciscans not only had a great veneration for their original founder, they also had sacred relics and a Holy Well. These were powerful organizational tools for an order which must exercise complete control over its members lest it should loose them to the secular world. In the insecurity of change the teaching congregation lost many of its sisters because they could not see why they should be in the organization when they could do just as well outside of it. The new situations in which some of the nuns found themselves rendered previously acceptable beliefs implausible and downright disadvantageous. Both the compliance relationship and the plausibility structure of religious beliefs broke down. But, as Shils points out, 'the drastic disjunctions which separate traditionally transmitted beliefs from new beliefs are often blurred by the reassertion of the traditionally transmitted beliefs in the idiom of the new beliefs, as well as by the anti-traditional rhetoric of "total" innovations.'[32] After the drastic alterations of the 1960s there has been some retrogression in the teaching order. The sisters were able to manipulate the ambiguity of ritual and symbols in their new context as they had in the old. The dialectical relationship between beliefs, the believers and the social structure persists.

CHAPTER NINE

Body Metaphors

When the teaching congregation changed their religious habit and the style of the houses they lived in, they were expressing, symbolically, the changes in their daily lives and religious orientations. Each element in the changes contains representations of their social situation. There is a sense in which the body acts as a medium of expression. Mary Douglas has summed this up with the words, 'The social body constrains the way the physical body is perceived. The physical experience of the body, always modified by the social categories through which it is known, sustains a particular view of society.'[1] The most obvious example is the contrast between the modern teaching nun and her counterpart in the 1930s, but this can also be contrasted with the founder's image of his religious women. Living in a time when women were wearing corsets and tight restrictive clothes, he was determined that his nuns should wear sensible clothes, have good posture and a smiling face. His image had been bastardized into a mechanical, self-conscious, controlled form by the 1930s when the early vibrancy of his religious foundation had given way to a rigid bureaucratic structure and a mechanistic ritualization of beliefs. The image of this standardized nun in her habit, hands folded under her scapular, feet never too far apart or too fast-moving, can be contrasted with the modern sister, free, arms swinging, eyes looking about her, full of curiosity and momentum. Body metaphors form part of the symbolic world-view in which changes in the structure of government are changes in the body politic, reflected in the boundaries of the collectivity, in architecture, in household arrangements, in body maintenance and in food.

The first sisters to reach England from the teaching congregation wore plain fustian dresses and velour cloaks. Their plain linen shifts, cotton stockings and plain shoes were an expression of the nun's renunciation of the world and her acceptance of herself as one of the religious group. The clothes also gave her body a measure of freedom which her married sisters lost in corsets, crinolines and buttoned boots. There was a case for regarding marriage to Christ as both a more exclusive career and one which gave greater personal freedom in the Victorian era. In the secular world wives had no responsibility under law and were classed with minors and idiots. When a woman married, her wedding ring literally bound her to her husband; even some champions of rights for women regarded themselves as second class, as slaves! Lady Mary Wortley Montague could say, 'We are a lower part of creation. We owe obedience and submission to the superior sex and any woman who suffers her vanity and folly to deny this rebels against the laws of the Creator and the indisputable order of nature.' The Victorian nun welcomed this attitude and adopted it towards her God; she was convinced that her place on earth was to fulfil God's will. The nuns in their plain fustian dresses joined the urban poor in those early days; they lived on the margins of society both in their Catholicism and their poverty. As the Catholic population grew in strength, became established as part of the society, so the congregation consolidated its organization with rules and bureaucratization, and the nuns began to wear the more restricted and carefully defined habit.

The Rule of 1891 set down the dress to be worn by choir sisters and the alternatives for lay sisters. The choir sister must wear a black dress, full-length scapular, a girdle round their waists and a long veil. Their faces must be enclosed by a foreheadband, chinband and gimp. In choir they must adopt a different-coloured veil and mantle. A rosary should hang from the girdle and a plain gold ring worn on the ring finger of the right hand should proclaim their profession. Choir novices should wear a similar habit, only the scapular was to be cut short at the waist and fastened by a leather belt and apron. The lay sisters were to wear a black dress, a heavier shorter veil and a differently shaped chinband and gimp. They should not wear a scapular but an apron fastened by a leather belt and their ring must be made of silver rather than gold.

Adherence to this habit was absolute; dressing and undressing were prescribed by the custom book, although the nuns invariably found ways round the rule. One of the old nuns told me that she used to tie all the bows and loops of the certet at the beginning of the week and then slip it off her head at night and wriggle back into it in the morning! The habits themselves were made by the lay sisters under the overall supervision of a lay sister called the 'linen sister'. Plain linen shifts, cotton stockings and lace-up shoes completed the garments.

The first Christians had not worn distinctive clothing, but with the build-up of the monastic orders the distinctive style and universal symbolism of the religious habit became the norm. The capuche symbolized innocence and simplicity, the linen tunic the renouncement of the works of this world and mortification, the scapular the willingness to labour, the mafors (a short cloak not worn by this congregation) humility and poverty, and the cincture purity. Both St Augustine and St Benedict agreed that clothes need not necessarily be identical but they should be utterly simple and without adornment. They were an outward sign of dedication to God and should show a 'respectable poverty'. The habit of the Victorian nuns (that of the teaching congregation was much the same as any other) had a recognized function. Within the congregation it revealed the distinctions between the various ranks—choir, lay, novices. The scapular enabled the hands to be hidden at all times when they were not usefully at work or prayer. The totally enclosed face repeated symbolically the enclosure of the nun, whose eyes were not meant to wander, whose ears were to hear only God's words. The anthropologist, Mauss, claims that one should always proceed from the concrete to the abstract when considering the ways in which people use their bodies.[2] He claims that there is no such thing as natural behaviour; every action takes the imprint of learning. He gives the example of a convent girl who walks with her fists closed and close to her body, while he himself always walked with his hands open and relaxed. The control of the body was certainly an important element in the socialization of the novice and in the continuing efforts of the nun to reach a degree of religious perfection. The 'imprinting' frequently matched the fashions of the times, particularly middle-class manners.

Of all the items of clothing the most striking and possibly the most symbolic of the nun's separation from the world was the enclosed face. When the habit was first changed it took the form of a long black dress with a white standing collar. The habit left the face and neck open and some hair showing round the veil. The revised habit had two important effects for the body, the face and neck were freed from enclosure and the hair was left to grow. With the opening of the face came the opening of the senses. The 'modesty of the eyes' was forgotten. The nuns could read books, watch television, look at the world around them. The emphasis of the religious life was on the world outside and the nun was given the freedom to act on it.

In almost any culture the treatment of head hair has immense symbolic power. It was not for nothing that the young people who joined the alternative society in the 1960s grew their hair to an unconscionable length. Raymond Firth devotes an entire chapter to the different aspects of hair symbolism.[3] The shaving of the head or close cutting of hair generally marks a transition from one social status to another; in particular it modifies the social status of that person. The tonsure, for example, is supposed to have derived from the Eastern custom of shaving the heads of slaves. The early monks shaved their heads as a symbolic acknowledgement of their service to God. Firth says of the Buddhist attitude to hair that long hair symbolizes the cosmic power of growth and no hair symbolizes the power of sub-jugation of the self to social rules. Leach and Malinowski put it even more forcibly:[4] the shaving of widows' heads during mourning cere-monies in the Trobriand islands symbolized their social death. After a long period of confinement they were allowed to grow their hair again and to remarry, their relationship with their former husband and his kin being declared formally at an end. This, to use Firth's distinction between public and private symbolism, is the public symbolism of a rite in contrast with the private symbolism that a Freudian analysis might reveal. An orthodox Freudian approach would equate head hair with the genital organs; by shaving or cutting the head hair you are undertaking a symbolic castration. The nuns cutting their hair close to their heads therefore symbolized the re-pressive nature of the chastity vow and the hiding of all sexuality. Like the Trobriand widow, she too withdraws from the world; she undergoes a form of social death when she enters the convent.

From 1965 the sisters had a choice of clothes and a choice of opting for an open face or an enclosed face. The new habits were more com-fortable and practical. Rather than being subjugated the needs of the body were pampered, with improvements in food standards and the installation of central heating in the convents. Donald MacRae has described the body as an expressive organ, 'the sum of its parts func-tioning in time'.[5] A glance at the sisters in the late 1960s revealed almost immediately how far their attempt at religious renewal had progressed. The most progressive wore ordinary clothes, sat and walked with careless ease and 'looked after' their bodies with talcs, deodorants and frequent baths. Just as the New Theology carried them out of themselves to find God in humanity, so they gave up their position as a religious élite and, dressing in ordinary clothes, joined the populace, a gesture legitimized both by the injunctions of their founder and the lifestyle of the earliest Christians. It was a gesture repeated in the renewed liturgy of the Eucharist. The sacramental meal was ritualized as an ordinary meal in the progressive convents; it had lost its traditional clothes, vestments, order and movement. Those sisters who continued to wear the old habit, and those who wore the revised version with an open face said that they did so because they felt more comfortable. The older sisters who were moving outside the convent for the first time felt vulnerable without the habit which identified them as nuns. Even the younger sisters sometimes felt that their position was ambiguous. They wore ordinary dress in order to look the same as the ordinary people, yet they were different—they led a life dedicated to God, chaste, virginal. Approaches from men were particularly difficult to handle. When the sisters first changed to ordinary dress they restricted themselves to sober colours, grey, white, navy blue, but as the changes in their routines, in the whole structure of their lives and beliefs grew more radical so they began experimenting with different colours. It was rumoured that one sister had knitted a bright pink jumper but had not yet dared to wear it! Many of the sisters now made their own clothes. To wear or not to wear a veil was an individual decision. Some wore a short veil all the time, others only to go outside the convent, and in one convent the sisters only put on their veils to open the door for visitors or when the priest visited them. The change to ordinary clothes not only reflected a change in self-perception but it affected every relationship inside and outside the convent.

In total contrast the Franciscan congregation wear virtually the same habit today as they did when they were first instituted in 1930— a habit which would not have looked too outrageous in the Middle Ages. They wear a white tunic made of washable material, which reaches the ankle and buttons at the wrists. Over that is a scapular of the same material. Round the waist they wear a woollen cord, looped twice round and hanging on the right side. The longer end has three knots placed at equal distances apart and on the left side the Franciscan symbol of the Seven Joys. On their heads the sisters wear a band and gimp and a white veil. Professed sisters wear a plain gold ring and a medal of the Virgin Mary round their necks. In choir they used to pull white detachable sleeves over their tunics and added a light-weight blue veil. The veil has been retained but the sleeves were dropped in 1968. Remembering that in the Franciscan congregation there was no lay/choir dichotomy, the detachable sleeves were supposed to make the sisters look cleaner for chapel in case they had become dirty doing housework or some grubby task. In the teaching congregation the lay sisters wore black habits, it was said, because they were engaged in dirty tasks like cleaning and washing. But when this segregation of roles was no longer valid all the sisters took the same habit. The only distinctions made in the Franciscan congregation were between the novices and professed; the novices wore a white rather than a blue veil in chapel. When travelling the sisters wore grey tunics and scapulars and a long woollen black cloak as an outer garment. Again, in 1968 the colour of the cloak was changed to blue and a white or blue working habit was adopted for messy tasks.

The Franciscans were very clear about the symbolism of their habit and the importance of wearing pure white. They regarded the habit as an external sign of their consecration of Christ of which the scapular was of particular symbolic significance. The veil symbolized their virginity, the Franciscan cord their faithfulness to their vows and acts of penance. The white habit symbolized chastity and also reminded them of the 'spotless purity' of Mary the Virgin Mother. The blue cord round their necks and the blue choir veil were also worn as a reminder of their special dedication to the Virgin Mary. This dedication was reflected in the apostolic work in which the congregation was engaged. The maternity work, the work with children, were specific goals symbolized and symbolizing the mother/child relationship of Mary and Jesus Christ.

The divine motherhood of the Virgin Mary was both a mystery for the sisters to take and accept as part of their religious beliefs and it was symbolic of the Church and the relationship between the concept of the Church and its members. The Franciscans recognized a dependency on the Church which though mature none the less existed. The disintegration of family life in the secular world was the impetus of the founder's charisma. Maternity nursing was the 'inspiration' of which 'spiritual motherhood' was the ultimate goal. 'Spiritual motherhood' is a package concept which carries the meaning of spreading the word of God, as well as of performing specific tasks. St Francis had a special devotion to the Virgin Mary. St Bonaventure records that at the Portiuncula, a shrine dedicated to Mary, St Francis conceived and brought forth the spirit of evangelical truth through the merits of the 'Mother of Mercy' (*Legenda Major*, 3, 1). The Virgin Mary's conception and the birth of Jesus Christ is equated with the idea of the true word of God—a belief in the Christian God. Some words of St Francis make this connection very clear: 'We are Christ's mothers when we carry him about in our heart and person by means of love and a clear and sincere conscience, and we give birth to Him by means of our holy actions' (*Letter to the Faithful*). All these complex associations served to reinforce the normative control of the Franciscan organization over its members. The habit serves as a symbolic representation of a number of complex ideological and sacred metaphors all of which are legitimated not only by reference to Christ but more specifically to the very 'Franciscan' spirit of this religious foundation. The retention of the habit to the present day is similarly an indication of the power of its symbolic qualities and the nature of the organization it represents.

The devotion of both congregations to the Virgin Mary and the white habit of the Franciscans embraced the Pauline doctrine of purity in which the body had to be mortified with violence and fasting. The *agape* of the early Christians was lost in an argument between pure and impure love, the sacred and profane. But whereas the teaching order restricted its body metaphors to the negative aspects of chastity, the Franciscans always carried the message of 'brotherly love' in their ideology. Their chapel was dedicated to Our Lady, but St Francis dominated. His were the glowing colours and mythical scenes painted on the walls. The Franciscan congregation had not been through a Jansenist phase; their vow of chastity went hand in hand with love of mankind and the notion of God in humanity. They even had a relic of St Francis in a glass dome in the chapel. Such a body relic is a powerful protection against evil; believers have a magical faith in the efficacy of the saint's body to ward off evil. The power of Franciscan symbols was present and they reaffirmed the congregation's connection with the supernatural. It is important that the Franciscans were able to reinstate a holy well in the grounds of one of their convents. They make regular candlelit pilgrimages to it. Holy well or magic spring, its function is a source of supernatural aid. The Franciscan congregation not only had a holy well, a sacred relic, the Mass, it also had a saint as a founder, a saint who was capable of miracles and carried the marks of the stigmata. The concern for purity and reliance on magical and mystical sources of protection against the evils of the world were also reflected in the devotion to the Sacred Heart.

The founder of the teaching congregation had encouraged this devotion in Victorian times, and I have already described the part it played in their prayers for reparation for the sins and wickedness of the world. The Franciscans did not give it up, though it remained secondary to their symbolic tributes to St Francis and the Virgin Mary in their chapels and convents. The Sacred Heart is an interesting symbol because it neatly bridges the gap between what Firth calls the private and the public. For centuries the Western world considered the heart to be the seat of the emotions, so it is not surprising that the Church recognized a potent symbol and adopted it. By the twentieth century, with a lot of help from the founder of the teaching congregation, there were cultic groups whose religious congregations and various colleges and universities associated with it. Popular iconography—and there were plenty of depictions to be seen in both the congregations' convents—showed a wounded heart, blood spurting from it, radiating light from under the cross and crown of thorns. The official interpretation of this as given by the *Catholic Encyclopaedia* states that 'in the devotion of the Sacred Heart the special object is Jesus's physical heart of flesh as the true natural symbol of his three-fold love.'[6] This interpretation is based on the testimony of the nun, Marie Alacoque, who claimed that her heart was received by Christ and returned to her surrounded by flames. The Church compounds the rest of the devotion by taking a private illusion and creating a concrete, public symbol from it. Further, the material object, the painted heart, is a symbol of a symbol; it stands for an abstract, conceptual heart, which in turn represents human and divine love and family solidarity.

Firth has made the interesting observation that it is the representations of the Sacred Heart themselves which are considered suitable receptacles for worship, yet aesthetic tastes vary and some of these representations have been withdrawn as 'unworthy'. This is precisely what happened in the teaching congregation where, with a great purge, literally hundreds of icons, pictures and representations were relegated to the dustbin or the loft. In one large convent, there are more than 240 assorted icons, statues and religious pictures in the attics although some still hang on their walls. The symbol had indeed lost its potency. It is a clear case of the connection between the content of the symbol and the people who share it. There is a familiar principle of aesthetics which says that where the medium and the message are appropriately related communication is easy. In language, verbal forms syntactically and lexically will correspond to their message, whether it is sublime, mundane, expressive of speed or lethargy. Critics of literary style have commented not only on the 'fit' of style to content, but also on the use of style itself as a non-verbal channel of meaning. Douglas quotes Barthes on this feature: 'imagery, delicacy, vocabulary spring from the body and the past of the writer and gradually becomes the very reflexes of his art.'[7] Style is either a conscious or unconscious response to social situations which will be culturally determined. The art historian James Laver confirms that fashions in clothes, decorations and architecture are dictated by the deepest unconscious desires of the people who wear or live in them. In the fifteenth century men's shoes were exactly comparable with the windows of their churches. When the windows flattened out in the sixteenth century do did the shoes, as shown in the portraits of Henry VIII's broad, embroidered shoes. The Tudor ladies' hats were the same shape as their fireplaces. When Queen Victoria went to open the Albert Hall, whose structure was basically a steel hooped dome, she wore steel hooped petticoats.[8] When the teaching order changed their religious habit and the style of the houses they lived in, when they threw out the icons and statuettes which decorated their convents, they were expressing, symbolically, the changes in their authority relationships and their religious orientations.

It was not only the style of decorations which changed but also the architecture of the convents and the usage of space. As one might expect, the Franciscans did not alter the style or usage of their convents. Their Mother House was a converted mansion but the extensions built on to it made it virtually custom-made. All the other buildings owned by the congregation were purpose-built—hospitals, mission houses, leprosariums, children's homes. Attached to every building were the nuns' quarters, recognizably poorer, built to a meaner standard of living. The Franciscans lived out their vows of poverty in taking plain cooked food and using hard chairs, beds and furniture. In the 1960s the nuns moved from dormitories to cells but the refectory retained its U-shaped seating, the nuns sitting in rank order just as they did in chapel, on hard benches. Spatial representations of the organization reflected, as they always had done, the hierarchy, the role structure, and the isolation of the Franciscan from the outside world. In contrast the teaching congregation saw fundamental changes in both the utilization of existing space and the design and habitat of their convents. Up to the Second World War the congregation in England consisted of four large houses each set in large grounds of up to ten acres. Without exception these convents were situated in prosperous middle-class areas, either in the green-belt around London or in seaside towns. The buildings were large and spacious, well-endowed, the chapels filled with ornaments and decorations. Each convent accommodated twenty to thirty sisters and boarding facilities for up to 200 girls. The buildings and land were owned by the congregation. They provided a considerable capital investment which could be mortgaged with the permission of the diocese. By 1974 all of these convents had been sold and in their place were a number of small houses accommodating from four to eight sisters each. The buildings were rarely purpose-built, and rarely owned by the Institute; leasing or renting was more likely. They were now situated in the less prosperous urban areas and lived in by sisters with a realistic approach to the needs of the people around them, whether they were young offenders, drug-addicts, down-and-outs or families in need. Teachers now went out to state primary schools. There was little difference between their convent and the homes of the children they taught. Before the change the convent building itself made a huge impact on the sensibilities of the inmates and particularly on new arrivals.

When a young girl entered the teaching congregation in an old-style convent the separation between the world outside and the inside world of the convent was emphasized by the architecture. One such convent had a wide flight of stone steps leading to an impressive wooden door imbedded with metal studs. To one side of the door was a small grille and a turning handle; every visitor was peered at through the grille before being let in. The entrance hall itself was huge and belittling, the ceiling three times the height of a woman. The nun, especially a young novice entering for the first time, would at once feel small, weak and vulnerable. In many *rites de passage* initiates are subjected to debilitating experiences before passing from one ritual status to another. The passage from the outside world to the convent enclosure had this psychological effect on anyone who entered. Once inside the experience was of imprisonment. Every window was covered with iron bars, every window was above peering height. The whole focus of the building was on the chapel, which was both centrally placed and higher (actually built higher and reached by steps) than any other part.

E. T. Hall coined the phrase, 'Time talks, space speaks'[9] to describe the impact of territoriality on culture and on people. Space itself is a message system and the convent communicated the obedience, the hierarchy, the closed communications which were a central feature of traditional convent life. Hall says, 'Fixed-feature space is one of the basic ways of organizing the activities of individuals and groups. It includes material manifestations as well as the hidden internalized designs that govern behaviour as man moves about this earth. Buildings are one expression of fixed-feature patterns, but buildings are also grouped together in characteristic ways as well as being divided internally according to culturally determined designs.'[10] To illustrate this ordering of space he gives the example of the specialization of rooms. In the seventeenth century houses had virtually no private rooms nor did rooms have fixed functions. In the eighteenth century houses altered their form and strangers and household members no longer wandered through rooms at will; the rooms were built off a corridor and each one had a function and a name—bedroom, living-room, dining-room etc. . . . The Western family pattern stabilized itself at the same time; the rooms were an expression of that stability. In the traditional convent the sisters ate at a horseshoe-shaped dining-table, in strict order of rank. The placing and the shape of the table were an expression of the rank order and the exact positioning of every sister within the convent according to seniority and status.

Within the convent, the functions of rooms were clear and formalized as were their positions both in relation to the outside walls and to the system of enclosure operating at the time. The main offices of the house—the Superior's office, the Headmistress's office—were placed on one side of the front door on the outer wall. The visitors' parlour and the priest's room (this was necessary because the priest generally had breakfast in the convent after morning Mass) were on the opposite side, also on the outer wall. The visitors' parlour was plushly decorated with woollen carpets, brocade curtains and chintz covers. It was a place to entertain the parents of children or nuns and was designed to make them feel at home. The inner part of the building facing on to the garden accommodated the sisters and their facilities, the outer parts the offices and classrooms. Thus, on the inner wall was the nuns' refectory, on the outer wall a staff dining-room for lay helpers. The kitchens were below stairs, just slightly below ground level, as clear an indication of the differentiation between lay and choir nun as the Victorian demarcations between the servants'

quarters and the rest of the house. From the kitchens was the only
other exit/entry point to the outside world. This was the back door
through which all the provisions were brought, and which was used
by domestic staff, lay sisters going on errands, tramps and beggars
calling for alms.

Religious enclosure was obtained by a system of internal passageways and staircases linking dining-room, community room, cells and
chapel. The cells were five feet by nine feet, one small window set high
in the wall. All the rooms were barely furnished, beds were iron-
framed, chairs hard-backed. Until the big purge in the 1960s every
room was decorated with holy pictures and plaster statues. At each
angle of the staircase there were huge statues of the Sacred Heart.
The garden too was dominated by a statue. Over every doorway were
castellated architraves and arches enclosing nooks for figurines of the
Holy Family or patron saints. The contrast between the sparse
furnishings of the nuns' rooms and the elaborate statues and pictures
was a function of the religious belief in the glory of God, the promise
of Heaven and the search for perfection by imperfect beings. The
colours employed emphasized this aspect. The chapel and religious
pictures were light; the ceiling of the Chapel was pale blue, the walls
white. The 'earthly' secular areas of the convent were dark red. All
the colours there were sombre and heavy; light and sunshine were
excluded, reserved for the brilliant stained glass of the chapel.

The chapel was full of formal, codified tributes to the Church and
to Christian tradition. The sister who entered it from the inner part
of the convent entered a world of calm tranquillity, the colours pastel
and cool; she entered a world of incense and sensuality. The statuettes,
the décor, the climbing ivy motif on the pews, the vaulted ceiling, all
celebrated art forms which were repressed in the rest of the building.
There the mode was castellation, here it was vaulting. There dark
and sombre, here light and bright. The separation of the altar spoke
of the ritualized relationship between the sister and her God; candles,
incense, vestments set the stage for the drama of the Eucharist, which
was celebrated against the ornate stucco backdrop of the high altar.
The style, ornamentation and seating arrangements in the Chapel
were an indication not only of the social relationships between the
sisters themselves or between sisters and outsiders, but also between
the sisters and their religion, their God. The spatial separation between the altar and the nuns, between the choir and the rest of the
congregation were representative of a prayer life governed by the
devotional prayers of the Church, by Benediction, Holy Hours, visits
to the Blessed Sacrament, etc. The sacrament itself occupied a central
position on the altar in a curtained tabernacle; it was a small and
distant point in the whole schema of the Chapel, yet one which was

emphasized by rows of candles and a huge crucifix of the suffering Christ above it. The eye was taken and held by this image, the heavenly spouse, the sacrificial victim, the Saviour to whom the daily prayers and the whole life of the nuns were dedicated.

The teaching congregation did have one purpose-built modern convent and it could hardly have been in greater contrast with the traditional ones. The convent was part of a tripartite Catholic diocesan plan for a church, presbytery and convent all linked. The congregation bought the convent from the diocese on a long leasehold, and the nuns co-operated with the priests in parish work and social work. It was built as part of a housing scheme initiated to rehouse people dispossessed by slum clearance. The convent incorporated the same design features as the houses on the estate. It had central heating, wood-block flooring, wall-to-wall carpets and bright furnishings. The walls were brightly painted, each room having an integrated colour scheme. The bedrooms had floral quilts and matching curtains. There was no separation between the style of the convent and the style of the houses around, just as the sisters who lived in the convent wore ordinary clothes and were not distinguished by a religious habit. There was no chapel in the convent itself but there was direct access to the parish church. Lay people were welcomed into the house, dined with the sisters and sat with them in the living-room. The living-room itself was big and comfortable with a television set, bookshelves, piano, guitars, comfortable armchairs and low coffee tables. There was a crucifix over the fireplace but no statuettes, no holy pictures. The nuns themselves justified their lifestyle by their way of life. If they were to be 'nuns in the world' then their living quarters should reflect it. But there were difficulties in blurring the boundaries to such an extent. The poverty vow was more easily justified than the chastity vow. One writer commented, 'Nuns living in ordinary housing areas can be sharply reminded of lay attitudes to their vows. . . . Sisters may live across the stairway or through the hall from a Catholic woman with four small children who has been deserted by her husband. Like the sisters, she has to be chaste. But her vow of chastity—that of monogamy—is not so easily dispensed as that of the sisters.'[11] When a nun worked side by side with a lay social worker and the only apparent difference between them was the chastity vow, it introduced an intolerable strain. Sisters in these small open communities found themselves asking 'Why am I a nun?' and the answer, frequently, was to seek a dispensation from their vows. Just as the boundary between the inside world of the convent and the outside world of the secular had been blurred, so too had the division between the nun and her God, between Heaven and earth. She could seek her God now by working in humanity.

In the convents of the teaching congregation the individual manipulated space in the group context. Every misfit could be observed
clinging to old ways in new convents or trying new ways in the old.
Some refused to redecorate their rooms, others simply ignored the
comfortable chairs, refused rich foods and went on avoiding change
by pretending it hadn't happened to them. Old altars were replaced
by a table standing in front of the altar rail close to the main part of
the congregation. Statuettes were thrown out, cubicles were constructed in dormitories, small dining-tables replaced the old horseshoe-shaped table. But these were individual instances; in general the
historical changes which had affected every aspect of their organization were represented in the relationship between architecture, dress,
lifestyle and ideology. Changes in the symbolic order were non-
verbal signals about changes in the fabric of their religious life. The
old habits enclosed the body just as the old closed convents cloistered
the sisters, and the dark, sombre colours of their living-quarters
cramped their imagination. The light, airy colours of the old convent
were restricted to the chapel, the freedom of graceful clothes kept on
the statues of saints and martyrs. The body which was enclosed and
mortified on earth would find restitution in Heaven. In the new, open
convents where outsiders were allowed in and sisters allowed out, the
clothes gave the body greater freedom of movement. The colours of
clothes and convents, brilliant and gay, expressed job and happiness
on earth. It is no accident that the Franciscans, who kept their old
habits, wore white, that their passageways were painted white, that
their chapel was open and full of tributes to St Francis, their charismatic leader. They kept alive a sense of the mysticism, the fellowship
and brotherhood of their founder and preserved their traditional
ways knowing them to be appropriate to the twentieth century.

All the changes I have described for the teaching congregation had
an effect, in very real terms as well as in symbolic ones, of blurring
boundaries, the boundaries between the convent and the outside
world, between the nun and her God, who was now much more
accessible. The idea that man regulates his experience of life by various
discreet boundaries is central to Mary Douglas's analysis of ritual and
belief systems. She says: 'The better defined and the more significant
the social boundaries, the more the bias I would expect in favour or
ritual. If the social groups are weakly structured and their membership weak and fluctuating, then I would expect low value to be set on
symbolic performance. Along this line of ritual variation appropriate
doctrinal differences would appear. With weak social boundaries and
weak ritualism, I would expect doctrinal emphasis on internal emotion states. Sin would be more a matter of affect than of transgression:
sacraments and magic would give way to direct, unmediated com-

munion, even to the sacralization of states of trance and bodily dissociated.'[12] The changes in the teaching congregation certainly affected the way in which they were grouped and the extent of their boundaries. In the traditional convent the focus was sharp; the isolation of the convent was abrupt and emphasized. In the modern convent the nuns have attempted to blend in with their surroundings, but the boundaries are still there; the focus has shifted. Chastity is still built like a high wall round every community. Further, the sisters are most anxious to protect themselves against any 'weakening' of their faith. If anything they need added strength and protection in the physical world and in fulfilling the demands of their chosen life. While none of the progressives and few of the younger sisters expressed any magical belief, in the efficacy of the sacraments, for example, none of them had attempted to replace their belief in ritual symbols by a search for more personal ecstatic states. One sister alone had made an attempt to communicate with God through physical mechanisms other than those recommended by the congregation, and that was by the use of simple yoga, slow rhythmic breathing. I was told, 'They are all much too sensible. Their lives are too bound in the every day.' One must take care not to confuse the lack of ritual, or disappearance of certain rituals with a weakening in ritual altogether. The ritual was still there only in a different form, carrying symbolic representations of alternative social groupings. While these sisters were not attracted to trance and ecstasy they were attracted to the Ignation spiritual exercises and the writings of mystics like St Thérèse of Ávila. Raymond Firth confirms that in all the writings on ritual and symbolism which he investigated he found 'a dichotomy of sphere, if not of interest, recognized between the symbol patterns of tightly knit groups, concerned for instance with protection of interest and transmission of codes, and those of looser social aggregates, concerned more with expressive forms of self-realization.'[13]

Somehow Douglas disapproves of 'anti-ritualism' as she sees it, whereas Victor Turner sees a degree of *communitas* or anti-structure as a necessary phase in the dialectical process of society. *Communitas* has an existential quality. It is the pattern sought by the progressive teaching sisters: man in fellowship with his fellow man, the stage reached by the teaching order at the end of their three years' experimentation. The sisters were approaching the boundaries of Roman Catholicism. They stretched the doctrines of the Church to their fullest extent in their search for a meaningful form for their religious life. The sisters in the north of England, with their more conservative approach to prayer, retained much of the formal structure of their lifestyle. They still lived in a Victorian purpose-built convent with its rigid differentiation of space; they still had a Mother Superior and many of the traditional roles and statues. The sisters on the missions were the most progressive. Not only did they live on the borderline of their own culture, isolated from other Europeans, they lived amongst other Catholics, Belgian priests in particular, who had adopted forms of ritual which were unfamiliar. 'In a liminal period society emerges as an unstructured or rudimentarily structured and relatively un-differentiated *comitatus*.'[14] But there is another sense in which the religious community, at whatever stage in its development, is 'mar-ginal' to the society, especially the Christian religious community.

The Christian monastic order institutionalizes liminality. Seen from the point of view of the practising Roman Catholic, the monk or nun is halfway to Heaven, not quite of this world yet not quite dead to the world either. The contemplatives have always had a higher status than the active religious, not only because they have been seen to make a greater sacrifice but also because they appear more 'holy'. Turner speaks of liminal or threshold people as 'dangerous' carriers of supra-human powers; institutionalized danger is also sacred; its bearers become special, gifted, spiritual. There is an element of 'pas-sage', of transition in monastic life which is captured in the *rites de passage* of entry to the order where the old world is stripped off and new accoutrements taken on. It is no coincidence that the important positions of sacristan and portress, those two tasks which mark the boundaries of the religious community, are held by lay sisters in the hierarchy of the traditional teaching order. Many times the nuns spoke to me of the spirituality and simplicity of the lay sisters; they were believed to hold qualities which brought them close to God. Turner remarks that threshold people are often those who occupy the lowest rungs of the status ladder, who rest on the margins of the group, who lie at the interstices of social structure. He distinguishes two types of rituals associated with liminality, those which characterize status elevation, and those of status reversal, where inferiors exercise ritual authority over their superiors. In the latter case a key social element to the ritual is the elevation of ritual subjects to positions of eminent authority.

In the teaching congregation, 1 January was traditionally a day when the youngest novice was elected Superior for the day and ordered an elaborate feast. After the feast an extravagant play was acted out which always had a king and queen who took precedence over all the sisters. The sisters would dress up in disguises for the plays, including the making of wigs out of wood shavings or feathers, to look more like princesses. In medieval times the Feast of Fools (now called the Holy Innocents) on 1 January was a time when ordi-nary pious priests and townsfolk put on bawdy masks and sang out-rageous songs. Minor clerics painted their faces and strutted about in the clothes of their superiors, mocking the stately rituals of Church and court. Nothing was left sacred, every custom and convention was open to ridicule. Harvey Cox[15] sees an implicitly radical dimension in these festivities; they enabled people to see that things need not always be as they are. He makes a useful distinction between fantasy and festivity. Fantasy is the faculty of envisaging radically alternative life-styles, festivity is the capacity for revelry and celebration. In the party and the play on 1 January one is witnessing a fantasy (in Cox's terminology) of structural superiority. Turner would add that such festivities are also an indication of the permanent inferior status of the participants.[16]

Anthropologists make a distinction between life-crises, ritual, calendrical rites and *rites de passage*. Life-crises, e.g. birth, puberty and death, affect the individual, but calendrical rites and *rites de passage* affect groups and even whole societies. Festivities of status reversal are most frequent in calendrical rites. Superiors often have to accept a degree of degradation on these occasions. The day after the Feast of the Holy Innocents the last nun into chapel has to do all the cleaning for the next day, whatever her position in the convent. It is noticeable that the Franciscan congregation do not celebrate these days in the same way, possibly because there is no lay/choir dichotomy and because every sister shares in unwelcome tasks. The Mother General takes her turn to clean the chapel and all lend a hand to painting and decorating and other mundane tasks. In rituals of status elevation the subject is generally irreversibly conveyed from a lower to a higher position, this passage being accompanied by a degree of demotion before promotion. The fate of the novice, secluded, stripped of status and rights to property, subjected to trials of humility, is well documented. In both congregations the sisters spoke of a feeling of helplessness before they took their vows, of being dependent on their fate. The Franciscans go through a ritual reminiscent of Christ's ordeal. They wear a crown of thorns before becoming brides of Christ when the thorns are replaced by the religious habit, the veil and a crown of white roses.

Turner makes another vital contribution to our understanding of the Franciscan congregation in his distinction between normative *communitas*, existential or spontaneous *communitas* and ideological *communitas*.[17] Existential *communitas* is the 'hippy happening', some spontaneous movement to reach utopia of fellowship. It inevitably undergoes some restructuring as the initial impetus becomes routinized. Normative *communitas* is the organization of existential *communitas* into an enduring social system, and ideological *communitas* is the model on which that system might be built. Religious movements tend to rise in times of radical social transition. The normative and

ideological *communitas* are symbolized by structurally inferior categories and members may often take on their attributes just as St
Francis assumed the clothing of a leper. In particular the equation
between equality and lack of property becomes a central tenet in
ideological communities. Poverty is a crucial element in the Franciscan ideology. Every Franciscan nun questioned about her vows and
the meaning of religious life mentioned poverty first, and described it
as the imperative dynamic in their life. To be truly poor was to be
truly open to God and free from earthly encumbrances. St Francis
himself always insisted that poverty should be taken to the limits of
human endurance. The early friars were deliberately both highly
mobile and economically insecure. They begged from door to door
and took irregular work like grave-digging and water-carrying.
Turner says that this was a deliberate attempt on the part of St
Francis to keep his friars on the fringes and interstices of the social
structure of his time, to keep them therefore in a liminal state and
hence in a condition for *communitas*.

St Francis obviously fits Turner's idea of the spontaneous creator
of *communitas*. His order was founded on dreams and visions. The
early friars not only lived in a time of social unrest, but lived on the
margins of their society. The symbolism of St Francis's visit to the
leper colony is made more relevant by the socio-structural position of
lepers in medieval times: outcasts from society. The saint's problem
was to sustain this spontaneous *communitas* as ever-increasing
numbers of men flocked to join him. The growth of the order saw the
diminution of the spontaneous *communitas* and the routinization of
St Francis's vision by legal precepts and institutional arrangements.
Yet in some way, right down to the present day, the memory of the
original *communitas* is kept alive. The power of the doctrine *usis
pauper*, setting poverty at odds with obedience, retained the possibility of structural conflict and hence change, long after the order had
thoroughly organized itself with a traditional authority structure
under the unmediated control of the Pope. One of the mechanisms
which preserved the ideological *communitas* through the centuries was
the use of myth and allegory, in the form of stories, songs and books.
The library of the Franciscan convents were full of books, their walls
and chapels full of tributes to St Francis. Turner points out that it is
characteristic of movements of this kind to have on the one hand a
'naked unaccommodated man', simple and poor, and on the other
hand a poetic outpouring of his vision linking the ultimate fate of man
and of the Church on earth with mysticism and asceticism; liminality,
other-worldliness is preserved through time. It is this element of
ideological *communitas* which leaves the Franciscan congregation quite
untroubled by the radical changes urged on them by Vatican II.

The Franciscan vow of poverty was the distinguishing characteristic of the organization in its early years; it was from that excess that the rest of the message took its meanings. Today the Franciscan nun takes with her vows that ideal of poverty exemplified by her founder saint, and with it the humanity and suffering for the poor and under-privileged which distinguishes his message for the world. The Franciscan nun chastizes her body with fasting and mortification and it is part of her personal sacrifice to the religious life. She also cele-brates her contribution in offering talents to the community, in feast-ing with her sisters on saints' days and on all those special occasions in the Church calendar. The teaching congregation also feast and fast, fasting being an individual affair and feasting a group enterprise. A feast may be an extra Mass in chapel and special concessions for the day, or as one old sister told me, 'You might get an Ave Maria to speak, or you might have marmalade for breakfast. But on very special days like a Jubilee for example there would be special food in the convent all day. One of the sisters might bake a cake and put bits of chocolate on it.' Feasting is often accompanied by music and dancing—a real party atmosphere! In the traditional teaching con-gregation the body and food were a medium for mortification and the expression of poverty rather than for celebration—remember the talent-stripping which went on in the traditional organization. The body, enclosed by the habit, mortified by the discipline, was also starved. At one time far too many sisters in the congregation caught T.B.; doctors attributed it to neglect and insufficient rest. With the opening of communications and the reappraisal of religious life in the 1950s the sisters came to realize that food was not a proper medium for poverty in the sense in which they had interpreted it. Much of the world was actually starving. Missionary sisters were forced to acknowledge that they were of no use to the poor around them when they themselves were ill and undernourished. Food was freed from poverty and the sisters joined the cooking revolution—escalope de veau and coq au vin featured on the convent menu. The evening meal acquired the status of a Mass, the Mass the symbolism of a meal in these small modern convents, where the gathering of a group round the table assumed a ritual significance for nuns whose daily life was spent in the bustle of the outside world.

The intimate relationship between architecture, dress, lifestyle and ideology produces a symbolic order. I could tell just by knocking at the door, at which stage in their revolution each convent in the teach-ing congregation had reached. The contrast between the old convents and the new is positively breathtaking. Instead of the chapel being the focal point there might well be no chapel at all. But this is under-standable when you consider that in the old days the spiritual nun was the nun who knelt straightest, who was 'close to heaven' in a chapel which reached to the heavens with the aid of spires and vaultings. Now the sister's aim was to find God in humanity, to appear as normal as possible to the people around her, yet to remain special in the way that Christ in the Bible is special—loving, joyful. You no longer gave your time to God by praying in the chapel, you gave it by working, by getting out of the convent and helping people. And you let people in. Instead of being enclosed the convents left their doors open—open to people, to the mass media, to new ideas.

CHAPTER TEN

Utopia Revisited

In what he calls a 'concluding unscientific postscript' to his book on the sociology of English religion, David Martin makes a plea for the 'schizoid vision' of the sociologist[1]—schizoid, because he must seem committed to the principle that nothing is ever as it appears to be and that everything must be looked at from several, possibly contrasting angles. To many the sociologist appears as 'a pessimist and a determinist, with an irritated, cynical and suspicious attitude towards whatever the bulk of humanity holds most dear'. In writing about the communities of nuns and particularly about their faith and the expression of that faith in ritual and symbolism I am only too well aware of the scepticism of my approach. But I am not a determinist, nor are most of my colleagues. I merely assume that social life has a pattern of regularity which is there to be found and that, as David Martin puts it, 'any genuine freedom depends on the wide dominion of hierarchies of habit.' These 'hierarchies of habit' are the rules and the roles, the authority and the compliance which go to make up the organization of society. The Franciscans remain 'in habit' in their retention of traditional forms of the religious life including the religious habit, the hierarchical organization, the rigid structuring of everyday life, and they are highly successful in maintaining that organization today. The teaching congregation made a bid for a radical alternative to the traditional religious life, shattering, for a time, the viability, stability and plausibility of the organization. Looking beyond the obvious contrast between stability and change there is a less obvious similarity between the processes of the two congregations. Until it is understood that stability is not static, that the 'mechanisms of persistence' are not utterly distinct from the mechanisms of change,[2] the innovatory characteristics of the Franciscan organization will not be recognized.

These two congregations have a typical bureaucratic form of organization set out in a legal framework in which the *Rule* establishes an *ordered hierarchy* within which the sisters act out their *vocation*. These three terms hold the key to the operation of a bureaucracy in which both the ultimate goals of the religious as well as more prag-matic goals have to be achieved to remain successful. The religious order could never be quite separate from the outside world or from its own Church, and the Rule acted as a nexus between the internal and external. The Franciscan Rule has been shown to be univer-salistic in ideology, wide in its aims, spiritual in its directives, humani-tarian and personal in its appeal. In contrast, the Rule of the teaching congregation is more pragmatic, directed to specific goals. Parti-cularistic and religious individualism is subordinate to obedience and the infrastructure of the organization. The contrasts between the Rules also reflect between the founders. St Francis owed obedience to the Pope and to God directly; he was a great individualist, a saint, a charismatic leader. The founder of the teaching congregation was a member of the Church hierarchy, dedicated to the constitutional development of Catholic bureaucracy. His foundation had a more restrictive charter than the Franciscans.

If authority in the bureaucratic organization is legitimated by a formal Rule, power is legitimated by high moral commitment of members to organizational goals and leaders; indeed a 'total' commit-ment is required. In the teaching congregation less than half the membership is actively engaged in teaching, which is a secondary goal in one sense, but is nevertheless vital both for resources and for further recruitment. All the time there was a demand for private education for Catholic girls there was no threat to the aim or the resource, but once state education became a realistic alternative and educational aims began to change, this highly specific pursuit was threatened, and with it the viability of the teaching congregation. It suffered a crisis of member commitment as well as a drop in demand for its services from the outside world, on which it depended for economic security.

In contrast the Franciscan congregation involves all its membership in some form of active apostolate; there is no class distinction and it is not committed to a single pragmatic goal. When the State took over hospitals but left work still to be done in nursery-nursing or geriatric care the Franciscans moved into those areas, which gave them a great strength in times of economic instability. The Franciscans also tend to be more dependent on ultimate values, even their vows were seen to be legitimated by the early Church and a seraphic saint rather than by the social values held at the time of their foundation. This meant they were both less open to the criticism of changing social values in the outside world and less rigidly constrained by the nature of their foundation, which was, crucially, the work of a charismatic leader. Michael Hill has produced perhaps the neatest definition of charis-matic, 'Charismatics proclaim a message: virtuosi proclaim a method.'[3]

G

The virtuoso follows a rigorous interpretation which already exists in a religious tradition, but the charismatic articulates something entirely new, possibly shattering what already exists. The Franciscan congregation contains an element of charismatic domination in their bureaucratic organization which, originating in St Francis, has been routinized throughout the organization in offices where decisions about ends are made. Charisma is positively functional and especially effective in the office of Mother General where she uses her charismatic authority to innovate and introduce new apostolic work and alternative forms of expression for primary religious goals in the performance of pilgrimages, feast-days and other rituals. The Franciscan congregation did not become ossified in nineteenth-century manners and morals because successive leaders were able to modify goals. Moreover they were able to depend on the special style of Franciscan spirituality which emphasized 'inner will', 'spirit' and 'ecstacy' to gain commitment of members to new goals, and to avoid the more stereotyped, devotional expression of religion common to other congregations.

The period 1940–60 was a period of expansion for the Franciscans. They achieved most of their goals and new goals were engendered. Their ability to innovate was crucial to their development. During this period the teaching congregation became increasingly rigid. They failed to maintain standards in their schools and were forced to take in non-Catholic pupils and lay-staff to keep them running. As the validity of their secondary goals was questioned the response was even greater rigidity. Conformity to the Rule became an end in itself; instrumental values tended to become terminal values. A group emerged and developed which pressed for change, but the breakthrough was achieved in 1958 with the election to the office of Superior General of a leader with 'charismatic' qualities. The reform movement now had the power to begin implementing change through traditional bureaucratic procedures. Rigorous questioning of values and goals revealed a fundamental incompatibility between the traditional beliefs, the Rule, the founder's precepts, and the demands of religious life and radical Catholicism in the 1960s. In amending the Rule so that the aims of the congregation could allow for a diversity of apostolic work, not only the material base but the structuring of everyday life was profoundly altered.

Whether the process of change in the teaching congregation can be called secularization is, I believe, open to question. The sisters have a belief in a supra-empirical reality which shares the real world with them. In their move from traditional practices to experimental living, the sisters experienced a shift in this relationship between the supra-empirical and the real world; a shift rather than a debasement or a reduction of one by the other. The justification for many of the developments in the teaching congregation was a move to establish 'God in humanity'. It indicates a switch from other-worldly to this-worldly orientations beloved by those who favour the secularization model. But it is beset by misunderstanding. The religious sisters saw the move as one which would bring them closer to God and which would strengthen the 'religious' element in their lives. Their explanation has to be considered in the context of changing ritual and beliefs which revised the relationship between the individual sister, her Church and her God. While previously she had been a dependent, now she was a mature individual. The importance of this move should not be minimized. It affected every aspect of the sister's life and commitment. The changes in the teaching congregation are better described by changes in a conceptual paradigm than by use of the secularization model. Vatican II shattered the Tridentine paradigm in which priests held the positions of mediators between God and humans. The breakdown of the Tridentine paradigm preceded the breakdown of the plausibility structure of the belief system in the teaching congregation. A plurality of forms and goals led to a confused acceptance of the new conceptual paradigm, hence the uncertainties and withdrawals of the late 1960s.

An anthropological study of the Carmel indicated that a Carmelite nun who spends sixty years in the convent would be in the same place at the same time in the chapel choir, 42,800 times during those years.[4] The use of ritual to structure time in daily life is a feature of all religious communities, but its importance in the contemplative order is that each day can be like a lifetime. Historical time, liturgical time and physical spacetime unfold through the days, months, years, enabling the nun to live her life in a cosmology quite unlike that of people in the world. When the teaching congregation revised its prayer life and axed many of the community prayers they freed the day but lost the reinforcement of organizational goals which the rigid structuring of time had ensured. In keeping these rituals the Franciscans not only preserved the boundaries of their collectivity but reaffirmed their position between God and humanity in general. The ability of the Franciscans to preserve this *liminality* through time was due largely to the ideology and symbolism of St Francis. Symbols, capable of both generating and receiving communication, have an ambiguity which can be seen as a strength in critical situations where they are subject to a plurality of interpretations, for example, the capability of the Mass to represent a hierarchical power structure in one context and the ideological concept of universal brotherhood in another. Changes in the symbolic order are signals about changes in the fabric of life; every aspect of architecture, dress, lifestyle and ideology is involved.

Franciscan ideology included a notion of brotherhood which was compatible with the new theology of the 1960s. Not only theologians but youth movements of the '60s stressed communitarian and utopian ideals and yet the impact of both was felt in different ways by the two congregations. It is important to recognize a crucial difference between the 'fraternalization' of the teaching congregation and the ideal of 'brotherhood' exalted by the Franciscans. Fraternalization implies a levelling process which was carried out to the logical conclusion of making all group members 'sister', of abolishing the office of local Superior, and of reducing the powers of the Superior General to those of a co-ordinator rather than a legislator, still less an innovator. Fraternalization meant, in effect, abolishing the family and the position of God the Father and replacing it with a polymorphous structure in which God was all things to all men. The idea of God and notions of fraternity and brotherhood borrow as much from concepts of the family as from philosophical and theological ideas. In Victorian times, when the teaching congregation established its group identity in relationship to God, the father was an awesome figure in the family. It followed that God should be an awesome figure in the religious family. When the position of the father changed and he became the loving father, the playful friend and companion, so, too, God the Father was worshipped with less awe and more ease.

The Franciscan 'brotherhood' never relinquished the notion of the family as the primary unit, with the father at its head. But the teaching congregation tried to banish the father. They confused brotherhood with communitarianism. 'The equality of brotherhood is a levelling in the presence of a father.'[5] Norman O'Brown uses Locke's writings on the absolute monarchy in the seventeenth century to explain this concept. He relates the Freudian concept of the archetypal father to the absolute monarchy and to Locke's idea of the equality and liberty of men as the 'sons of God'. Where brotherhood is a social contract rather than a familial relationship there are elaborate initiation rites which define the group of brothers. The principle of fraternal equality will be combined with paternal domination in a taut relationship. The threat of upheaval is ever-present in the Freudian opposition of father/son. But where the father is elevated to a heavenly Father this fundamental opposition is alleviated. The band of brothers can remain united under the heavenly Father and he can even become the symbolic representation of group unity. Where he has a direct representative on earth, in the form of Jesus Christ or St Francis, it is important for that representative to have 'special' qualities, not owned by ordinary men, or the threat of opposition arises once again. St Francis carried the markings of the supernatural as well as the charisma to attract and bind followers to his cause. His nuns today continue to have an elaborate initiation ceremony, they continue in their hierarchical system of government, they continue to think of God as a super-elevated father-figure, in control, patronizing, powerful. Locke was opposed to the absolute monarchy of the seventeenth century because he argued that no man could be elevated above another. Similarly he argued against primogeniture; all brothers should share an estate; for one only to inherit was to perpetuate an inequality. In the relationship between the Franciscans and their leader these issues were side-stepped by the notion of charisma, where personal devotion to the leader was the primary motivation of the follower. The equality of brotherhood was preserved not only in relation to the heavenly Father but in relation to the head of their organization.

The teaching congregation wanted not to be equal *under* the father (Mother Superior) but equal *with* their God and their superiors. From its inception their organization lacked the Franciscan ideal of the equality of brotherhood. The Augustinian priest who was its founder was more interested in the techniques by which goals might be reached than by universalistic values like love and brotherhood. The stratified 'class' structure of the teaching congregation, in which a lower order of sisters were responsible for menial work, were denied votes or executive opportunity and had their status affirmed daily by their dress and rank order in church and in the refectory, would have been unthinkable in the Franciscan congregation. The Augustinian Canon, unlike St Francis who stripped himself of worldly values before taking on the religious life, held an elevated social position throughout his life. His work in the foundation of educational establishments was located in the middle classes. The help he extended to the poor was both separate and different; he taught them to work, not to acquire an education. This class differentiation, carried into the convent, had important implications not only for the ideology but also for the legitimation of values and the institutionalization of power (who controls who). The location of power and control has been seen to be crucial to an understanding of the variation between these two bureaucratically organized congregations. Political sociologists have attempted to reveal the distribution of values and the consensus or lack of consensus in values in class-differentiated societies.[6] One school of thought maintains that there is a general consensus on values which are simply held in varying degrees of commitment. Another school holds that there is never a unified moral order, that one is constantly confronted with 'two nations' in which explicit contrasts can be found between working-class and middle-class values. Certainly an us-and-them attitude existed in the convents of the teaching congregation.

Class differentiation was a criterion in the allocation of tasks and orientation to goals present in the teaching congregation and absent in the Franciscan. Its historical antecedents and the effects of its abolition contribute to the importance of class as a variable in both the ideological make-up and the organizational structure of the teaching congregation. The lay sister had no opportunity at all to display her natural talents; one of the first effects of the abolition of lay-status was the flowering of those many talents so long buried. The lay sister accepted her lot without complaining because she was doing it 'for God'. Moreover she was not expected to admit even to the thought of dissatisfaction, and to accept a penance in the weekly Chapter and perform it, whether it was saying more prayers or undertaking an unpleasant task. The humility of the lay sisters often endeared her to those seculars with whom she came in contact and to the choir nuns in her convent. The lay sister was on the boundary between the outside world and the convent; children talked to her; she was the portress and the refectorian; she took the groceries from the back door of the convent. But the lay sister accepted her place in the organization because she accepted its values, not because she existed in some sort of sub-culture. If she had truly been a member of a highly differentiated class system, including subscription to a separate code of morals, then it would have taken coercive or utilitarian modes of control to gain her acceptance of that position. It did not. Her position was sustained by the holders of institutionalized power operating normative sanctions: censure, deprivation of symbolic awards, symbolic punishments (saying extra prayers) or verbal appeals for cooperation and self-discipline—in other words the same sanctions as were applied to the dominant class. 'Values are much more likely to flow in a downward than in an upward direction.'[7] The explanation of why the lay sister status lasted so long, and why it was possible to abolish it 'in one stroke' lies in the alacrity with which values are accepted by subordinates when they are passed down by the holders of institutionalized power. When it came to wholesale change the lay sister accepted it as readily as she had her subordinate status earlier.

It was the choir nun who referred to the change in status with some regret, the choir nun who felt the change keenly and in personal terms. Now the lay sisters were out on training courses in preparation for more 'fulfilling' work, the gaps had either to be filled with seculars, both inconvenient and expensive, or by sharing out tasks between themselves. Initially the novices did much of the work but they rebelled and showed their dissatisfaction by leaving the order or appearing very unhappy. In some convents ex-lay sisters ran the household but with the rights and privileges of the rest of the community. Not one ex-lay sister appeared in the vanguard of the reforming group.

Several of the more elderly sisters refused to change, including one who kept to all the old routines, refusing to speak, wearing a rosary, saying all the traditional prayers in chapel. She was regarded as slightly mad by her fellow sisters who left her in peace. When the progressive sisters, who came from the dominant class, questioned the validity of stratification they also undermined the values on which the system was based, and the structure of day-to-day living.

The Franciscans had always been one class of sisters under the leadership of the Mother General and her officials. When these officials ceased to hold office they lost the title of 'Mother' and returned to 'sister'. Egalitarianism was a feature of Franciscan organization from its foundation. There was no loss of talent. Every sister was treated as an individual with a contribution to make to the group. There is a parallel here with the communitarian idealism of the 1960s.[8] Communitarians stressed the free development of the self and the creation of honest, creative human relationships within the context of the commune. Because they already contained these elements in their ideology they were no threat to their value system and they remained staunchly conservative in their beliefs. The Eucharist remained a celebration of Christ's supreme sacrifice; it was not reinterpreted as a fraternal meal. They still became the brides of Christ when they entered the convent. But the teaching congregation lacked these elements in their ideology and when Vatican II added its voice to the call for communitarianism it was bound to leave the isolation of its nineteenth-century value system where every brother had a younger brother and every father was feared. *Perfectae Caritatis* 15 laid the guidelines which the sisters, leaving their enclosed convents, could follow. 'The primitive Church provided an example of community life when the multitude of believers were of one heart and one mind, and found nourishment in the teaching of the gospel and in the sacred liturgy, especially the Eucharist. As Christ's members living fraternally together, let them excel one another in showing respect, and let each carry the other's burdens. For thanks to God's love poured into hearts by the Holy Spirit, a religious community is a true family gathered together in the Lord's name and rejoicing in His presence. For love is the fulfilment of the law and the bond of perfection, where it exists we know we have been taken from death to life. In fact, brotherly unity shows that Christ has come; from it results great apostolic influence.' Not quite the millennium arrived but certainly a Utopian script! The communitarian ideal, as proclaimed by the Vatican Council, claimed legitimacy, like St Francis's before it, in the early Church, referring to the 'pure' form of Christian living in the original bands of brothers. When the radical nuns of the teaching congregation took this ideal they acted out the notion of sharing, of love, of poverty, in the modern living liturgy of the Church. Group meditations were seen to deepen the sisters' union with God and their solidarity towards one another. Personal relationships would now be a key element in the liturgy as they were in human life. They were a far remove from the devotional prayers of the past.

The emphasis on understanding each other, on recognizing the individual, on thinking about their shared commitment to the religious life, had a profound effect on the way in which the teaching nuns interpreted their vows. Up to the Second World War individual friendships were regarded as a breach of chastity. Nuns could be friendly but this was kept outside the bounds of personal friendships. With the change in the 1960s came the possibility of close personal friendships not only between the sisters but between the sisters and outsiders and with priests. Since God, too, was their friend, they saw the experience of human friendship as an aid to their relationship with God. They recognized that to become a nun they had renounced the fulness of that friendship in the sacrament of marriage, but justified the loss by saying that to become a nun in 1970 meant that the idea of marriage was welcomed and understood, but that it was foregone, by passed, in order to remain free for everybody. Their chastity was regarded as a positive contribution to the community of religious. This is in strong contrast to the earlier interpretation which had emphasized chastity as a practical barrier against human weakness. It is a significant indication of the breakdown in the dualistic philosophy which had accompanied their traditional belief system. The sisters had regarded themselves as an élite in their Church, not one of a band of brothers in Christ as had the Franciscans. They preserved their élitism with the physical barriers of enclosure and the normative constraints of the vows.

The progressives began to stress the inner psychological commitment of sisters to their religious life; it was yet another feature in the change which brought them closer to the Franciscans who had not only recognized their importance but enshrined them in the cult of the seraphic saint. The sisters' vocation was now defined as listening to the moving of the spirit within her. One sister described it as feeling free to move as the spirit moves you (a contrast to the control of bells and schedules). The special consecration of her life was, she claimed, the attachment which kept the religious community together. They did not need external constraints, only communication through intense and meaningful relationships which in themselves were a sacrament—the sacrament of unity. Here is an explicit use of the concept of charisma to invoke normative compliance to a set of organizational goals, including the stability of an amorphous small group.

Like the Franciscans the teaching congregation now had a number of secondary goals, they could even move out of teaching and related professions and into social work. The sisters who were, as late as 1968, still involved in the education of middle-class girls in boarding schools far removed from the reality of urban parishes, questioned the validity of their apostolate, not only in relation to human needs and Christian ideals, but also in relation to their own vows. A sister who had remained sheltered by religious enclosures and the spacious grounds of her environment found that her vow of poverty and even chastity meant nothing in the context of urban poverty, deserted wives and the maladjusted or needy. They could see that state education had taken over their role as educators and that their role as instructors in the Catholic faith could be equally well combined with social work and nursing. Several qualified teachers with many years' experience gave up school-teaching and took up social work, going to live in derelict parts of the cities. Sister Columba was one of those sisters. She said: 'I would be happy teaching bright children in a nice school, as a sister I could enjoy it very much. But I could never content myself doing it any more because I know too much about the needs of the individual children and the needs of the families. I couldn't help noticing on some children's faces that there's enough worry and trouble there—so what I'm trying to do is to make life have some sense for them, and incidentally for myself as well. It's one of the ways of making the religious life applicable to 1969.' In giving up teaching and going into social work Sister Columba changed her whole way of life. Soon she left the convent and lived and worked on her own in a run-down part of the city. She found that she was needed at all times of the day, not just from 9 to 5. But she was attached to a nearby community of religious and returned there at least once a week to refresh herself and to take community prayers with her fellow sisters.

Sister Columba was very practical and well adjusted to the changes in her life; others found it very difficult. In 1968 a hostel for 'lost girls' was set up by the congregation in Dublin. It was geared to rehabilitating girls who had run into trouble, drugs, alcoholism, prostitution, unmarried motherhood. The sisters were determined to bring the girls back to the Church as well as back into society. They were picked up from the dock area at night and taken to the hostel where they were given food, a bed and clothes. The sisters tried to find them jobs and lodgings, and psychiatric or medical help if necessary. To nursing sisters used to the tough life of the missions the work was a challenge; to other sisters used to the shelter of the big convent it was a shattering experience. Sister Mary Anne described how terrified she was at first. She arrived at the house to find that she was expected to cope on her own until the relief arrived the next day.

H

She was taken on a tour of the house and kitchens and then left. She was so frightened that she stayed in her room until another nun arrived for the night. She was frightened, she said, because she had never met a prostitute before, but she had heard about them and how evil they were. From her room she could hear loud voices and foul language, bangings and raucous drunken behaviour. She was so terrified that she left the house and went to a relative in another part of the city. But the next day she returned and in the company of another nun began cooking and serving meals. Within the week she lost her fear; she could see that they were human, she said. Within another week she was responding naturally to her charges and only left the hostel to take a course in social work in order, she said, to learn how best to help them. She also campaigned for more sex education in the convents so that other nuns might be better prepared than she was for the rougher elements in society.

The question that has to be asked about the teaching congregation is, what were its chances of survival in the new form? Not only was there a loss of capital from the sale of the big houses and schools but their income was scarcely matched by the salaries of social workers and schoolteachers in state education. Recruitment fell off and a number of sisters left the congregation during the period of rapid change, but now that a novitiate has been re-established and the number of communities has stabilized there should be no further loss of personnel. The history of monasticism in Western Christendom has innumerable examples of groups which hive off when reform of the traditional structure becomes impossible, until the developmental cycle of growth, consolidation, stagnation and revolution repeats itself. There are those who think that monasticism is doomed, that the new-style convents are halfway houses to allow the gradual phasing-out of religious life as it has been known. Others talk of fluid communities with no formal vows but a temporary commitment based on the acceptance of a general aim.[9] There is another possibility which is that here, in the latter half of the twentieth century, the form of religious life is completely changing and that these small, unstructured groups, in which the teaching congregation put so much hope and love and commitment, will become a witness to the Christian ideal in our society. Unfortunately that very scepticism which makes me, as David Martin says, 'chronically suspicious of all the solemn paraphernalia of patriotism, the puppetry of law, the phraseology of religion . . . also means a suspicion of "openness" when this is prescribed either as a precondition of "authentic" social living or of the Church being its true self.'[10] The sociologist cannot be a utopian. The small modern houses in which the nuns now live are open in relation to the old convents with their enclosure, silence, discipline and

authority, but they are not unstructured. When the nuns talk inces-
santly about community, how to create a community mentality, it
may be new to them, but it is a theme as old as civilization itself. The
nuns are sharing in a communitarian tradition which goes back twenty
centuries to the Qmran community in the Dead Sea.

The communiatrianism of the 1950s and 1960s has been variously
described as a response to the rapid advance of technology and
mechanization. People finding themselves isolated return to the idea
of small groups. 'People living in an impersonal milieu move into
groups, seeking ties in common interests, love, recreation, books,
records, drugs, crafts, religion . . . they search for the integrity of the
gemeinschaft on the one hand, and the flowering of the identity of the
individual in the group on the other.'[11] It can equally well be explained
by Victor Turner's notion of communitas, communitas being a community or even a communion of equal individuals who submit together to the general authority of the ritual elders, for example, the
early bands of Franciscan brothers which originated the ideal of
brotherhood preserved in Franciscan ideology. The emergence of a
relatively unstructured or undifferentiated communitas tends to occur
in liminal periods or transitionary stages in the history of a society or
organization. In the Christian tradition the state of liminality or
transition can become a permanent condition—'the Christian is a
stranger to the world, a pilgrim, a traveller, with no place to rest his
head.'[12] The great monastic and mendicant traditions of the medieval
Church institutionalized this liminality. Similarly, utopian sects tend
to emerge in periods when value patterns and institutions are in a
state of flux. Utopian sectarians believe themselves to be endowed
with the power of the Holy Spirit which in part enables them to see
that the corruption of men is the product of corrupt institutions.
They see themselves as divinely commissioned to establish the kingdom of God on earth. This is somewhat similar to the efforts of the
teaching congregation to demolish the dualistic theology of which
their institution had been a perpetrator and to establish new communities as witness to the charisma of the Holy Spirit. The response
of the young nuns was similar to that of the youth of Western society
who spoke out their criticism and disillusionment. They took up their
folk guitars, asked for greater poverty in their daily life and celebrated
their small communities as a sacral fellowship—with the Church's
sacrament of the Eucharist as their principal ritual. Further, by giving
their vocation the name and characteristics of a spiritual charisma,
they idealized their world to create a 'kingdom on earth' like so many
other communitarians before them.

The first Christian communities of the first and second centuries
were communes in the sense that they shared all things including

fraternal love. In the twelfth and thirteenth centuries Europe was overrun with 'wandering fanatics, militants, flower people—most of whom preached brotherhood and poverty.'[13] Some of these groups routinized and became sects like the Bohemian Brethren or the Taborites, until the Lutheran reformation and the Anabaptist movement in the sixteenth century. Norman Cohn has shown the links between the spiritual leaders and the restless poor of the Middle Ages, a fusion which produced the millennial sects and the great mendicant orders. Muntzer, regarded as founder of the Anabaptist movement, is described by Cohn as 'a propheta obsessed by eschatological phantasies which he attempted to translate into reality by exploiting social discontent.'[14] Hence his veneration by Engels and other Marxists who see him as a 'prodigious hero in the history of the class war.' The Anabaptists were anti-Church; they believed in direct inspiration from God and in ethical values such as active brotherly love. Their way of life was legitimated by the New Testament and the early Church. Like the first Franciscans and the progressive teaching nuns of 1960 they were questioning the Church and seeking direct inspiration, a key feature in charismatic appeal.

In the eighteenth century a new type of communitarianism developed, that of the *philosophes* and Saint-Simon. The backwoods of America were peppered by experiments in fraternal living. They still are today; by the hippie communes, the rural co-operatives, urban communal residential schemes, in which sharing and commitment to the group takes precedence over more material aims and competitive interests. Direct comparisons have been made between the hippie-flower children of the late 1960s and the itinerant and semi-itinerant communities and bands wandering the countryside in the Middle Ages. . . . 'Drop-outs from a hierarchical society devoted to war and vainglory and churchly pretence and corruption.'[15] The progressive teaching sisters were more like Cohn's millennial sects than the itinerant communities, above all in the appeal to the simple life, work amongst the poor and lowly and the philosophy of egalitarianism. The nuns of the teaching congregation wanted to continue working within the Church. They criticized it but they were not anti-Church (nor was St Francis in his time). All the changes had carefully worked out theological justifications which kept them within the bounds of Church dogma and doctrine and which received further confirmation by a time-honoured reference back to the founder. By selective reference to his writings they could justify even the most progressive moves.

The very catholicity of the Roman Catholic Church has always been one of its great strengths as an organization. It has always managed to absorb a variety of beliefs and organizations, while holding the power of excommunication to control truly dissident elements. Hugh Trevor-Roper describes a religious attitude of the fifteenth and sixteenth centuries as Erasmianism, not because it projects the views of Erasmus but because it contains many very general beliefs of which Erasmus's were a clearly projected form. Erasmus stressed in particular 'the real inner piety of the active layman above the complacency of the indolent monks who assume a greater holiness because of the costume they wear or the "mechanical devotions" they practise.'[16] The Erasmians were both Christians and Catholic yet they rejected or ignored a great deal of the external apparatus of official Catholicism and the mechanical religion of monasticism. Inevitably Erasmians were forced into full Protestantism when the Counter-Reformation demanded more rigid adherence to Catholic doctrine. The Catholic Church post-Vatican II is in a position not unlike that described by Trevor-Roper. Priests remain priests, yet they allow birth control and admit to Papal fallibility. Polygamous marriage is permitted in Africa. There are a number of widely held beliefs which under Canon Law would lead to withdrawal of the sacraments if not excommunication, but these constraints are not brought into force. Protestant theologians are read and quoted by Catholic nuns, but the Church is still the sole introitus and institute of the supernatural; man and God might be brought together in humanity but the Church sacraments will preside, at baptism, at the Mass.

The contemporary convents of the teaching congregation emphasize spirit. They ritualize their community in the small group gathered round their dining-table sharing a Communion supper. They share hopes for an ideal society. Harvey Cox describes Utopian thinking as being to the corporate community what fantasy is to the individual person. 'It provides the images by which existing societies can be cracked open and recreated. It prevents societies like thought systems from becoming closed and ossified.'[17] If he is right, and the evidence of this research would suggest that he is, then the teaching congregation will, like the Franciscans, succeed. They will succeed because they have kept alive *communitas* and not allowed it to become bounded and rigid, in a kind of totalitarianism of the sacred.[18] Utopian thinking has its expression in play. The radical dimension of the festivities in the old convents when lay sisters took roles as Superiors, and singing, dancing and acting broke the routine, is now contained in ideology and in a re-interpretation of beliefs. The sisters who had abolished the big convents, the enclosure, silence, uniformity of dress and routine, the formal constraints on behaviour, the coulpe, the mortifications, the discipline, the leaders, bureaucratic hierarchy, had not lost their reasons for being religious, chaste and bound by the vows of chastity, poverty and obedience. They were still bound by a belief in a supra-empirical reality which embraced the notion of an eternal life. Paul Tillich comments, 'Most religious are full of mythological, usually very fanciful images of hope. Taken literally in any sense, they appear as pale but beautiful images of our daily experienced world.'[19] These images are, he says, the key to the eternal life and their acceptance means joy in today. Life takes on a dimension which gives it trans-temporal meaning. In keeping God alive in their communities the religious sisters were witness to the promise of eternal life which is the Christian message. It was one which accorded with the radical Catholic thinkers of the 1950s and 1960s for it embraced a form of communitarianism which was both Utopian, idealistic and capable of innovation. The teaching congregation arrived in 1974 with an organization radically different in form from that of the Franciscans, but similar in ideology.

In the process of change the teaching congregation had destroyed the mechanisms for gaining commitment from its membership and attempted to replace them with an adherence to a universal system of values. In practice they had to replace some of the traditional mechanisms, especially those of Novitiate. But theoretically at least the value system combined with religious beliefs and rituals provided not only consensus on the normative goals of the organization but also on the operational norms of each sub-group. I can illustrate this with a fine example: the changing attitude of sisters towards the sacrament of confession. Indeed confession provides an excellent summary of all those aspects of change, personal, social, in ritual and in belief which have characterized the development of these religious groups and organizations within the Church and the outside world. In the nineteenth century the sisters went to confession weekly and confessed their sins to a confessor appointed by the Papal ordinary. He might well be the chaplain to the convent who, though living in a separate house, would celebrate the offices with the sisters and give catechism to the pupils of the schools. He would be appointed for a period of three years after which he would be replaced. Four times a year and on Ember days the sisters presented themselves to an extra-ordinary confessor, also brought in by the Papal Ordinary. No latitude of choice was allowed. Confession was not supposed to be in any way connected with the government of the Institute. Sisters were instructed by their Rule to confess matters of conscience only. The danger of interference in the internal affairs of the institute was recognized in Canon Law as was the individual's right to the secrecy of the confessional—Superiors were instructed not to ask what had taken place and sisters were forbidden to talk about it among themselves. The Rule also included advice to the sisters on how to compose themselves for the confessional. The convents either had a confessional built into the chapel, or they had black screens which they set up at the back of the nave. There was a physical separation between nun and confessor. The confessor, the nun was told, holds the place of Our Lord Jesus Christ. She must therefore avoid any human feelings for or against him. His concern must be for the purity of her soul and the purity of her heart; her affections should be for God and for her Rule. She should compare one week with the last and honestly see if there was any improvement in her behaviour. If she could find fault then she should set it out as simply as possible, accept the absolution offered and fuss over it no further.

In the 1930s some latitude was allowed, but sisters were still bound to present themselves to the extraordinary confessor four times a year. They still went to confession once a week on the ringing of a bell. Their confessions were devotional, in that they were horrified at the thought of committing a mortal sin. Confession was to help you keep away from sin. The sisters recognized how mechanical confession had become for them, but they did still believe in Heaven and Hell at this time and it did keep the soul alive. They presented themselves for confession every week whether they had anything to confess or not, received absolution and said a few set prayers. Underlying these mechanical devotional confessions was a schema of beliefs which dramatized the awfulness of wrongdoing and the sanctity of goodness and right. Confession illustrates not only the belief system but also the normative power of those beliefs and the institutionalization of those beliefs.

In the 1960s not only the Canon Law on confession changed, but the whole attitude of the teaching congregation towards this sacrament underwent a radical transformation. Instead of going to confession once a week on the ringing of a bell, the sister now had one special confessor whom she could choose herself and who was called a 'spiritual director'. Any priest who was known to the sister and who was reasonably accessible was suitable, though he was supposed to have reached a certain age. The sisters said, with some amusement, that young priests couldn't hear the confessions of nuns, it wasn't proper. The extent to which the sisters utilized the new ruling varied according to how radical/conservative were their religious beliefs. The more conservative went to the parish priest or asked the Superior in charge for advice. The more radical went to a lot of trouble to find someone with whom they felt at ease, often travelling to London to visit a particular priest. Whereas previously the sister had been separated from the priest by the confessional box or a black curtain, she now had not only visual contact but human contact. The priest would be someone she knew very well with whom she could sit down and 'talk things over'. Confession was not a weekly event; it might be a meeting once a month or every six weeks or even longer. The process of confession, if there was a problem to be talked over, might take months, after which absolution was given in liturgical form. Many of the sisters found that the ability to talk to a sympathetic priest saved their vocation and sometimes even their faith. It was an inner crisis of a psychological or emotional nature rather than some exterior fault which sent the modern sister to her confessor. In some cases it was an actual crisis of faith, in which the nun had ceased to believe. Some expressed it as a 'turning away from God' for which help was required and forthcoming at confession.

By these changes the sacrament of confession was taken out of the jurisdiction of the convent and established as an individual responsibility. To some extent, it is true, the confessional had always acted on the individual rather than on the group, but the organization had made all the arrangements and had held a central place in the 'sufficient matter' she might find to confess. Now it was the relationship with God which received the most attention, and the individual had a more direct and unmediated relationship both with her confessor and with her God.

In comparison the Franciscans exhibit all those contrasts to the teaching congregation which have held for beliefs, ritual and organization. They did not engage in a radical reappraisal of the sacrament of confession during the 1960s, the alterations in Canon Law produced no real conflict with existing structures of belief or operation. The Rule of 1927 stated, as in the teaching congregation, that sisters should attend confession once a week. But the Franciscans, even at this time, had a choice of confessor within the bounds of Canon Law. In other words the sisters could go to any 'qualified' priest they like and could not be questioned by the Mother Superior of their house about their choice. In general they tried to go to confessors who were Fathers of the Franciscan Order, because, the Rule said, they were aware of the Franciscan spirit, and the need for its preservation. The special Chapter in 1968 did not alter this but suggested that sisters be given some clarification on the meaning of confession. It said, 'the sacrament of Penance is our personal encounter with Christ the Good Shepherd, where we obtain pardon from the mercy of God . . .' Thus the Franciscans preserved their 'Franciscan' ideology even in the sacrament of confession, ensuring that it would not be diluted by contact with a priest from outside the order in this important area of normative control. They also stressed the personal links with Jesus Christ and (through the Franciscan father) with St Francis, which reaffirmed the charismatic nature of their responses. The responsibility lay in the individual now as it had done fifty years earlier. The Franciscan organization achieved normative compliance with fewer mechanistic controls than the teaching congregation. It was also more successful in preserving both compliance and the plausibility of beliefs in the face of the questioning assaults made on both in the 1960s.

Cardinal Suenens, one of the progressive forces whose views were prominent in the Vatican Council, always emphasized that the world the religious leaves behind on professing her vows is in a supernatural way the very heart of her vocation. 'She wants to go from God to God in prayer, and from God himself to God in her fellow-creatures in the apostolate.' It was he who particularly criticized the retention of out-worn practices and the medievalism of the habit. Nuns he said, 'raise at best an ironical smile when a nun is seen on her way to tend a sick person, flapping through the streets on her scooter with her habit and veil streaming behind her to the imminent danger of herself and other traffic.'[20] He would be proud of the teaching nuns, swinging down the street in smart 'ordinary' clothes, dedicated religious working for God in humanity. In a decade when Women's Liberation has lost its strident voice and negotiates with a Royal Commission behind it, the experience of the nuns is particularly relevant. The teaching nun is once more in step with society, she exercises her religious belief in harmony with twentieth-century existential philosophy. Her organiza-tion once more attracts recruits from committed young Catholic women who are prepared to dedicate their lives to bear witness to Christ in the world. By their very existence they are keeping their God alive and they are witness to the promise of eternal life—which is the Christian message. Now, as in the time of their founder, the nuns may have a better deal than their married sisters. They have re-nounced sexual relationships in exchange for a useful, fulfilled life, with all modern comforts and the values of brotherhood, love and sharing which have always been a Utopian ideal. They belong to a large community, spreading far beyond the walls of their houses, they are not isolated, they enjoy relationships with a wide variety of people, they have the possibility of changing their situation constantly within their grasp.

A young girl, or even an older woman, who wants to become a nun can go to an organization like the Vocation sisters and find there such a variety of congregations, performing such a variety of functions in today's society that she will at first become bewildered by the choice. I have described two congregations; others will have different prac-tices, different ideals, but their organization will have been the same, at least until the late 1960s. There is a tendency for outsiders to see nuns in terms of extremes, living, like Diderot's Sister Suzanne, in a darkness relieved only by candlelight or the faint glimmer of altar-lamps, living lives of claustrophobic unhealthiness, mental instability,

illness, anxiety and febrile intensity.[21] Or they remember the head-
liners like the singing nun or Mother Thérèse of Calcutta. I hope I
have revealed the very ordinary nun whose life can be bogged down
in bureaucratic organization, whose communities face all the problems of commitment and faith in ideals and economic viability which
haunt all small groups. Their struggles with change and their search
for stability have lessons for any organization which relies on normative
compliance to achieve its goals. And why become a nun? Bearing in
mind that every Christian believer is committed to a set of religious
beliefs, and that the Catholic has the colourful backdrop of centuries
behind her, I end with this account of a vision. There was 'a superb
procession of Apostles, Saints and Martyrs, with the Blessed Virgin
at their head, all walking carefully and scrutinizing the ground with
much earnestness, that they might tread as nearly as possible in the
very footsteps of Christ. At the end of this pageant of the Church
Triumphant came the little shabby figure of Francis, barefoot and
brown-robed; and he alone was walking easily and steadily in the
actual footprints of our Lord.'[22]

ACKNOWLEDGEMENTS

First thanks must go to the nuns, whose names of course have been changed and the identity of their congregation disguised. To the Mothers General who courageously gave permission and to every sister who co-operated in the research, my heartfelt thanks.

My researches originated when I was a graduate student in the anthropology department of University College, London, and were completed while preparing a doctoral thesis in the sociology department of the London School of Economics. I am grateful for the stimulating atmosphere and helpful criticisms of colleagues in both those institutions.

Professor Mary Douglas first interested me in the nuns and it was under her supervision that the first report on the teaching congregation was prepared for the Social Sciences Research Council. I am thankful to her also for my 'awakening' as an anthropologist.

The second stage of my research and the achievement of my doctoral thesis were due to the encouragement of Professor Michael Hill whose inspiration and confidence in my sometimes rather 'wild' ideas was unflagging. I am enormously grateful to him.

The views in this book are not necessarily shared by my teachers and I take full responsibility for any errors or omissions.

NOTES

CHAPTER ONE

1. O'Neill, J., *Sociology as a Skin Trade*, p. 10, Heinemann Educational Books, London, 1972.
2. Lewis, I. M., *Social Anthropology in Perspective*, p. 26, Penguin Books, 1976.
3. Malinowski, B., *A Diary in the Strict Sense of the Term*, Routledge and Kegan Paul, 1967.
4. Lewis, *op. cit.*, p. 16.
5. Pears, D., *Wittgenstein*, p. 174, Fontana Paperbacks, Collins, 1971.
6. Gellner, E., *Cause and Meaning in the Social Sciences*, p. 20, Routledge and Kegan Paul, 1973.
7. Mannheim, K., 'Man attains objectivity . . . not by giving up his will to action and holding his evaluations in abeyance but in confronting and examining himself. The criterion of such self-illumination is that not only the object but we ourselves fall squarely within our field of vision.' *Ideology and Utopia*, pp. 42–3, first published 1936, Routledge and Kegan Paul, 1960.
8. Goffman, E., *Asylums*, p. 17, Pelican Books, 1968.
9. Research on the entrants to seminaries has shown that while recruits are seen to enter voluntarily and they are told the 'gate is always open for withdrawal', they are reminded that they have not chosen their vocation but that they have been chosen by God. There was even greater pressure on sons to become priests in societies where, at one time, every third son was destined for the Church. Cf. Moore, J., *Some Aspects of the Sociology of Priesthood*, M.Sc. Dissertation, London School of Economics, 1973.
10. Hill, M., *The Religious Order*, Heinemann Educational Books, 1973, Chapter 1, gives a definition and a typology of the characteristics of a religious order virtually all of which apply to the religious congregation.
11. Berger, P., *Invitation to Sociology, A humanistic Perspective*, p. 134, Penguin Books, 1966.
12. O'Neill is referring here to a Kwaitiutl Indian belief that the three cosmic levels of their world (underworld, earth, sky) were pierced by a copper pole which provided a doorway to the world above.
13. O'Neill, *op. cit.*, p. 24.

CHAPTER TWO

1. *Life of the Founder*, unpublished.
2. *Ibid.*, p. 50.
3. Hill, *The Religious Order, op. cit.*, p. 22.
4. Southern, R. W., *Western Society and the Church in the Middle Ages*, p. 247, Penguin Books, 1970.
5. Reeves, J. B., *The Dominicans*, p. 117, Sheed and Ward, 1931.
6. Nisbet, R., *The Social Philosophers*, p. 225, Paladin Paperbacks, Granada, 1976.
7. de Tocqueville, A., *The Old Régime and the French Revolution*, p. 149, Doubleday and Co., New York, 1955.
8. Courthope Bowen, H., *Froebel and Education by Self-Activity*, p. 92, Heinemann, 1903.
9. *Life of the Founder*, p. 117.
10. Best, G., *Mid-Victorian Britain 1851–1875*, pp. 161–2, Weidenfeld and Nicolson, 1971.
11. Marks, P., 'Femininity in the Classroom', pp. 176–99, in *The Rights and Wrongs of Women*, ed., Juliet Mitchell and Ann Oakley, Penguin Books, 1976.
12. *Ibid.*, p. 182.
13. Davidoff, L., L'Esperance, J. and Newby, H., 'Landscape with Figures', in *The Rights and Wrongs of Women, op. cit.*, p. 155.
14. *Ibid.*, p. 155, quoting Ruskin, J., *Sesame and Lilies*, p. 145, 1868.
15. Nisbet, *op. cit.*, p. 226.
16. Harrison, J. F. C., *The Early Victorians 1832–51*, p. 122, Weidenfeld and Nicolson, 1971.
17. Marx, K., 'Towards the Critique of Hegel's Philosophy of Right'; in *Marx and Engels, Basic Writings*, ed. Feuer, L. S., p. 304, Fontana Paperbacks, Collins, 1971.
18. Crow, D., *The Victorian Woman*, p. 59, Allen and Unwin, London, 1971.
19. Marks, P., *op. cit.*, quoting the report from the select committee on the education of the poorer classes, p. 13, 1838.
20. *Ibid.*, p. 186.
21. Battersby in Beck, G. A., *The English Catholics 1850–1950*, p. 337, Burns and Oates, 1950.
22. Hughes, P., in Beck, *op. cit.*, p. 44.
23. *Ibid.*
24. Murphy, J., *Terra Incognita or the Convents of the United Kingdom*, 1873.
25. Hill, *op. cit.*, p. 36.
26. Constitutions, 1891, unpublished.
27. Davidoff *et al.*, *op. cit.*, p. 157.
28. Woodham-Smith, C., *Florence Nightingale*, p. 364, Fontana Paperbacks, Collins, 1977.
29. Beale, D., *The Organization of Girls' Day Schools*, a paper read at the Social Science Congress, 1873.

CHAPTER THREE

1. Moorman, J. R. H., *St Francis of Assisi*, p. 7, S.P.C.K., 1963.
2. Dubois, Leo, *St Francis of Assisi: Social Reformer*, p. 62, 1906.
3. Steiner, Rudolf, *Anthroposophical Ethics*, lecture, May 1912.
4. Augustine, OFM, Capuchin, *Some Loves of the Seraphic Saint*, p. 6, Dublin, 1944.
5. Douie, D. L., *The Nature and Effect of the Heresy of the Fraticelli*, p. 49, Manchester University Press, 1932.
6. Knowles, D., *The Religious Orders in England*, p. 115, Cambridge University Press, 1950.
7. Cuthbert, Fa., *The Romanticism of St Francis*, p. 19, Longmans, 1915.
8. Theobald, R., *Charisma: Some Empirical Problems Considered*, p. 3, occasional paper of the Polytechnic of Central London, 1975.
9. Weber, M., *Economy and Society: an outline of Interpretive Sociology*, p. 1111, ed. Roth and Wittich, Bedminster Press, N.Y., 1968.
10. *Ibid.*, p. 1115.
11. Cohn, N., *Pursuit of the Millennium*, p. 268, Paladin Paperbacks, Granada, 1970.
12. Weber, *op. cit.*, p. 1121.
13. Wach, J., *Master and Disciple*, p. 5, *Journal of Religion*, Vol. XLII, January 1962.
14. Weber, *op. cit.*, p. 1139.
15. *Ibid.*, p. 1141.
16. Moorman, J., *History of the Franciscan Order*, p. 18, Oxford, Clarendon Press, 1968.
17. *Ibid.*, p. 13.
18. Etzioni, A., *Complex Organizations*, p. 243, Free Press, N.Y., 1961.
19. Mecklin, J. M., *The Passing of the Saint, American Journal of Sociology*. Supplement, LX, 1955.
20. Papal Pronouncement 'de beatificatione et canonization sanctorum', Pope Benedict XIV.
21. Hill, *The Religious Order*, *op. cit.*, p. 100.
22. Hill, M., *A Sociology of Religion*, p. 141, Heinemann Educational Books, 1973, quoting Talcott-Parsons, 'Authority, Legitimation and political action', in *Authority*, ed., Friedrick, American Sociology Political & Legal Philosophy, Harvard University Press, 1968.
23. Hill, *The Religious Order*, *op. cit.*, p. 97.
24. Matthew, 16.13, Revised Standard Version.
25. Southern, *Western Society and the Church in the Middle Ages*, *op. cit.*, p. 24.
26. *Ibid.*, p. 95.
27. Moulin, L., 'Policy Making in the Religious Orders', p. 32, fn., in *Government and Opposition*, Vol. I, No. 1, October 1965.
28. Sorokin, P. A., *Altruistic Love. A study of American 'Good Neighbours and Christian Saints'*, Beacon Press, Boston, 1950.
29. Mecklin, *op. cit.*, p. 50.
30. Moorman, J., *The Franciscans in England*, p. 29, Mowbrays, 1974.

CHAPTER FOUR

1. Coser, L. A., *Greedy Institutions, Patterns of Undivided Commitment,* Free Press, N.Y., 1974.
2. The compliance relationship is a word coined from Max Weber by Amitai Etzioni. See Etzioni, *Complex Organizations,* Free Press, N.Y., 1961.
3. Diderot, D., *The Nun,* Penguin Classics, 1977.
4. Etzioni, *op. cit.,* pp. 4–6.
5. Thompson, F., *Lark Rise to Candleford,* Penguin Classics.
6. Holdsworth, W. A., *The Married Women's Property Act, 1882,* Routledge and Kegan Paul, Legal Handbook, 1882.
7. Bernstein, M., *Nuns,* p. 302, Collins, 1976.
8. Merton, T., *The Monastic Journey,* p. 31, Sheldon Press, 1977.
9. Crow, *The Victorian Woman, op. cit.,* p. 294.
10. Valentine, O. P., *All for the King's Delight,* p. 121, Burns and Oates, 1958.
11. Baldwin, M., *I Leap over the Wall,* p. 199, Pan Books, 1949.
12. Knox, R. A., *Enthusiasm: A Chapter in the History of Religion,* Oxford, Clarendon Press, 1950. See Chapter 9 for the impact of Jansenism on French Catholicism.
13. Baldwin, *op. cit.*
14. Hill, *The Religious Order, op. cit., p.* 76.

CHAPTER FIVE

1. Goffman, E., *Asylums, Essays on the social situation of Mental Patients and other inmates,* p. 17, Pelican Books, 1961.
2. Newitt, H., *Women must Choose,* p. 30, Left Book Club Edition, Gollancz, 1937, gives a vivid description of social conditions between the wars.
3. *Ibid.,* p. 260.
4. Taylor, A. J. P., *English History 1914–45,* p. 305, Oxford, Clarendon Press, 1965.
5. Branson, N. and Heinemann, M., *Britain in the Nineteen-Thirties,* Weidenfeld and Nicolson, 1961.
6. *Ibid.,* p. 158.
7. Mitchison, N., *The Home and a changing civilization,* John Lane, Bodley Head, 1934.
8. Newitt, *op. cit.,* p. 38, quoting Hitler speech 1934.
9. Sargent, W., *Battle for the Mind,* p. 128, Pan Books, 1957.
10. Newitt, *op. cit.,* p. 79.
11. Examples of devotional prayers are the Angelus and the Regina Coeli. The Angelus: The Angel of the Lord declared unto Mary
    And she conceived by the Holy Ghost, Hail Mary, rept.,

> Behold the handmaid of the Lord:
> Be it done unto me according to the Word,
> Hail Mary, rept.,
> And the Word was made Flesh
> And dwelt among us.
> Hail Mary, rept.,

The prayers involved much repetition.

The Regina Coeli: Joy to Thee, O Queen of Heaven, Alleluia
He whom thou wast meet to bear, Alleluia
As he promised has arisen, Alleluia
Pour forth for us to Him thy prayer, Alleluia
Rejoice and be glad, O Virgin Mary, Alleluia
For the Lord has truly risen. Alleluia.

12. Shils, E., 'Tradition', p. 137, *American Sociological Review*, pp. 123–57, 1971.
13. Valentine, *All for the King's Delight*, *op. cit.*, p. 192.
14. Douglas, M., *Purity and Danger*, Routledge and Kegan Paul, 1966. These ideas are elaborated in her later book, *Natural Symbols*, Barrie and Rockcliffe, 1970.
15. Douglas, *Purity and Danger*, *op. cit.*, p. 3.
16. For a full interpretation of the expressive function of danger beliefs, see Campbell-Jones, S. A. unpublished M.Phil. thesis, University of London.
17. Hill, *The Religious Order*, *op. cit.*, p. 22.
18. Yang, C. K., 'Some Characteristics of Chinese Bureaucratic Behaviour', in *Confucianism in Action*, ed., D. S. Nivison and A. P. Wright, pp. 134–64, Stanford University Press, 1959.
19. Albrow, M., *Bureaucracy*, p. 42, Pall Mall Press, 1970.
20. Gerth and Mills, *From Max Weber*, p. 126, Routledge and Kegan Paul, paperback edition, 1970.
21. Hill, *The Religious Order*, *op. cit.*, p. 24.

CHAPTER SIX

1. Arendt, H., *On Revolution*, p. 29, Penguin Books, 1973.
2. *Ibid.*, p. 33.
3. Russell, B., *On Changing the World*, an essay quoted in Chomsky, N., *Problems of Knowledge and Freedom*, p. 47, Fontana, 1977.
4. Hopkins, H., *The New Looks*, Secker and Warburg, 1963.
5. Longmate, N., *How We Lived Then*, p. 23, Hutchinson, 1971.
6. *Ibid.*, p. 71.
7. *Ibid.*, p. 142.
8. Thompson, D., *England in the Twentieth Century, 1914–1963*, p. 172, Jonathan Cape, 1964.
9. *Ibid.*, p. 182.
10. Cruikshand, M., *Church and State in English Education, 1870–Present Day*, p. 136, Macmillan, 1964.

11. *Ibid.*, p. 142, *Quoting the Green Book*, 1941.
12. *Ibid.*, p. 157.
13. Courthope-Bowen, H., *Froebel and Educational by Self-Activity*, pp. 92 and 101, Heinemann, 1907.
14. Blackie, J., *Inside the Primary School*, H.M.S.O., 1967.
15. Blau, P., *Dynamics of Bureaucracy*, p. 232, University of Chicago Press, 1955.
16. Suenens, Cardinal, *The Nun in the World*, Burnes and Oates, 1961.
17. Merton, R. K., *Social Theory and Social Structure* (revised edn.), pp. 199–200, Free Press, N.Y. Glencoe, 1957.
18. *Life of the Founder*, p. 112.
19. Suenens, *op. cit.*, p. 162.

CHAPTER SEVEN

1. Akers and Quinney, *Differential Organization of Health Professions*, *American Sociological Review*, Vol. 33, No. 1, February 1968.
2. Volmer, H. M., *Member Commitment and Organizational Competence in Religious Orders*, p. 20, *Berkeley Publications in Society and Institutions*, Vol. 3 No. 1, Spring, 1957.
3. Etzioni, *Complex Organizations, op. cit.*, p. 243.
4. Theobald, R., *Charisma: Some Empirical Problems considered*, p. 3, occasional paper of the Polytechnic of Central London, 1975.
5. Etzioni, *op. cit.*, p. 205.
6. Eisenstadt, S. N., *Introduction to Max Weber: On Charisma*, p. xlv, University of Chicago Press, 1968.
7. Gerth, H., *The Nazi Party: its leadership and Composition*, p. 541, *American Journal of Sociology*, Vol. XLV, January 1940.
8. Etzioni, *op. cit.*, p. 205.
9. Worsley, P., *The Trumpet Shall Sound*, pp. 274–80, Paladin, 1970.
10. Latourette, K. S., *The Twentieth Century in Europe*, p. 96, Eyre and Spottiswoode, 1961.
11. Willer and Zollschan, *Prolegomenon to a Theory of Revolutions*, eds. Zollschan and Hirsh, p. 142, Routledge and Kegan Paul, 1964.
12. Hill, *The Religious Order, op. cit.*, pp. 85–100.
13. Crozier, M., *The Bureaucratic Phenomenon*, pp. 194–6, Tavistock Publications, 1964.
14. Blau, *Dynamics of Bureaucracy, op. cit.*
15. Abbott, W. M., *Documents of Vatican II*, Geoffrey Chapman, 1967. The promulgations which most affected religious were: *Perfectae Caritatis*, October 1965, *Ecclesiae Sanctae*, August 1966, and the *Decrees on Religious Formation*, January 1969. I am indebted for the interpretation of these decrees to *The Way*, No. 4, November 1967, *Supplement on Religious Renewal*, and an interview with the Secretary of Council for Religious Superiors.
16. This was the St Catherine's Centre, a Roman Catholic theological centre set up in London as part of a general move on the behalf of

educational orders to revitalize religious training. It was subsequently closed down, some say because it became too radical!

17. Suenens, Cardinal, *Co-Responsibility in the Church*, Burns and Oates, 1968.
18. Blau, *op. cit.*, p. 264.
19. Hill, *The Religious Order, op. cit.*, p. 229.
20. Shiner, L., *The Concept of Secularization in Empirical Research*, pp. 207–20, *Journal for the Scientific Study of Religion*, Vol. VL, No. 2, 1967.
21. Cox, H., *The Secular City*, p. 31, Pelican Books, 1968.
22. Hill, *The Religious Order, op. cit.*, p. 238.
23. Moore, J., *Some Aspects of the Sociology of Priesthood*, M.Sc. Dissertation, London University, 1974.
24. Kuhn, T. S., *The Structures of Scientific Revolutions* (2nd edn.), p. 174, Vol. II, No. 2, *International Encyclopaedia of Unified Science*, 1962, 1970.
25. Berger, P., *The Homeless Mind*, p. 77, Penguin Books, 1973.

CHAPTER EIGHT

1. Evans-Pritchard, *Nuer Religion*, Oxford, Clarendon Press, 1956.
2. Thomas, K., *Religion and the Decline of Magic*, p. 33, Weidenfeld and Nicolson, 1971.
3. Berger, P., *The Social Reality of Religion*, p. 41, Faber and Faber, 1969.
4. O'Neill, *Sociology as a Skin Trade, op. cit.*, p. 217.
5. Berger, *op. cit.*, p. 26.
6. *Ibid.*, p. 33.
7. Hill, *A Sociology of Religion, op. cit.*, pp. 262–3.
8. Douglas, *Natural Symbols, op. cit.*, p. 161.
9. As described in Moorhouse, G., *Against All Reason*, p. 121, Weidenfeld and Nicolson, 1969.
10. Vinjhof, in Brothers, J., *Readings in the Sociology of Religion*, p. 52, Pergamon Press, 1967.
11. Robinson, J. A. T., *Honest to God*, S.C.M., 1963.
12. Gellner, E., *Time and Theory in Social Anthropology*, p. 190n., *MIND*, 1968.
13. Sister Anne had rationalized the events at Calvary with her readings of modern theologians such as Sebastian Moore. In *No Exit* he describes Christ as a political revolutionary and Calvary as a political execution.
14. Firth, R., *Symbols Public and Private*, p. 197, Allen and Unwin, 1973. I rely heavily on Professor Firth's scholarship in reaching some appropriate definition of symbolism. His recent book contains a definitive summary of all the possible definitions of symbolism and their application.
15. *Ibid.*, p. 57.

16. Langer, D., *Philosophical Sketches*, p. 55, Baltimore, 1962.
17. Geertz, C., *Anthropological Approaches to the Study of Religion*, p. 4, Tavistock Publications, 1966.
18. Firth, *op. cit.*, p. 130.
19. *Ibid.*, p. 195.
20. *Ibid.*, p. 419.
21. *Ibid.*, p. 419.
22. Leach, E., 'The Structure of Symbolism', in Fountain, J. S. L., *The Interpretation of Ritual*, Tavistock, 1972.
23. *Ibid.*, p. 266.
24. Huisinga, J., *Homo Ludens: a Study of the Play Element in Culture*, p. 15, Routledge and Kegan Paul, 1949.
25. Firth, *op. cit.*, p. 425.
26. Douglas, *Natural Symbols*, *op. cit.*, p. 49.
27. O'Brown, N., *Love's Body*, p. 167, Vintage Books, N.Y., 1966.
28. Lash, N., *His Presence in the World, A study of Eucharistic Worship and Theology*, Sheed and Ward Stagbooks, London, 1968.
29. *Ibid.*, p. 100.
30. Cohen, A., *2 Dimensional Man*, p. 66, Routledge and Kegan Paul, 1974.
31. Shils, 'Tradition', *op. cit.*, p. 140.
32. *Ibid.*, p. 157.

CHAPTER NINE

1. Douglas, *Natural Symbols*, *op. cit.*
2. Mauss, M., *Sociologie et Anthropologie*, Presses Universitaires de France, 1960.
3. Firth, *Symbols Public and Private*, *op. cit.*, Chapter 8, pp. 262–98.
4. Leach, E., 'Magical Hair', in Middleton (ed.), *Myth and Cosmos, Readings in Mythology and Symbolism*, Natural History Press, 1967.
5. MacRae, D. G., *The Body and Social Metaphor*, Allen Lane, 1975.
6. Firth, *op. cit.*, p. 234.
7. Douglas, *Natural Symbols*, *op. cit.*, p. 69.
8. Laver, J., Lecture at the Institute of Contemporary Art, Autumn, 1972, unpublished.
9. Hall, E. T., *Silent Language*, p. 51, Doubleday, N.Y., 1959.
10. Hall, E. T., *Hidden Dimension*, p. 97, Bodley Head, 1966.
11. Rice, D., 'Nuns in a New World', *New Society*, no. 410, 4 June 1970.
12. Douglas, *Natural Symbols*, *op. cit.*, p. 14.
13. Firth, *op. cit.*, p. 197.
14. Turner, V. W., *The Ritual Process*, p. 96, Routledge and Kegan Paul, 1969.
15. Cox, H., *The Feast of Fools: a theological essay in Festivity and Fantasy*, Harvard University Press, 1969.
16. Turner, V. W., *op. cit.*, p. 168.
17. Drawn from Chapter 4 in Turner, V. W., *op. cit.*

CHAPTER TEN

1. Martin, D., *A Sociology of English Religion*, p. 139, Heinemann, Educational Books, 1967.
2. Shils, E., 'Tradition', *op. cit.*, p. 122.
3. Hill, M., *The Religious Order*, *op. cit.*, p. 2.
4. Williams, D., 'The Bridge of Christ', pp. 105–25, in Ardener, S. (ed.), *Perceiving Women*, Malaby Press, 1976.
5. Brown, Norman O., *Love's Body*, pp. 3–6, Random House, N.Y., 1966.
6. Parkin, F., *Class Inequality and Political Order*, Chapter 3, Granada Publications, 1972.
7. *Ibid.*, p. 81.
8. Rigby, A., *Alternative Realities*, p. 304, Routledge and Kegan Paul, 1974.
9. Rice, D., 'Nuns in a New World', *ast. cit.* Reports on conversations with male and female religious.
10. Martin, *op. cit.*, p. 143.
11. Bennett, J. W., *Cultural Integrity and Personal Identity: a Communitarian response*: a paper for the Smithsonian Institution's Fourth International Symposium, 1970.
12. Turner, V. W., *The Ritual Process*, op. cit.
13. Bennett, *op. cit.*, 1970.
14. Cohn, N., *Pursuit of the Millennium*, p. 251, Paladin Paperbacks, 1970.
15. Bennett, *op. cit.*, 1970.
16. Trevor-Roper, R. H., *Religion, the Reformation and Social Change*, p. 24, Macmillan, 1967.
17. Cox, H., *The Feast of Fools*, op. cit.
18. Myerhof, B., 'Organization & Fantasy', p. 65, in Myerhof and Falk Moore, *Symbol and Politics in Communal Ideology*, Cornell University Press, 1975.
19. Tillich, P., *From Two Types of Philosophy of Religion*, 1964, reprinted in Harold A. Basilus (ed.), *Contemporary Problems in Religion*, Detroit University Press, 1956.
20. Suenens, *A Nun in the World*, *op. cit.*, pp. 162 and 20.
21. Tancock, L., Introduction to Diderot, *The Nun*, *op. cit.*
22. Moorman, J. R. H., *St Francis of Assisi*, p. 42, S.P.C.K., London, 1963.

INDEX